VOICE OF A NATIVE SON

VOICE
OF A
NATIVE
SON

The Poetics of Richard Wright

Eugene E. Miller

University Press of Mississippi
Jackson and London

Copyright © 1990 by the University Press of Mississippi
Manufactured in the United States of America
93 92 91 90   4 3 2
The paper in this book meets the guidelines for permanence and
durability of the Committee on Production Guidelines for Book Lon-
gevity of the Council on Library Resources.

Library of Congress Cataloging-in-Publication Data

Miller, Eugene E.
    Voice of a native son : the poetics of Richard Wright / Eugene E.
Miller.
        p.   cm.
    Includes bibliographical references.
    ISBN 0-87805-399-9 (alk. paper)
    1. Wright, Richard, 1908-1960—Criticism and interpretation.
    2. Afro-Americans in literature.   I. Title.
    PS3545.R815Z77   1990   89-37374
    813'.52—dc20   CIP

British Library Cataloguing-in-Publication data available

To Margaret, Amy, and Cara

CONTENTS

Acknowledgments

My deepest gratitude: to Seetha Srinivasan and her University Press staff for their advice and diligence in steering this work through the publication process; to the NEH Summer Seminar and Summer Stipend programs, during which this project was initiated and furthered; to the Albion College library staff, not only for their skill and dispatch in obtaining many research materials, but also for their provision of a lovely work space, numerous cups of coffee, and other cures for bouts of writer's block; to Michael G. Cooke of Yale and Houston Baker, Jr., of Pennsylvania for encouraging me to begin, providing insights into Richard Wright and practical publication advice; to the Beinecke Library and especially to Ellen Wright for permitting me generous use of unpublished Wright materials on which this work is based.

Introduction

In the Western world, from Plato to the present, distance from reality has been seen as an inherent, problematic characteristic of art. Artists, in their attempts to justify art, have dealt with this distance between art and reality in two basic ways. Afro-American culture has evolved in the midst of these aesthetic attitudes: the older states the classical notion of art as artifice and the validity of artifice because it reflects human involvement with an ultraphysical reality, and the newer stubbornly attempts to create an actual world in its own image. Afro-American sympathies have been decidedly with the latter. The well-articulated mystique of Afro-American music, for example, has long proclaimed an identity between the jazz musician and his instrument and between the musician and what he produces by means of that instrument. Something similar is attributed also to the Afro-American who can and does dance, or who can and does excel in a sport: they are so very good at these because they are what they do (which is not saying that all black people are naturally singers, dancers, or athletes). And in Afro-American literature since the Civil War, the development has been in the direction of a form or forms that deal as directly as possible with black American life—physical, emotional, psychological—as it actually is, to put on paper the very consciousness of black Americans.

This movement in Afro-American literature has been particularly self-conscious for at least sixty-five years. Hughes's "The Negro Artist and the Racial Mountain" expressed the desire to bring art and life together; Johnson's "Preface" to *The Book of Negro Poetry*, with its call for capturing the special flavor more accurately by "symbols from within rather than by symbols from without," was in some ways an even clearer example. The Black Aesthetic of the 1960s and early 1970s was only the most recent and the most explicit. In the 1980s, emerging theorists of Afro-American literature are devoting their attention to what black American writers have long been working towards.

Afro-American artists and thinkers in the twentieth century have taken increasingly to the idea that Euro-American languages are not their own. These are languages developed not from the Afro-American experience but from and by a culture-defining sensibility that had separated their ancestors from their own cultures and denied them any language of their own. Dexter Fischer and Robert Stepto, in *Afro-American Literature: The Reconstruction of Instruction*, refer to this Afro-American awareness of no specfic language, of the need to create a language of its own in order to avoid being enslaved by that of another, as the "pregeneric myth" of Afro-American literary tradition—the antecedent quest for literacy *and* freedom which lies behind the generation of all Afro-American literary forms.

And Richard Wright sits in the midst of these cultures, these awarenesses, and this quest.

The objective of this study is to describe Wright's poetics. "Poetics" here is defined according to Kenneth Burke: "the formulation of the critical precepts implicit in the poet's practice." The meaning of "practice" is expanded to include Wright's theoretical writings as well as his imaginative and journalistic works. Formulating these precepts involves bringing into relief an often semi-conscious, often seemingly abeyant pattern of his conceptualizations and justifications of what he wanted to do as a writer. That such a pattern should exist in his works is suggested in his penchant for explanatory essays to preface his own fiction. If a writer is, even post facto, so self-conscious of what he was attempting in individual works, we should not be surprised to find that he had an even broader overview, one concerning what he was about as a writer in general.

This pattern in Wright's thought is manifested in various ways throughout the corpus of his works. Sometimes, especially early in his career, it is quite explicitly discussed in both published essays and unpublished fragments; at other times, in his midcareer, it assumes less obvious wording and even seems to disappear completely; at the end, as though he were returning to a book he had once read but barely remembered, the pattern returns in plans for projected fictional works as well as in his actual nonfiction writings and poetry. This present study views only certain of his writings from these different periods. Its intention is first to establish that this was indeed Wright's perspective and is not solely my own creative rewriting of Wright. Second, it hopes to bring about a fuller understanding of these works by looking at them from the perspective of Wright's own poetics. Finally, it asks the reader to complete the study by utilizing the poetics depicted here as he reads other of Wright's works. But even beyond these, it offers a perspective that, because of the potency of some of Wright's insights, is applicable to the fruitful study of other Afro-American literary works. It is also a chapter in the study of Afro-American literary theory and asks to be critiqued in light of other investigations into the distinctive nature of Afro-American literature.

We have had good biographies and autobiographies of Richard Wright. What is missing from these works is an account of his artistic principles. Granted that these life studies, as well as studies by a number of other Wright scholars, do touch on his reactions to, and his influence by, the literary works of other artists, but a complex search went on in this poet's mind for at least twenty-five years, a search ended by his death not by his sense that he had attained a final grasp of what he wanted to do or felt he should be doing as an artist. This search is partially revealed in such of his published essays as "A Blueprint for Negro Writing" and "Negro Literature in the United States." A more common view of Wright as artist and literary theorist is reflected in Edward Margolies's comment, in his somewhat misnamed *The Art of Richard Wright*, that

Wright has not ever been considered as a literary innovator. His best-known published fiction, *Uncle Tom's Children* and *Native Son*, were heralded for the impact of their content. The creation of this impact was also notable, but the creative principles of Wright's work seem to have been considered generally well accounted for by placing him and his writings (a placement admittedly questioned by Fabre in his esssay "Beyond Naturalism?") in the school of the Realists or the Naturalists or, later, the Existentialists. As Margolies points out, Wright's posthumously published, though written early, novel *Lawd Today* reveals a novelist who is extremely self-conscious about literary form, one willing to experiment with literary arrangements, trying to combine them into something distinctly his own. In "Richard Wright's First Hundred Books," Fabre has made the statement, based on the paucity of books on the subject in Wright's early library, that Wright "knew comparatively little about the theory of literature" (p. 474); yet he has also indicated that as early as 1933 Wright was reading books on aesthetics (*The Unfinished Quest of Richard Wright*, p. 93), which demonstrates Wright's interest in the subject. Among such works was Kenneth Burke's *Permanence and Change*, which Wright owned and presumably had read by 1940. That book contains many ideas concerning creative thought and expression that parallel Wright's, most notably the idea of "perspective by incongruity."

The present study owes much to Burke, more than I realized when I began. It develops Wright from an incongruous perspective. Some of the material, notably that on the voodoo parallels in *Native Son*, has already appeared in print and been judged by some scholars as an attempt to rewrite Wright. Burke makes one aware that, in fact, all criticism is a rewriting. If the "re-," the incongruous viewpoint, is meshed with the "writing" (the older, established view of the subject), a validly new awareness of the subject can be obtained. However much one tries to integrate his "re-" with what has already been "written," old pieties will undoubtedly be offended. I have had to struggle against a kind of guilty sense that my study was not in accord with the pragmatic, utilitarian, political Richard Wright that Fabre's masterful biography so convincingly creates, and that my intuitive, emotional, even visionary and semi-mystical Wright seems to fly in the face of it. Part of my trepidation in opening negotiations for the use of material from Wright's unpublished papers came from my wondering what Mrs. Wright would think of the Richard Wright I was trying to bring to the fore. At times I found myself even asking Richard what *he* thought of it.

In scattered published writings other than *Lawd Today*, both journalistic and literary, Wright left us further clues to the nature of his concern with art. In his unpublished papers, he has left us an even fuller record of his tentative, probing experiments, not just with literary forms but with a philosophy or theory. His philosophy attempts to explain, at least to himself, (and eventually like Henry James, whose book of prefaces he much admired) to others, just what it was that he was attempting, or actually doing, or should be doing in and with his art. His earliest statement concerning literary theory, or more exactly, his own poetics, is found in his unpublished essay "Personalism," written in 1935. It amounts to a kind of manifesto and contains a number of the ideas about artistic expression that were to recur to one degree or another throughout the rest of his life.

He states that, like the work of Emerson, Thoreau, Whitman, Twain, Drieser, Anderson, and Lewis, which he had been voraciously reading, "Mid-Western artistic expression, especially . . . literature . . . should have as its main burden and theme the posing of the problem of the individual in relation to society." Interestingly enough, in light of his involvement with the Communist party at the time, his approach to exploring this relationship leads him to attempt an aesthetic theory that is based not in what he considered the two "major camps" of the day—the one concerned with "proletarian," the other with "fascist" themes—but in the "domain of the petty bourgeoisie." This "petty bourgeoisie" basis is "a sort of twilight region, a No Man's Land, an unexplored ground" on which frequently and "strangely" the other two, superficially opposing "camps" come together. As a foundation upon which to build an artistic theory, a program for one's own literary expression, it sounds none too promising; yet it is like the intermediate stage between orientations that Burke discusses and compares to "the stage of 'rending and tearing' . . . in tragic ritual" and equates with the "process in the Hegelian dialectic . . . called a 'log-onomical purgatory'." (*Permanence and Change*, p. 69). In Wright's "Personalism," it is "a dream-like domain where theories sprout like mushrooms. It is a ground strewn with . . . human statues striking unusual and outlandish poses. Its psychology is fluid and uncertain. . . . In short, it is a land [of] self-consciousness, of nervousness, of questioning, of seeking, of trial and of wandering." But it is clearly Wright's kind of milieu: radically free.

Beyond the surrealistic quality that the expressive language gives to this domain, another note sounded that was to reverberate throughout his career concerning what lifted this "petty bourgeois" stance and the aesthetic theory it fostered above both the proletarian and the fascist "tendencies." This was the "one thing it has in abundance—emotional consciousness, intense emotional consciousness." This emotional intensity develops from the petty bourgeoisie's very indeterminate condition of existence, "likened to . . . a man holding above his head a great weight which he dares not turn loose lest it should crush him." The lack of anything in the objective world that speaks to him, that unequivocally calls forth his energies, his devotion, his love—"no definite heritage, no definite ideology, no definite psychology, no firm economic buttress"—leaves the artist based in a "non-class" only with himself. This, of course, sets up something akin to a feeling of guilt, as well as a "tendency" toward what a dozen years later would be called Existentialism.

Such an apparently empty condition would seem to lead to despair, to suicide, but Wright's artistic credo leads him to, of all things, "art for art's sake," to the idea of creating one's own world: "The petty bourgeois artist seeks to pour into his artistic expression all the meaning of religion, all the denied satisfaction of social life . . . art becomes the vessel which contains those values without which he feels he cannot live (Proust, Eliot, etc.). In other words, he holds that art is for the sake of art." Once in this chosen aesthetic alternative, Wright returns to his original theme: how such a position in a self-created world can be used "in a class conscious sense;" how art for art's sake can be used to explore, express the relationship of the individual to society. The antithetic nature of the terms involved in this question is another feature that was to recur in Wright's ruminations on his artistic processes and motives.

One of his answers (in "Personalism") is that the new art for art's sake will be different from the older version in that the older was used to bolster "the collapsing spiritual values of the 17th and 18th centuries," the view that art reflected a reality transcendent of the physical but was integral to the essence of humanness. Those values, Wright says, are now long past resuscitation, and the nineteenth-century world that tried to save them by the use of art is itself moribund. Personalism and its use of art for art's sake will differ, apparently, in the greater stress on "personal protest." Wright's view of art for its own sake is a homuncular version of Ellison's later and clearer statement that the very consideration of a work of art as important in itself makes that work a social action. The idea is partly that a work of art is like an individual person, valuable in itself; a society that can accept art for its own sake is also one that can accept the individual person as valuable beyond his mere functionary role in that society, but foremostly the work of art and the individual must be true to themselves, to their own natures. Again and again throughout his writings on artistic expression, Wright stresses that all he could know— and hence express—were his own intense subjective responses to objective conditions. Such a view, that the individual alone, expressing the emotions stirring in him, is the only way in which a relationship between the individual and society can be explored or stated, does not encourage any notion of a "school" of writing. Personalism is, he states, a theory of "extreme individualism." For Wright, with his empirical outlook, reality exists only in the particular, and his poetics looks to a way of "naming," without generalizing, what he has found or experienced in the particular, himself.

Personalism seems an anarchistic aesthetic. Rather than fomenting cohesiveness, it not only stresses "that all values, save the bare organic ones are dead" but emphasizes "tendency rather than form or content." It "represents all forms of revolt in writing," including "the revolt of the petty bourgeoisie against the petty bourgeoisie," as well as "the forces of reaction as they crush the petty bourgeoisie between the bourgeoisie and the working class." Wright wants to produce an "art of attack" as well as of defence. These notions of fluidity, of contending movements and impermanences also recur throughout the search that is his poetics.

Another lasting motif of his poetics and its concern with overcoming the distance between art and reality is indicated in his statement that Personalism will produce an art that will be "anti-literature," that it "will be anti-aesthetic in so far as it will seek to push art beyond mere contemplation. In short, its expression must become an objective act, having immediacy as its aim." Part ot this "immediacy" will be the work's "having implications and consequences in the social sphere," seeking not merely to move readers emotionally but also "to make those who come in contact with it take sides for or against certain *moral* issues." Wright's search always assumes that art can do this only insofar as it coincides with reality as grasped by individuals.

Wright also provides some specifics as to how a personalist writer would achieve these ends, indicating at the same time his cognizance of current artistic theories and also touching on ideas that were to reappear in his later poeticistic musings. Personalism, reflecting its extreme individualism and allegiance to nothing, would be free to "use . . . part or wholes of [all] techniques, such as imagism, symbolism, realism, dadaism, surrealism, etc., as vehicles of expression." But the most emphatic characteristic of personalist method, one he stressed in the text of the typescript essay and also in handwritten notes on the final page, is that

> the basic unit of personalist creation will be the image, that is an emotional perception of reality. The unity, emotional and philosophic, of these images will constitute the ruling symbol of the work. This symbol . . . will carry organically embedded within it the message or judgement of the writer . . . this symbol can be as simple as that used by Japanese writers in their short stories; it can be as complex as that used by Block in his "—and Co.". . . . One of the primary aims of personalism is the integration and resolution of discordant and conflicting impulses . . .
>
> The hallmark of personalism is the audacity of conception. . . . The warring, conflicting, paralyzed, and frustrated impulses of the reader and the writer are . . . postulated in an imaginative, ideal realm where through exaggeration, intensity and manipulation they are resolved into a new, fructifying and positive experience . . .

one of the main sources of strength in a personalist writer lies in his ability to grasp those defeated impulses in the collective individual consciousness which are most important and resolve them in *readily accessible* images, images taken from the common life of the people.

Personalism is a reassertion of the will to live.

That the unity of disparate images is itself a symbol, despite his earlier suggestion that a personalist work would be a chaos, is a seminal notion that runs through all of Wright's later poetics. It is also an idea akin to Burke's definition of symbol in *Counter-Statement:* the symbol of the lyrical *The Tempest,* while "more nearly condensed in the sayings and doings of Ariel," is "essentially a complex attitude that pervades the setting, plot, and characters." Such a symbol is also more intimately related in Wright's thought to the "will to live" than his notes on Personalism indicate. Finally, the references to "images taken from the common life of the people" obviously foreshadow his recommendations regarding folklore in "Blueprint for Negro Writing," and the allusion to the methods of Japanese "short stories" is a portent of his interest in haiku at the end of his life and writing career.

While Wright was never again to use the term "personalism," what these remarks, and others in both unpublished and published form, indicate is that Wright was aware of the need to articulate in a theoretic mode just what his own "voice" was. What his various, uncollated expressions regarding literature and art were attempting also exemplifies a problem faced by all artists—and certainly by black writers.

Wright was explicitly aware of the problem. In the early 1940s, he wrote that one of the first books by a Communist authority to gain his attention in the 1930s was what he calls Stalin's *The National and Colonial Question (Marxism and the National and Colonial Question).* What specifically "enthralled" him was Stalin's account of the Soviet method of gathering the many "backward peoples" of the country into a national unity:

> . . . the Communists had sent phonetic experts . . . to listen to the stammering dialects of peoples oppressed for centuries. . . . I had made the first total emotional commitment of my life when I read how the phonetic experts had given these tongueless people a

language, newspapers, institutions . . . how these forgotten folk had been encouraged to keep their old cultures, to see in their ancient customs meanings and satisfactions as deep as those contained in supposedly superior ways of living . . . how different this was from the way in which Negroes were sneered at in America. (*American Hunger*, p. 82)

In the late 1950s, while emphasizing less the retention of "ancient customs," he still deplored, and spelled out more fully, the language problem:

> The elite of Asia and Africa are truly men without language. . . . It is a psychological language that I speak of. . . . The seizure of his country, its subjugation, the introduction of military rule, another language, another religion—all of these events existed without his interpretation of them. . . . The Asian-African recoil and withdrawal [from "bruising contacts" with whites] have many determinations, the most distinctive and powerful of which is to reorganize their lives in accordance with their own basic feelings. ("The Psychological Reactions of Oppressed People," in *White Man, Listen!*, pp. 36-37, 39)

His published and unpublished expressions of what might be considered a literary theory of his own are obviously attempts to find a "psychological language," a code that did aesthetic justice to his connatural, affective, experiential knowledge of reality, his "basic feelings" that sprang from his existence in a repressed minority group.

Simultaneously, in part because of the canon of literature that had influenced his early literary awareness and whose affect became stronger as he grew older, the sought-after language had also to be one true to his individualistic self. Wright wanted no more to be locked into a prefabricated black language than into a white one, but this was not because of any rejection of black language.

Rather than just the double vision DuBois spoke of as a double-edged attribute of black Americans, Wright was possessed of a triple characteristic: his very strong sense of himself and his freedom to control that self, and his double awareness of the two cultural milieux in which that self had to exist. His titanic impulse was to expropriate the three rather than to be expropriated by them. Only in his agony to shape these could his self be perpetuated.

The practice he advocated for black writers in "A Blueprint for Negro Writing" explicitly indicates such a tripodal stance: "The Negro writer who seeks to function within his race as a purposeful agent has a serious responsibility. In order to do justice to his subject matter, in order to depict Negro life in all its manifold and intricate relationships, a deep, informed, and complex consciousness is necessary; a consciousness which draws for its strength upon the fluid lore of a great people, and moulds this lore with the concepts that move and direct the forces of history today." (p. 57) His formulation of this stance epitomizes Wright's poetics and the focus of this book.

Appearing originally in print where and when it did, this statement obviously seems to refer to a Marxist revamping of Afro-American folklore, but it is on Wright's more purely literary "concepts that move and direct the forces of history today" that our study will dwell. Communism occurs in only a most ideal, philosophical way, as shall be indicated. Early in his self-education, he was awed by the power of language as used by a number of Euro-American masters of prose from Doestoevsky to Dreiser, many of whom he refers to in the "Blueprint" article. We are not equally aware, because he never expressed it in a context as popular or as memorable as *Black Boy*, of the authors and movements that gained his attention because they struck his imaginative perception as having some kind of strange affinity with the system of values and concepts—the schema—which he had experientially assimilated from his southern black American culture. His concern with self and with the two cultures he must deal with led to a dialectical poetics that had three terms: the folkloristic, the avant garde, and the "mood."

As with all classification systems, these categories are devised mostly for the sake of discussion. In actuality, Wright's ruminations concerning a code, a metaphor, or a voice, his interest in the matters of literary expression and the relationship of literature to reality, were more of a gyral, intellectual probing of something central to his psyche, something he felt that he needed to tap if his art were to carry "the air of finality and conviction in every word," if it were to have the impact that the writing of Mencken, Dreiser, and all the others had had on him. It was also something he felt he needed to discover if his work were truly to realize himself in the reality of his apprehension of black American reality. This "something" seems to have remained a recurring mystery for him, although his several attempts to solve it—attempts that fall along one or the other of the three vectors mentioned above—sometimes seemed successful to him.

As Keats said of Coleridge, many might say of Wright: he lacked the quality, essential in a poet, of negative capability. He could not let a fine simile, metaphor, or narrative stand on its own. His complex consciousness needed to be searching after fact and reason to clarify any half-lights or mysteries, whether they involved the motivation of his characters or whether they concerned his own experience. Yet for all his almost passionate public espousal of reason and rational exposition and his practice of rational analysis, Wright was always fascinated by the irrational aspects of life.

His earliest extant published short story, "Superstition," is relevant to this introduction because of its subject matter and its ending. A "holiday" story in the tradition of Dickens's "A Christmas Carol," it deals with the visit on two successive Christmases of an implausible narrator-character to an equally implausible family over which, for no specified reason, there hangs a kind of curse: one of the family will die if ever they all gather under the same roof. During the narrator's two visits, all of the clan does gather, and each time one of them does die. When mentioned at all by Wright scholars and critics, the story is seen as implying a rational explanation of the apparent validity of the superstition: the curse has become a self-fulfilling prophecy, effective on already physically debilitated individuals because of the power given it by the person who dies because of irrational fear. That is the thrust of the story within the story. The enveloping story ends on a much more ambiguous note:

> "In that silence . . . was revealed . . . the fearful hearts of a primitive folk—fearful hearts bowing abjectly to the terror of an unknown created by their own imaginations. . . . The unreasoning fear of death. . . ."
>
> [The narrator] brought his tale to an end. [His audience] simply gazed at him in silence. [The] story allowed no comment; it carried the air of finality and conviction in every word. His two skeptical

listeners sat still and silent, touched to depths . . . by wonder and awe, by something profound and greater than themselves. (p. 73)

Although Wright practically repudiated this piece later in his career, it presents us with his earliest view of his ideal storyteller. It is also notable in that the attitudes behind both the stated and the implied interpretations of the story's curse remained with him. The awareness of "something" greater than anyone can fully grasp, but that is, nevertheless, present in both the "primitive folk" and the more sophisticated narrator and that gives the power to their projections, was at the root of his rational search for a code and for an explanation of what imaginative literature really was for him. The "something" he pursued and the expressive form he sought both to derive from and mould to it are related, in his psyche, to his condition as an Afro-American. That he had such an interest and that it extended to a deep literary form indicates a dimension to his genius that has been overlooked in favor of studying him as a polemicist for the desires, attitudes, and injustices bourne by black Americans and people of color throughout the world. His sense of obligation to use his talents to speak out explicitly on social issues, promoted by the Communist groups that first encouraged his intellectual and writing gifts, and the role of spokesman that literary celebrity afforded him distracted him from his more personal inquisitiveness concerning even deeper questions regarding art.

Distracted him, but never competely deflected him, since he clung to the imperfectly conceivable realization that the subjective personal goal he sought was united to those that were more external. Among his papers in the Beinecke Library are two passages obliquely indicative that, to the end of his life, Wright kept an inner eye on this quest to formulate the power that gave reality to verbal worlds. The first is in a long letter he wrote in 1955 to Edward Aswell, his long-time editor, outlining a plan for an ambitious multi-volume work to be titled "Celebration of Life." It stresses artistic concerns he had iterated in his 1935 manifesto "Personalism" and 1937 "Blueprint." Society, he says, is a human creation and is therefore not some foreign imposition on mankind, yet perversely we as individuals seem to have used our creative powers to produce something that increasingly drains our individuality with its claims, restricting freedom of imagination, feeling and action. We find in his reassertion of this interest a pattern parallel to the complex consciousness—fluid lore—historically effective concepts triad he had outlined in "A Blueprint for Negro Writing." Like that 1937 trivium, this 1955 one is also typically Wrightian in the priority it gives to the individual. In its equally neo-Romantic view of all society as a structure circumscribing the individual, this passage underscores the durability of Wright's abiding concern that he be "named" by no system other than one of his own creation.

The second passage Wright took from Colin Wilson's 1959 book, *Age of Defeat (The Stature of Man)*:

> the answer Faust missed lay in subjectivity, in turning inwards. But it must be immediately admitted that this is only half a solution. . . . The problem of the hero goes deeper than this. It is not simply a question of turning inwards, but of coming to terms with the interior problems *and then turning outwards again*. [Wright's emphasis]. . . . The "new hero" . . . has to learn to heal his self-division. The final hero will be the man who has healed . . . self-division, and is again prepared to fling himself back into the social struggle. (pp. 81-82)

The emphasis he gave to that one phrase reveals his persistent commitment to his life-long, identity-giving struggle with the two external cultures that marked his existence. His copying the rest of the passage suggests his awareness that the tripartite division of a self facing two cultures—of a complex consciousness drawing strength from "the fluid lore of a great people" which it "moulds . . . with [the rationalizations,] the concepts that move and direct the forces of history today" derived from another mode of thought—also existed within himself. Wright did not admire some of the very "lore" he felt he needed to draw his strength from as an artist; he clearly considered it debilitating superstition, an ignorance that restricted Afro-American development. On the other hand, the rational concepts with which he also felt he had to mold that superstition, the impersonal, systematic ways of Euro-American culture that he saw as energizing and controlling modern human behavior were, he came increasingly to realize, themselves debilitating, limiting the free play of the mind and heart. Yet both of these cultures were inveterately ingrained in his character. Wright was not uncritical of the two cultures, cultures that existed not only outside himself but within his psychological makeup and produced a dilemma that was surfacing again in his middle (-life) passage, an ambiguity, ambivalence, or contradiction that had to be reconciled before he could be "again prepared to fling himself . . . into the social struggle" as the dominant hero he wanted to be in that arena.

Insofar as the terms of this inner division, which he had to deal with in order to "write" himself, are analogous to, or metaphoric of, those involved in the blueprint he had verbalized for writing authentic Afro-American literature, this quotation from Wilson's book is symbolic of just how central and continuing, albeit inchoate, his interest in a poetics was. This parallel between the "writing" of himself and the writing of literary works is, however, only one such parallel, for Wright's poetics appears implicitly in at least three of his works that are concerned with neither himself nor with imaginative literature. His concern about the expressive morphology of human creations manifested itself, especially in the later years of his career, in a concern about political forms that expressed the reality of and to the peoples involved. Whether dealing with literature or other mind-made entities, he wanted forms that were products of and amenable to a fixating, Euro-American type of human intelligence and that were still somehow identical to the motile, living, organic versions generated by the minds of "folk," especially as he had encountered the latter in Afro-American culture.

VOICE OF A NATIVE SON

1

POLITICAL FORMS

The root of Richard Wright's poetics is in his Afro-American heritage. It was within him before he had access to the Memphis public library, before his discovery of Mencken's *A Book of Prefaces* and the numerous writers who were revealed to him there, prior even to his decision to be a writer. It was not, however, a root he clearly knew he possessed. Not until after his writing career was well launched did he state, in a preface of his own, the very personal basis of his concern with expressive form.

In 1941, he wrote an essay intended as a preface to his just then completed manuscript, *The Man Who Lived Underground*. This piece of fiction in its original form was almost novel length, and the preface-essay was to relate to it as "How Bigger Was Born" was tied to *Native Son* and "How Uncle Tom's Children Grew" was related to that collection of stories, explaining origins and wider-reaching implications. Judging from what Wright says in this essay, it seems to be, more than either of the earlier prefaces, a spontaneous overflow of feelings resulting from a number of mind-expanding intuitions that occurred as he wrote the novella. Longer than "How Uncle Tom's Children Grew," and less concerned than "How Bigger Was Born" with external conditions, this later essay attempts to sketch more fully Wright's aesthetic development, his interest in language, and his imaginative outlook during the drafting of *The Man Who Lived Underground*.

The publication history of *The Man Who Lived Underground*,

a result of editorial opinions differing from Wright's evalua- tion of it as the most inspired and satisfying piece he had written, obviated the need for a preface to the narrative. The essay, entitled "Memories of My Grandmother," exists there- fore only in manuscript and typescript versions among Wright's unpublished papers. In its unfinished condition, it is a provocative, seminal exposition of experiences and specula- tions concerning Wright's search for the secret of how to pro- duce verbal structures that had the ring of authenticity, a search that was inextricably intertwined with a regard for folk levels of expression.

The essay begins with Wright's stating that the manuscript version of *The Man Who Lived Underground* was most satisfy- ing to him because he felt it to be a work produced more from creative exhilaration than anything he had done. What was inspiring him and finding its way into his writing was a par- ticular something that he could sense but not really define. It was a multi-dimensional and multi-implicational yet single spirit, floating throughout the novella just behind the surface figures and episodes. It melded and, especially, informed them, as the steady throb of the bass fiddle informs all the variations within a jazz piece. This notion of a dominant chord was as central to his experience of his grandmother as she was to a whole chain of semiperceptions that he felt crystalized in this story. There was an indefinable something about her that had reached his semiconsciousness on and off for sixteen years, something that puzzled and often surprised him with the awarenesses it gave him of himself and of his milieu.

The grandmother was Margaret Wilson, his mother's moth- er, the redoubtable little woman with whom Wright lived, at different times, for a number of years and whom he was to make vividly known to readers of *Black Boy*. His paramount remembrance of her was her religious view of life, a Seventh Day Adventist's "other world" orientation. In complete combat with "this world" reality, in her constant struggle to keep it from her and yet to enable her to cope with it, she looked at her environment through the lense of the Old Testament, classify- ing things according to highly undoctrinaire categories she believed derived from that source. Things and events that struck Wright as not being related were often vitally, if fuzzily, blended for her. Obversely, things, ideas, and behaviors that were united for Wright were just as often quite unrelated to her. Radios were the work of the devil, since sounds did not travel through the air unapprehended by human ears. Talking at the table during meals was a sin. Her life seemed unreal to him in a way because she derived meaning, not from objectively experienced relationships or values, but from something outside and alien to experiential reality.

Eugene Genovese, in *Roll, Jordan, Roll*, significantly subtitled *The World the Slaves Made*, gives a kind of reverse example from slavery documents of an attitude similar to what Wright observed in his grandmother and that he eventually attributed to Afro-American folk in general. Slaves, converted to Methodism, which considered dancing sinful, continued to perform the "ring shout" at the "praise house." This looked like dancing to white observers, but "the blacks convinced themselves that they did not dance the shout, for as everyone knows, you cross your feet when you dance; . . . since they did not tolerate crossing of feet, they clearly were not dancing." This alteration of dancing involved as much of an adjustment of Methodism as the slaves "adjusted every other creed, to their own way of life." (p. 234)

Although enraged by the high-handed effect it frequently had on his own life and repulsed by the religious, illogical format in which her attitude was manifested, Wright was also fascinatedly baffled by this trait at the core of his grandmother's personality. It was not just simply religion. What motivated her, he felt, was something that lay behind her obvious and pervasive religious consciousness. In trying to name what he sensed but could not fully grasp, he sought for years to go "nudist," as Kenneth Burke would put it, to strip away phenomenal stereotypic Negro religious behavior, to get at the essentials of it. The striping was also a reclothing of this essential something, not in an already established literary form, but in a kind of verbal ceremony, a dynamic outline that would inevitably veil yet reveal it, like the bandages on the movies' Invisible Man. In terms of current literary theory, he sought to rewrite/revise her text.

Leading to his sense that it was not her religious encoding of experience that was the ultimately important thing, and perhaps feeding the mildly obsessive fascination-revulsion syndrome that characterized his relationship with his grandmother, was his discernment of the paradox that this same conceptual and verbal behavior he had attributed to his grandmother's strict religious outlook was also evident in the blues. These songs, earthy and definitely of this world, completely anathema to her, consisted of verses that in themselves said little, had nothing in common with each other, and were included in the same song for no apparent reason. Something extrinsic to them, an emotional atmosphere, was brought to bear on the verses and give them meaning.

This function, Wright says of his grandmother and, by extension, of all Afro-American folk, indicated some mysterious necessity in her, to the extent that he saw it as one defining characteristic of Afro-American thought and emotional processes. Unremarked by Wright, although the impulse behind the essay up to this point is apparent, is that he did not possess it sufficiently. It was something in the spontaneous black American "folk psyche." To his perception, he was not able to manifest it satisfactorily until *The Man Who Lived Underground*, a story that brought together, although not in autobiographical garb (not in sensory forms mimetic of those in which they had first entered his consciousness), a variety of his disparate experiences.

In addition to his sense of having created or arrived at some kind of dynamic contour adequately expressive of his grandmother's personality, a contour also connected with the blues and hence one that gave him a closer approximation to their essence and to the essence of the black American psyche, his writing of *The Man Who Lived Underground* further enlightened him regarding what he calls his early attraction to "The Invisible Man" movies. Since he would have been about twenty-five when the first of these movies was made, his statement raises some questions about this remembrance and perhaps about the entire memoir. Wright was aware of these questions and includes a caveat regarding the sequential accuracy of these memories that were written some time after the fact. In any case, he was fascinated with these movies, and he links his fascination to his impression of his grandmother's belief in unseen realities, in "other world" verities, despite his early rejection of her overt religious dogmas. He came to realize that these movies, which greatly stimulated his feelings and his imagination, were related to folkloric interpretations of life as told to him by his mother and grandmother. This lore spoke of an unseen world that impacted on the visible, a kind of invisible gallery one could occupy to view this world.

Although later in the essay he speaks of more direct literary and aesthetic theories (which we shall take up in a subsquent chapter) that also came to fruition in the drafting of *The Man Who Lived Underground*, it is clear from his references to religion, to the blues, to traits of thinking found in Negroes generally, and, above all, to folklore, that what was at the basis of his satisfaction with his novella was that he felt he had tapped something at the heart of folk expression, something that gives such expression, or at least Afro-American folk expression, its power. He tells us in *American Hunger* that, when he was beginning his apprenticeship as a writer in Chicago, one thing he desparingly sought was "a level of expression that matched those of the novels [he] read," a level of expression that captured "a physical state or movement that carried a strong subjective impression." (pp. 21-22) He wanted to produce a "vast, delicate, intricate, and psychological structure" equal in thoroughness to what he found in Proust, for one, but he wanted "to write of the people in [his own] environment." (p. 24)

The "something" that he describes in "Memories of My Grandmother," that lay behind his grandmother's attitude toward life and the attitude of black folk in general, was therefore essential to this goal. This "something" was necessary to give his work a power of expression equal to what he detected in the classical works of fiction he was reading, an oxymoronic emotion-concept that would give meaning to the assemblage of words and images he put on paper. His grandmother had it, as did the anonymous blues composers, and it enabled them to give a reality to the very worlds they created, the kind of reality he strove to give his works: "I strove to master words, to make them disappear, to make them important by making them new, to make them melt into a rising spirit of emotional stimuli, each greater than the other, each feeding and reinforcing the other, and all ending in an emotional climax that would drench the reader with a sense of a new world." (*American Hunger*, p. 22) Such a passage, read with knowledge of his grandmother's influence on his poetic development, underscores religious ritual rather than physical sex as the analog of his ideal of literary creativity.

While the memoir poses some problems of credibility, Wright's interest and belief in a subjective folk power to create worlds, religious or secular, was expressed before this 1941 essay in his 1936 review of Arna Bontemps's *Black Thunder*, a novel dealing with Gabriel Prosser's slave revolt in 1800:

> Gabriel . . . is convinced that God and the universe are on his side. He believes he will lead the Negro people to freedom. . . . he believes even when he is caught; even when the black cowl is capped about his head, even when the ax swings, he believes. Why?
> . . . the cardinal value of Bontemps' book . . . is the answer to that question . . . we have in *Black Thunder* a revelation of the very origin and source of folk values in literature . . . [in Gabriel's attitude] is something which transcends the limits of immediate consciousness . . . He hopes when there are no objective reasons or grounds for hope. . . . Bontemps endows Gabriel with a mythlike and deathless quality. ("A Tale of Folk Courage," p. 31)

His story "Superstition" is an additional and even earlier testament to this belief in the efficacy of subjective power and its presence in the folk psyche. While seeming to deplore this capacity because it is irrational, the story ends by paying tribute to it. The "sceptical listeners," as well as, one assumes, the tale's teller who had given "conviction" to the story, are moved to "wonder and awe." Wright has them acknowledging the existence of something very deep and "greater than themselves." In this story, this "something" is clearly labled an emotion; it is the "terror of the unknown," and the "unknown" here is "death." The "unreasoning fear of death" is so powerful that it is able to overcome life. It not only creates the very form of the thing unknown but a form that has a concretely real existence (insofar as death can be said to have existence), just as his grandmother's outlook was able to shape, for her, a wholly new world out of elements whose actual existence she refused to acknowledge.

Although told by a character who is purportedly a sophisticated, urbane businessman and dealing with a family composed likewise of business people, a family that lives in a house large enough to accommodate not only the entire reunited family but also a guest, occupying rooms with individual fireplaces, a family that has dinner at eight every evening, the story is a kind of folktale, updated and adapted for Wright's own purposes. The superstition-ridden family, in spite of the attributes and amenities listed above, is referred to by the narrator as "these primitive folk." Even the tale's fictional audience, supposedly educated and worldly, as well as the enlightened narrator, recognize their lives as grounded in mystery, the mystery of intense feeling, the mystery that human beings could be capable of creating such a real force. It is as though these individuals had a kind of emotional hydrogen bomb within them and were capable of releasing prodigeous energies; that they were deplorable in their ability to exceed all bounds and yet admirable for the creativity implict in that same ability.

This intense energy, manifested in a feeling, was not something Wright sought or was interested in only in his younger years. Nor, in spite of his reference to its giving rise to "Forms of Things Unknown" in a context discussing the literature of the Negro in the United States, did he restrict it only to manifestation in artistic expression or verbal and musical artifacts of black Americans. His use of the phrase, "Forms of Things Unknown," indicates that he was envisioning behind these forms a power that frequently bears another label. As Shakespeare put it,

> . . . as imagination bodies forth
> The forms of things unknown, the poet's pen
> Turns them to shapes, and gives to airy nothing
> A local habitation and a name.
> Such tricks hath strong imagination,
> That, if it would but apprehend some joy,
> It comprehends some bringer of that joy;
> Or in the night, imagining some fear,
> How easy is a bush supposed a bear!
> (*A Midsummer Night's Dream*, Act V, sc. 1)

Wright believed, as Shakespeare seemed to, in a two stage manifestion of this power. First is its ability to "body forth" what for want of a better term can be called notions: intimations, anterior to language of any sort, of "more than cool reason ever comprehends." This operation, reinforced by the context in which Shakespeare has Theseus make such a comment, Wright saw as a power well known to uneducated folk. The second stage, the idolization of these intimations, according to Shakespeare, requires a poet, a lunatic, or a lover. Important to our understanding of Wright's poetics is a study of how he lengthened, or at least altered, this list of shapers. As his references to his grandmother indicate, one of the strongest and most common of these additional shapers is the priest or the religious zealot. Still another is the politician or statesman. In the last decade of his life, Wright's continuing interest in this "something" was revealed in his concern with these latter two shapers.

In the mid-1950s, he wrote three works—*Black Power, The Color Curtain*, and *Pagan Spain*—journalistic, analytic travelogues of journies to three countries, countries he knew little about and that he chose, at least on two occasions, rather randomly and impulsively. These books suggest that he was somewhat less than open-minded. Coming to these countries with the mind-set that is his poetics, he reads these countries— or, perhaps, "writes" them—in terms similar to those he had used regarding his grandmother and her importance in his search for the "something" that would enable him to give authenticity to his writings. Ghana, Indonesia (indeed, all of Asia at the Bandung conference) and Spain readily lent themselves to the kind of analysis he had applied to his grandmother because of the prominence of religion in their cultures, a fact Wright must have been aware of initially when briefing himself for the visits. In each of the books, he focuses on religion and politics. In each of these studies, as in his memoir of his grandmother which was written fifteen years earlier, he is concerned with what lies behind the obvious forms that highlight the personality of the entity, whether human or political, being experienced. In each case, he found "something" very much like what he had discerned in her—an energetic force perceived as an intense feeling, with which national leaders must rationally find or devise the contour, but in governmental forms.

At the heart of *Black Power: A Record of Reactions in a Land of Pathos*—indeed, implicit in the book's title—are constant references to a quality manifest in black folk, although in this case they are African rather than Afro-American. From the moment he sets foot in Ghana, and even while on his way to that country, he speaks in terms of a strong religous element in Africans, an element that he comes to see eventually in the masses of Ghanaians in a more basic form: intense emotion that is the foundation of their lives. The book, because it was hastily edited from a journal of his trip, gives the impression that he needed only a day or two, one quick auto tour of Accra, and attendance at a brief politcal rally to bring home to him the "wild and liquid emotion" (p. 56) that he saw as the source of Nkrumah's political power. The crowds of children, men, and "washerwomen, cooks, housewives" who spontaneously flock around Nkrumah's auto are "passionate" in their cries of "Free-doom!" and "Kwame!" and "Welcome!" and in their loyalty.

Kwame Nkrumah had not created this power. Later in the book, Wright speaks of it as a "primal attitude" (p. 267) that had given rise to a tribal culture, a formulation that seemed to provide meaning to the lives of the people but really only gave a local habitation to its real meaning, their affective, subjective knowledge. In Wright's view, as expressed in *Black Power*, this "primal attitude" owes nothing to a mystical or metaphysical origin. The "persistence and vitality of primal attitudes" are the result of social causes, but they also seem to have, for Wright, some basis in biological nature. Awed by the African climate and the lush, free, open life it spawns, most sublimely in the sixty-foot-high walls of jungle that lie just beyond Ghana's barren coastal plains, he was led to the conclusion that "Life in Africa must handle life; life here is just bare, sentient life; life is all that life has in Africa. . . . Here instinct ruled and flowered without being concerned with the nature of the physical structure of the world; man lived without too much effort; there was nothing to distract him from concentrating upon the currents and countercurrents of his heart." (p. 159)

Wright finds that these "currents and countercurrents" of feeling are closely allied to "association of images": "The tribal mind is sensuous: loving images, not concepts; personalities, not abstractions; movement, not form.". . . . System is the enemy of the tribal mind; action proceeds on the basis of association of images; if feeling is absent, the tribal African mind is in doubt." (pp. 264-65)

The African reacted to his sense of reality as feeling, as emotional subjectivity, by projecting "out of himself what he thought he was" and so established a social world: "There is no way to check one's perceptions or feelings against any objective standard [in this setting]. What one feels, one's neighbor also feels instantaneously by the mere fact of communication, for, in that state, to feel something is to make it true. What one imagines, instantly exists. What one fears comes immediately into being. Thought and feeling become omnipotent." (p. 257)

As in his grandmother and the blues composer, Wright saw in the tribal African "a deep predilection toward the omnipotence of thought, of spirit acting on spirit (pp. 223-24) . . . [he] transforms that which he touches into something else which is his and his alone." (p. 265) He also was seen by Wright as possessing "an intuitive grasp of life dictated by endemic wisdom, tracing relationships between objects that really had no relations, but establishing such relations." (p. 336) And, again like Grandmother Wilson, the "African had projected an invisible world out of himself and he was living in and reacting to that world." (p. 245)

In a discussion of African survivals in the New World, Wright makes a further connection, this time much more explicit, between such a folk impulse and that which motivates formal artistic creations. Just how African traits could have survived after several hundred years of transplantation in a new cultural area such as the United States is a question that surfaced in his mind in the motorcade with Nkruma. He noticed many of the African women along the route performing a kind of foot-shuffling dance that struck him as very familiar: "I'd seen these same snakelike, veering dances before . . . in America, in storefront churches, in Holy Roller Tabernacles, in God's Temples, in unpainted wooden prayer-meeting houses on the plantations of the Deep South. . . . How could that be?" (pp. 56-57)

Later, he comes up with an answer that avoids metaphysics

as well as typing Negroes as peculiar, exotic primitives; it assigns a universality to these primal attitudes:

> The African attitude toward life springs from a natural and poetic grasp of existence and all the emotional implications that such an attitude carries; . . . what the anthropologists have been trying to explain are not "African survivals" at all—they are but the retention of basic and primal attitudes toward life. . . . The question of how much African culture an African retains when transplanted to a new environment is not a social, but a cultural problem.
>
> . . . There is no reason why an African or a person of African descent—in America, England, or France—should abandon his primal outlook upon life if he finds that no other way of life is available, or if he is intimidated in his attempt to grasp the new way. . . . The tribal African's culture *is* primarily human; that *all* men once had as their warm, indigenous way of living . . .
>
> If the American Negro retained, in part and for a time, remnants of his background of traditional African attitude, it was because he couldn't see or feel or trust (at that moment in history) any other system of value or belief that could interpret the world and make it meaningful enough for him to act and rely upon it . . . The social scientist . . . would discover that the same primal attitudes exist among other people; after all, what are the basic promptings of artists, poets, and actors but primal attitudes consciously held? (pp. 266-67)

While Wright, in these passages, seems to approve this "primal attitude," he was no more sympathetic to the extrinsic forms in which it had been realized, or to which it had given validity to traditional African culture, than he had been to the forms it took in his grandmother's life. At best, he showed the same ambivalence toward this attitude that he had written in "Superstition." Insofar as the formal tribal culture this "primal attitude" gave rise to was essentially religious, Wright, at times, seems to be finding fault with the attitude itself. He was indignant, however, at the British and other European outrageous "imperialist actions" and "crimes of the highest order," subjugating the Africans, that had ruined forever the traditional lives of these people, "slain something that they could never rekindle" (p. 60). Christianity, colonial government, and, to some extent, modern commerce and education had irrevocably undermined the older forms, derived from and commanding a certitude of passion, that had given the culture its shape. Furthermore, what the foreign tenets and practices had supplied instead were not forms to which the Africans could—or, in most cases, were allowed to—give themselves totally.

On the positive side, the Europeans' smashing of this tribal culture, especially that form of it which invested the chiefs with political power derived from supposedly supernatural sources and ancestors, opened up a way for the Ghanaians to enter into the twentieth century. Nkrumah's genius, and the reason for Wright's hope in him as the man capable of shaping his country and perhaps all of Africa into a bright future along lines distinctly non-Western, lay in his ability and willingness to identify with the African folk, to realize their motivating "something." The Europeans, whether secular government individuals or religious missionaries, because of a sense of their own racial or cultural superiority, had been unable to relate the political and religious forms they supplied to this force. They never realized that they "had created a vacuum in these people's hearts," leaving an imagination/emotional/"spiritual" wasteland for them to inhabit, the kind of wasteland typical of Western culture itself, devoid of social forms intimately linked to the vitality of the people. Nkrumah had "the intellectual daring" to realize that such a vacuum existed and showed promise of projecting a "new structure for the lives of these people," a structure of twentieth-century caliber but one that to a large extent bore enough resemblance to this "something" to command the heartfelt allegiance of the masses: "Nkruma was tapping the abandoned emotional reservoir that Christian religon had no use for." (p. 61)

In Nkrumah, Wright seems to have sensed a man who was aware of the need to seek the dynamic outline of religion's interior reality, as Wright had tried to do in the case of his grandmother in an effort to shape a fiction that was real. Nkrumah's relationship to this reservoir is presented in terms highly reminiscent of those Wright had used to picture his attempts to understand what drove his grandmother:

> Behind Nkrumah's successful political organizing was something much deeper and more potent than the mere influence of Marxist thought . . . the twentieth century was throwing up these

mass patterns of behavior out of the compulsiveness of men's disin-
herited lives. These men were not being so much guided as they
were being provoked by elements deep in their own personalities,
elements which they could not have ignored even if they had tried
. . . there burned in these black hearts a hunger to regain control
over their lives and create a new sense of their identities. . . .

What I had seen was not politics proper . . . it bordered upon
religion; it involved a total and basic response to reality; it smacked
of the dream-like, of the stuff of which art and myths were made.
. . . Nkrumah himself was but an *agent provocateur* to the emotions
of millions—emotions which even he did not quite grasp or understand in all their ramifications. (pp. 91-92)

Another person he writes of, the British educated Ghanaian,
Dr. J. B. Danquah, also sounds much like a version, albeit
negative, of Wright himself in his search for authentic expressive form. Dr. Danquah, author of *The Akan Doctrine of God*, a
study of the area's native religion, would seem to be, like
Nkrumah, an ideal candidate to derive this "contour." He
seems to possess two of the traits necessary for producing a
truly Negro political "literature," for "writing" a truly black
African state. Formally educated, he would have had access to
"the concepts that move and direct the forces of history today."
Also, he would have maintained a closeness to the "fluid lore of
a great people" by his intellectual analysis of it. In terms that
echo those that Wright used to outline the development of an
authentic American Negro literature, the shortcomings of this
Ghanaian are laid out: "The good doctor's grasp of life was
essentially poetic; it was close to that which our fantasies and
day dreams would have reality be; its essence was woven out of
what we call human traits. Yet, he would pit himself against
his political adversaries, if he would win a struggle for the
liberation of his country, he would have to lay aside such poetic
preoccupations and adopt more realistic measures." (p. 222)

The term "poetic," which Wright uses to characterize the
doctor's mind, is not a completely approbative designation.
This "poetic" level of mentality, as he indicates in the above
passage and the earlier one dealing with Nkrumah, borders on
being a religious mentality, but it is secularized by a permeation of varying intensities of reason. One problem with "the

good doctor," which makes him both the reverse image of Wright and unsuitable as a leader in Wright's estimation, is that, in spite of his official Christianity and his intellectualization of Akan religion, he still practices it to some extent. That is, he still is caught in the "outer processes" of religion. While the doctor's "outer processes" of religion might be more intellectual, they are removed from the irrationality of the religious form only to the level of being "poetic." That degree of secularization still leaves the doctor's mentality, in Wright's view, too close to the "fluidity" of the folk mind and hence unlikely to create a truly black nation of the twentieth century, according to the blueprint Wright had laid out for literature and was repeating in this book on African politics.

Wright is not without respect for the doctor, just as he was not without a certain regard for his grandmother, in spite of the irrationality of the outer forms that they adopted to express this inner "something" that is the core of reality for humans. He seems to feel that while all such religious forms are faulty expressions or contours of this reality, the one held by the doctor has more merit than the one manifested in his grandmother's life because the doctor's higher degree of intellectualization contains a higher potential for compassion: "It's rare in our world today to feel that the sky has value over and above that of space to be conquered, and that the earth means something more than an object out of which to dig minerals, or that human personality is something beyond a mere consumptive-productive unit." (p. 222)

The element of compassion that Wright implies here as an integral strand of the poetic outlook is definitely the result of an influx of humanistic reasoning into the religious attitude. His grandmother possessed no such compassion; one of her remarkable irrationalities in his opinion was that she had no sensitivity to individuals while professing a devotion to the salvation of souls in general.

Compassion does not mold or interpret the fluid "something" rightly enough, however; it is not one of the "concepts" that moves and directs the forces of history today. Wright makes his view on this matter clear in *The Color Curtain*, describing a young Asian who sounds very similar to the Ghanaian Dr. Danquah. This young man was also given a formal, Western, but humanistic education, one that fostered rationality only to a certain "poetic" level. The result, with all its inadequacies to the task of creating an authentically "colored" and authentically modern nation, was that "compassion was this Asian's hallmark. If the future of the masses of Asia were to be in the hands of aristocratic spirits such as this Indonesian educator, then one could say that the bridge between lives anchored in mysticism and lives built on a secular and industrial reason could be erected with a minimum of tragedy and human waste. But neither Asia nor Africa nor Europe was . . . likely to be ruled by compassionate aristocrats." (p. 54)

In the case of this Asian, unlike that of Dr. Dunquah, the problem with the "poetic" mind is summed up in the adjective "aristocratic." A "poetic" mind is rational enough to be too distant from the primal attitude for its constructs to have the exact contour of that attitude and so command the allegiance of the folk. Instead of such aristocratic mentalities leading these new nations, it is more likely to be, in Wright's opinion, false prophets, "messianic men" who will present the masses with "irresponsible interpretations" of their condition—offer them pseudo-religious forms that are closer to the religious mentality the folk are used to but that can be used to manipulate the masses for the benefit of the messiahs.

In the passages on Dr. Danquah and Nkrumah quoted above, Wright indicates that the "poetic" mind, depending on the admixture of reason, is capable of producing, in addition to compassion, such forms as "the dream-like," "fantasies and day dreams," "art and myths." Such forms, however, while they might permit bankers' daughters to weep over them, are not true enough to the essence of what they attempt to name; they do not, Wright might have said, justify, or are not worthy of justification by, that "something" in either a literature or a nation of the modern era. What he seems to be reaching for is a form produced by a modern rationality that is at the opposite extreme from the irrationality that produces the religious form expressive of this a-rational primal reality-sense. Yet in a Mobius-strip-like way, this ideal Wrightian rationality is a double of that irrationality, as it is of the a-rationality behind the whole human psyche. This sameness-with-a-difference

17

renders it capable of producing a rational form that corresponds to the a-rational reality-sense, but it is a form free of "superstition," a form equal not only to this primal human "something" but also in conformity with the forces directing modern history.

The significance and the persistence of the pattern of Wright's thought which amounts to his poetics is further demonstrated by the appearance of that pattern in both *The Color Curtain* (1955) and *Pagan Spain* (1956). In both books, he focuses on a subsurface element in the cultures. If the main title of *The Color Curtain: A Report on the Bandung Conference* means anything, it is the power at the base of the predominately Asian culture, distinguishing that culture from the West and making it difficult for the West to understand, a power that bears a strong resemblance to the force that Wright half-saw and half-created as motivating his grandmother and the Ghanaians.

The subject of Wright's book, the 1955 international conference of Asian and African leaders called to discuss the direction their recently decolonized countries should go, "represented mankind negatively freed from its traditions and customs." (p. 207) By these "traditions and customs," he seems to mean those cultural forms that developed during three hundred years of alien domination. Deprived of these, however willingly, and now unable to give credence to those that had anciently seemed to give phenomenal reality to his existence, the "uprooted Easterner" is "rendered psychologically uncertain as to motive" and does "everything self-consciously, watching himself, as it were." The removal of these cultural forms reveals the basic, central power or "something" that make the Asian "tick": "Behavior was spontaneous only when passionate action lifted him to the place of self-forgetfulness. Hence to feel a thing deeply made that thing the worthwhile thing to do, indeed, made it the *right* thing to do." (p. 75)

This deep feeling that confers reality is, however, also loosed from more rational expressive forms, "loosed in terms of defensive, *irrational feelings*." (p. 207) Wright certainly recognized that these Western forms never affected greatly the expressive forms of this "something" held or created by the folk people. His concern here is with Asians who, like himself, stood between two worlds—the energetic, physical world of the unedu-

18

cated, indigenous masses and the abstract, logical one of the European-influenced and educated elite. His kindest references to the native cultures are that they are "poetic," indicating for Wright, as we have seen, an inferior degree of rationality, one that leaves these cultures quite opaque to the more, but not fully or optimally, rational gaze of Westerners. This deep feeling, having disengaged its realizing power for the elite from the folk forms of culture, but having kept it there for the masses whom the elite hoped to govern, was therefore in Wright's view too encoded for both groups in the highly irrational religious expressive form. The strength of Hinduism, Buddhism, and Mohammedism in the lives of these nations and representatives at Bandung was overwhelmingly apparent. Along with this irrational form, however, Wright discerned another: race. Both, he feared, would render these people incapable of creating twentieth-century states that would be strong and real:

> Have racial and religious feelings already set in so deeply in Asia and Africa that it would be impractical to transform and attach them to secular and practical goals? What would be the ultimate results of welding this Asian consciousness with its present content of race and religion on to techniques of the twentieth century? Was not Japanese Fascism the flower of such incongruous grafting of plants of different genres? There is no indication that the Japanese abandoned any of their earlier mystical notions when they embraced the disciplines of science and the techniques of modern industrial production. It is not difficult to imagine Moslems, Hindus, Buddhists, and Shintoists launching vast crusades, armed with modern weapons, to make the world safe for their mystical notions. (p. 218)

But this elemental force, heeded most closely by the folk, was definitely something that had to be answered, if any of the social, economic, and governmental forms devised by the leaders of these nations were to have a reality for, and hence the allegiance of, the masses: "Who can harness this force? . . . Bandung was not concerned with how to take power. ALL THE MEN THERE REPRESENTED GOVERNMENTS THAT HAD ALREADY SEIZED POWER AND THEY DID NOT KNOW WHAT TO DO WITH IT." (p. 208) They did not, in other words, have a poetics, and rather clearly not Wright's own poetics.

The essential, reality-creating or conferring power that establishes the need for a poetics in a fitting expressive form also underlies Wright's thinking in *Pagan Spain*. This book's reflections of the ideology and themes of *The Color Curtain* are no doubt so obvious because Wright interrupted his study of Spain to attend the Bandung conference. *Pagan Spain's* relationship to the studies of his grandmother and of Ghana is more remote than that of the other two, but it is no less extant and provides still further insight into his poetics and the persistence of his mind-set.

Like his grandmother, Spain, in whatever historical period, had always been "beleaguered by modern ideas, stormed by the forces of social and political progress . . . [and] had had to withdraw . . . [to] find some acceptable forms of endurable life." (p. 240) Like his grandmother also, Spain had, over the years, devised a form that could come to terms with and unite an array of disparate elements. Like his grandmother, it had come up with a form so dear to people who were close to a folk level of (ir-) rationality—religion: "All of [Spain] . . . had come from one (and perhaps unrepeatable) historical accident . . . compounded in Rome from Greek science and love of the human personality, from the Jewish notions of a One and Indivisible God, from Roman conceptions of law and order and property, and from a perhaps never-to-be-unraveled amalgamation of Eastern and African religions with their endless gods who were sacrificed and their virgins who gave birth perennially." (p. 240)

To encompass all of this, "the Inquisition" had provided an all-inclusive, if irrational, form. It was a form, however, that, like his grandmother's religion, also kept intact what Wright calls "the muddy residue of an irrational paganism that lurked at the bottom of the Spanish heart." (p. 240) As with his grandmother, Wright "soon discovered . . . and to his own dismay, that calling things by their right names in the area of Spanish reality, an area charged with passion and the quicksands of subjectivity, was no easy matter." (p. 194) Like his grandmother, the Spanish Falange and Catholic church started from "idiotic" and "metphysical assumptions" totally alien to anyone who "accepted living in an even somewhat rational world." (p. 194)

Like the ideal modern Negro writer, described by Wright in

1937, "who seeks to function within his race as a purposeful agent," the government of Spain in the mid-twentieth century is seen by Wright as having the responsibility of molding its "paganism," the fluid core of the Spanish people, with concepts driving the forces of history today. Unfortunately, in Wright's view, while twentieth-century Spain, that is "the Falange, the State, the Army and the Church . . . had been shaped by, and [was] drawing [its] vitality from some deep irrational core that made up the heart of Spanish reality" (p. 192), it was not seeking a mobile contour of this fluid emotion, a flexible contour of twentieth-century concepts that directed the way of the modern world yet breathed this dynamism. Instead of thus producing a new-old, rationally irrational form with the ring of authenticity, which the educated as well as the folk masses could respond to with their reality-giving belief, Spain had withdrawn into a fixed and highly irrational lore, yet not, even in these terms, adequate to express the ultimate reality-sense:

> Spain was a holy nation, a sacred state—a state as sacred and as irrational as the sacred state of the Akan in the African jungle. . . . *All was religion in Spain.* . . . The boundaries of Spanish religiosity went *beyond* the Church. . . . An early and victorious Catholicism, itself burdened with deep traits of a paganism that it had sought vainly to digest, had here been sucked into the maw of a paganism buried in the hearts of the people. (pp. 192-93)

As in the other countries he had visited, Wright did find evidence of the "poetic," but rather than allowing it to mark a small degree of rationality, flawed by a distance from reality, he interpreted it to reinforce his view that everything in Spain was religious. He discovered the term "poetic" used in a Falangist political tract that was styled as a catechism for young girls:

WHAT DO WE MEAN BY POETIC IMPERATIVE?
An inward force that always leads us to prefer the beauty of things.
AND BY THE MERE FACT OF CHOOSING THE BEAUTIFUL, THIS PREFERENCE WILL BE MANIFEST?
Yes, for all that is beautiful tends toward perfection and in choosing the beautiful we also choose what is perfect.
BUT IS THE AIM PERFECTION?

Certainly, for what is perfect is just, what is just is good, and what is good is fit and proper.
WHY MUST FALANGISTS OBEY THE POETIC IMPERATIVE TO BE REAL FALANGISTS?
Because the Falange is, in itself, a poetic movement. . . . The Falange does not seek ornament in poetry, but seeks in poetry, or in superior creation, the solution of all its problems. (pp. 231-32)

The Falange's strategy as depicted here was close to what his own mind-set called for; disturbingly close, no doubt, for this was a Fascist regime. He had also read *The Mass Psychology of Fascism* by Wilhelm Reich, about whom more will be said in chapter 8.

Such a passage reveals Wright's poetics in even more subtle ways. The more obscure relations to the pattern of his own poetic thought are in his handling of this and other passages from this catechism. Throughout *Pagan Spain* he inserted selections from it, often with no commentary on the selections and without their seeming to have any obvious connection with the surrounding context. This technique, in addition to its resemblance to the way, in his view, his grandmother and the blues composers worked, is similar to a device he had outlined, just before setting out for Ghana, to his agent and his editor, a literary device that was to tie together his proposed multi-volume magnum opus. More will be said about this device in a later chapter dealing with the "mood" vector of his poetics. Of immediate relevance here, and demonstrating the more obvious way in which the passage relates to his own poetics, is that it shows his own awareness of the analogy between the formation of a state and the formation of a literary work. Given his view of the "poetic" in the earlier works discussed here, we can see how he found in this selection further evidence of Spain's and the "poetic" literary artist's inadequate approach to the problem of creating a modern and attractive form, a form that was credible and would sweep the people up into the modern world, a new world.

In September 1956, after his return to France from his Third World travels, the presence of this thought pattern was also reflected in a question he raised at the First Congress of Negro Artists and Writers concerning the extent to which folk religious beliefs and tribal customs could be used in the African struggle against Western colonization: "'What could have been done to protect [African culture], perhaps changing the elements which seemed too subjective in that culture [,] purging it to make it more objective, and hence a more useful as a tool.'" (Fabre, *Unfinished Quest*, p. 436) This question hardly seems the rejection of his "Blueprint for Negro Writing" that conference participants and scholars have since alleged. Fabre, furthermore, states that Wright was disappointed that no "concrete action [was] planned to blend national traditions with modern rationalism." (p. 4) Unlike Wright, however, the Congress seems to have been held back by its own strong African sense of negritude, in his eyes a "too mystical" and hence politically ineffective clinging to unalloyed folk forms. These black minds could offer him no path in his renewed search for a "black form", whether political or literary, and, like the confreres at Bandung, they revealed their own lack of a poetics.

Whether early or late in his career, whether concerned with literary or social forms of expressing it—whether he called it "black power," "a primal attitude," a "curtain," or "paganism"—this "something" that he first encounters in his grandmother and that is at the basis of his poetics, this fluid, intense feeling at the center of human mental life which provides the touchstone of reality, is also alluded to by Wright in another writing. These scattered remarks give his more explicit conceptual sense of the internal nature of this "something" than do any "contour" of it he might have embodied in his fiction.

As indicated above, in his earliest (1931) extant published work, "Superstition," he dwelled quite openly on this emotion, calling it a "terror"—the unknown, death. In *How Bigger Was Born*, he was able to be more direct. He describes trying to develop more clearly "the shadowy outlines" (p. 16) of his folk protagonist, a figure that was "shadowy" and practically raw since "the civilization which had given birth to Bigger contained no spiritual sustenance, had created no culture that could hold and claim his allegiance and faith" (p. 18). In literary terms, no expressive form existed for Wright to use to contour this emotion. It was what he was trying to create. Unlike Wright's grandmother, Bigger is without even the irrational but formulating rituals and symbols of black folk culture. He is the most direct, the fullest, literary contour of that "something" which Wright was able to produce at that point in his career. Bigger, like the later Ghanaians and Indonesians, was negatively freed by Wright (who saw it as society's work) from all traditional forms and customs so that Wright could start with "another level of Bigger's life . . . a level as elusive to discuss as it was to grasp in writing." (p. 26) Even the fluidity of speech, let alone the fixed, stationary nature of writing, is scarcely up to expressing the "something" that "seems to hover somewhere in that dark part of all our lives, in some more than others, an objectless, timeless, spaceless element of primal fear and dread . . . a fear and dread which exercises an impelling influence upon our lives all out of proportion to its obscurity." (pp. 26-27)

In this context Wright allows, parenthetically, that perhaps the Freudian birth trauma offers an explanation for the origin of this fear, but he does not indicate his acceptance of such an explanation. He does continue with a characterization of this "fear" which ties it to his account of his grandmother and Gabriel Prosser and to what he would say in the future about the basis of the lives of Ghanains, Indonesians, and Spanish: "Accompanying this *first fear* is, for want of a better name, a reflex urge toward ecstacy, complete submission, and trust. The springs of religion are here, and also the origins of rebellion." (p. 27)

While Wright did not refer explicitly to the motivating force in his grandmother's psychic life or to what lay behind the blues composers' constructs as "primal fear," his comments on that force's effect, especially on her behavior, is comparable to what he said about the people of Ghana and the "primal attitude" behind their animistic, religious outlook. In *Black Power*, he makes an implicit link between the "primal attitude" of his grandmother and the "primal fear" motivating Bigger. Observing an African funeral that impressed him even as it disconcerted him with the wildness of its irrational symbolism, he shortly thereafter visited an African Christian service whose pallidness appalled him even more. He speculated that "if religion partakes of the terror stemming from the proximity of human life to eternity, to an absolute otherness, then there was . . . much more genuine religion in that barbaric pagan funeral than I could find in this quiet, bourgeois Christian church!" (p. 133)

Wright mused no further here about the nature of this "absolute otherness" in whose face the human being's sense of reality is triplet-born along with its emotional equivalent, terror, and its simultaneous action, creativity. Elsewhere in his writings, it appears as "the unknown," "death," "something greater" than ourselves. The "other," in the form of a hostile, alienating white society, confrontation that inspires in black Americans a terrified sense of their own reality is, of course, a staple of his best-known works. The path of his thinking does not lead, however, to the conclusion that white society is an absolute, except insofar as it is associated with death. Wright's thinking on this point, although it started with something observed in black Americans and black American culture, clearly expanded to the degree that objective racial confrontation was seen as one manifestation of a deeper, more subjective reality, as a very real response to this subjective confrontation and one that is, in most instances, as irrational and faulty a response as is religion. That is why his later novels—*The Outsider* and *Savage Holiday,* as well as his contemplated magnum opus—made less of purely racial matters and became more "existential" as he attempted to deal with this "other" in a more absolute sense in his fiction.

In any case, Wright remained constant in his view of this "something," this basic, intense, fluid, reality-conferring sense that was mingled with fear and creative reponse. Bigger's action, labeled "creative" by Boris Max, is a response not only to the white world but to some condition, some truth about himself so deep and so terrifying that he cannot, without some shielding formulation, face it. In *Pagan Spain,* Wright recounts his Hemingwayesque discovery that this fear in the face of "an absolute otherness" was the progenitor of a folk form that is almost synonymous with the country itself; it is so refined and ritualized that its folkloric quality has been all but obliterated:

> Bullfighting [has been characterized as] "fundamentally a spiritual exercise and not merely a sport. . . ."
> But what is this mysterious "spiritual exercise" . . . ? Is there something hidden here? If there is something hidden, why are bullfights enacted out in the open, before thousands of spectators?

The answer is not often recognized even when one is directly confronted with it. It is the conquering of fear, the making of a religion of the conquering of fear. (p. 113)

Wright also read ("wrote") Bandung in terms of this confrontation-response, if not a confrontation with and a response to an absolute, at least with and to an "other" that he imagines to be sufficiently greater than the conferees, making him see not only the present meeting but perhaps an even more important historical confrontation:

> Listening to the delegates rise and make their speeches, I got a belated glimpse, couched in terms of concrete history, of the compulsive terror that must have gripped the hearts of the Bolsheviks in Russia in 1920. . . . Lenin, no matter what we may think of him today, was faced with a half-starving nation of 160,000,000 partly tribalized people and he and his cohorts felt that they could trust nobody; they were afraid of losing their newly gained power, their control over the destinies of their country. . . .
>
> Seen through the perspective of Bandung, I think that it can be said that FEAR of a loss of their power, FEAR of re-enslavement, FEAR of attack was the key to the actions of the Russian Stalinists who felt that any and all efforts to modernize their nation would be preferable to a return to the *status quo. (Color Curtain,* p. 221)

Wright, as he traveled to Africa in 1953, not forgetful of Joseph Conrad, recorded a confrontation of his own with a vast "other" just before his disembarking at Ghana. Experiencing a feeling fostered alike by beauty and by fear, he observes the terror he found characteristic of such encounters: "As I watched the sea and the sky I knew that it was from feelings such as these floating in me now that man had got his sense of God, for, when such feelings stated themselves in him, he felt that some powerful but invisible spirit was speaking to him; and he fell on his face, asking to be saved from the emotion that claimed him, afraid, not so much of the sea or the sky, but of the fantastic commotion that bubbled in his heart." (*Black Power,* p. 21)

A dozen years after Wright recorded this experience, Robert Bone was to comment on James Baldwin in similar terms:

> The primal stuff of human personality is undifferentiated: "He was, briefly and horribly, in a region where there were no definitions of

any kind, neither of color nor of male and female". . . . One must face this formlessness, however, before one can hope to achieve form.

At the core of Baldwin's fiction is an existential psychology. In a passage whose language is reminiscent of Genesis, he describes Vivaldo's struggle to define himself: "And beneath all this was the void where anguish lived and questions crouched, which referred only to Vivaldo. . . . " As music depends ultimately on silence, so being is achieved in tension with nothingness . . . all identity . . . emerges from the void. (*The Negro Novel in America*, p. 233)

Wright's response to this formlessness, typified in the murky sea and sky, is creative and significantly idiosyncratic:

> But I stood still, detached, watching the sea and sky and at the same time hearing the echoing declarations that they roused in me. . . . I do not know why they are such as they are, what they really mean, but I stand before them with the same attention that I stand before this sea and this sky. I refuse to make a religion out of that which I do not know. I too can feel the limit of my reactions, can feel where my puny self ends, can savor the terror of it; but it does not make me want to impose that sense of my terror on others, or to rear it into a compulsive system. Detached, I contain my terror, look at it and wonder about it in the same way that I marvel about the sea and sky. (p. 21)

Trying to close his eyes in holy dread of the flashing, floating emotion within him, Wright reveals, in this blend of strong subjective emotional response with an equally strong—or even stronger—objective, rational outlook, both an attitude toward phenomena which is very much that of a modernist man of the twentieth century (and perhaps also very characteristically American) and a peculiar version of his own poetics as outlined sixteen years earlier.

All of the components of his "blueprint" are present in this experience, as well as qualities he had attributed to the essential "something" that was first observed in his grandmother and that was at the basis of his poetics. His complex consciousness is described as being primarily generic "feelings;" these are more specifically referred to as "wonder" and "marvel," and also in terms of fluid action: "floating" and "bubbled," "fantastic commotion," "declarations." He is aware of confronting "that which I do not know;" he does not know what these feelings mean, does not yet imagine what brings them, has not yet formulated a name for this unknown, although he does not say the feelings have no meaning, no referent, no ulterior cause. This consciousness is thus filled with a sense of reaching limits of self, of normal, conventional responsive capability—a reaching of the boundaries of that complexity; of sailing, appropriately in light of the context of the experience, in strange seas of thought, beyond or close to the ends of the known world, of reaching and perhaps going over the edge in a surrender of self, an ecstasy. Coequally present with this consciousness is, therefore, a terror. At first, Wright speaks of it as clearly distinguishable from the primary, generic "feelings." It is a fear of the "commotion that bubbled in his heart," a fear that would appear to be the first response of the consciousness to this unknown, a sharp withdrawal from the brink. This fear leads Wright to see the possibility of creating a habitation and a name for this amorphous agitation—the folk form or lore, religion—as a barrier, a protection from this unknown and from absorbtion by it.

Instead, Wright's will and his powers of detachment step in and provide a container for the terror. It is kept, as are the original feelings, his animated awe at the sea and sky, but the form or name created for them is not "God." The fear he turns into a natural object, like the sea and the sky, an object that in its turn feeds his sense of the wonderful. Now he knows the agent cause of the wonder as himself. The positivism inherent in this last step, leading into a circular thought pattern, obviates the need for considering anything like an ultimate cause or meaning. This is certainly an example of how the folk "fluid lore"—the primal attitude and the fear that is its correlative—can be molded or channeled into a concept that is moving the current forces of history, or at least what most modern thinkers believe should be controlling the world's energies. It is a positivist creativity that also preserves and enhances the emotions, especially the primal attitude. Wright ends the record of his experience saying: "I admit the reality of the feeling [of wonder]; but I would not rig up devious forms of sacrifice to rid myself of it, for that would be the surest way of stifling it, killing it for all time." (p. 21)

In so preserving this attitude, the form devised supplies a

need of the psyche, a need to feel deeply, a need that is ignored or at least not fulfilled by modern Western society. The modern world in the West may be rational, but it is so in an arid way, not permeated by the right attitude and stifling what Wright calls "wonder" or a sense of the marvelous.

Hints of other versions of the kind of form that Wright's poetics led him to envision, particularly in the area of politics, are also found in his writings. In *How Bigger Was Born*, Wright speaks of the form called nationalism and describes how it appealed to Bigger's prototypes, especially in the person of Marcus Garvey. However unsubstantial his movement might appear to many people, its nonreligious quality was no doubt acceptable to Wright, and its appeal to the Afro-American folk population testified to its compatability, or apparent compatability, with the primal attitude Wright descerned in the human psyche. At the end of *Black Power*, in his nervy, preaching open letter to Nkrumah, he exhorts "Kwame" to "militarize" his people. He appears somewhat less concerned about the matter of sacrifice involved in the creation of such a political form than he was in creating a form to contain and yet express his own essential "something," but still the political form is to enhance, not kill, the primal feelings. The militarization he calls for will produce "a degree of suffering, of trial, of tribulation," but also it will produce a "hardness" that African life needs, presumably to eliminate or compensate for the softer "poetic" forms it had traditionally developed. If such advice calls up visions of the massive Nazi rallies in the 1930s and, from a clinical perspective, the hysterical loyalty of the masses that allowed Hitler to rebuild a Germany shattered by World War I and economic depression, Wright is aware of the parallel, as he was of the parallels between Garveyism and nazism. Wright seems to have envisioned a political form that, reversing what he had tried to do with regard to his grandmother, kept the outer but not the inner processes or spirit of Western totalitarian states:

> Keep the fires of passion burning in your movement; don't let Westerners turn you away from the only force that can . . . knit your people together. It's a secular religion that you must slowly create.
> . . .
> There will be those who will try to frighten you by telling you that

29

the organization you are forging looks like Communism, Fascism, Nazism; but, Kwame, the form of organization that you need will be dictated by the needs, emotional and material, of your people. (p. 349)

This form, as Wright thinks of it at Bandung, undoubtedly owes much to the emotional reverberations that the conference had set up in him concerning his response in the 1930s to the Communist efforts to encode folk languages and customs in forms suited to modern means of communication. In *The Color Curtain*, the political form he sees most likely to emerge is that of the Communists, for reasons very close to his own poetics: "Mr. Chou En-Lai . . . can dredge down and rake up the hidden reserves of a people, can shake them, rip them out of the traditional and customary soil in which they have stagnated for centuries." (p. 221)

However, the violence of his language indicates Wright's awareness of the great stresses involved in adjusting an entire nation to a rationally irrational form of its traditional and largely folk culture. He is also aware that it is one of the great flaws in the already existing form of European communism, a flaw that presumably a political form in the pattern of his own poetics would not possess:

But can Stalinism repeat in Asia and Africa what it did in Russia, leaving aside for the moment the question of its aspects of limitless murder and terror, its wholesale sacrifices of human freedom and human life? . . . Today the Russians can feel bitterly, defiantly satisfied that they did what was brutally necessary, no matter how hard, inhuman and terrible, to keep their power and industrialize their country. BUT MUST THIS TRAGIC METHOD, WITH ITS SECULAR RELIGIOSITY OF HORROR AND BLOOD, BE REPEATED ON THE BODY OF THE HUMAN RACE? Is there no stand-in for these sacrifices, no substitute for these sufferings? (p. 221)

In the passage from *Black Power* recording his dealings with his own creation of a modern form to express the very real "something" that was manifesting itself in him vis-a-vis the tropic sunset, he expressed his repugnance to formulating any kind of compulsive system that would enable him to control his fear by foisting it on to others or that would require the stifling of any of his responses. In that context, his poetics worked with a minimum of privation to his individual self, but in a political context, the steeliness of will and the impassiveness of detachment involved in this rational form have to be accountable to more than just one's own fear. In addition to being the fear of many, the fear might even be of the twentieth century form itself. In *Black Power*, Wright speaks of the rational concepts driving and directing the twentieth century as pragmatism, mechanization, and industrialization, all three posing a great unknown "other" for people in folk cultures.

As "industrialization," "mechanization" and his advice to "militarize" imply, there is a harshness to the form he envisions, a rigidity, a systemization—a patterning or programming that is, in his view, apparently characteristic of all pragmatically productive, rational, contemporary concepts. This hardness was a quality he also wanted to build into *Native Son* so that readers could not simply cry over Bigger's condition and feel that they had responded adequately, a quality he would give this work that would allow readers no consolation, no "poetic" way to avoid its portent.

What Wright objected to about the Communist political form was not, therefore, its adamancy. What it possessed that Wright's envisioned form would not have was the power, the constitutive potential, of imposing. Imposition is a "tragic method." Any part of the body politic that falls beyond the circumference of the prescribed form is cut off willy-nilly. It becomes "the other" and, in that sense, is "sacrificed"—made "holy" or the cause of fear—but the acceptance of the prescribed form protects and saves. Wright's own creations—his stories and novels—are, to be sure, filled with characters imposing their "systems" on others, with the attendant plethora of "horror and blood." But within the fictions, the violence and bloodshed, whether he deplores them or understands them, are always presented as faulty consequences or implications but of a valid surge of a primal attitude inexplicably one with human reality. They result, these secularized versions of the more socially accepted but just as faulty religious forms, because the right conditions, the right concepts, the right rationality are not available, for whatever reasons, to the characters.

31

With specific relation to Wright's poetics and its roots presented thus far, such imposition is antithetic to Wright, the individualist par excellence, and involves the arbitrariness he had witnessed in his grandmother, in her dictatorial enforcement of her religious beliefs with a severity intent on cutting off his responses. The theoretical directions of his poetics, as implied in remarks in *American Hunger* and "Blueprint," would create "a physical state or movement" in words to provide a vehicle for a "strong subjective impression," a twentieth-century concept that contains and expresses the reality-conferring "something" in human being. This supremely valuable form would then so attract the reader, engage his deepest feeling so strongly, that the form—the words—would "disappear"; their old associations and connotations would "melt," and the reader would be aware of a newness, of being in a new world, but only in and through consciousness of his own responses. The form Wright envisions does not impose anything on, or take anything from, the individual but spirals what he has onto new levels.

Paralleling this view of the workings of the ideal literary form, Wright's ideal political form, as he suggests it in *The Color Curtain*, might involve the loss of human life—even "wholesale" losses—or the loss of freedom as in the dictatorship of the proletariat, but these "sacrifices" will be not so much losses as transcendencies "if the populations involved are made to feel that such a bloody path is preferable to a new loss of their freedom. (Men will give up their lives to save their freedom, just as they will give their lives to save their lives!) Indeed, I think that the very intensity of their racial and religious conditioning would lead these masses to accept such a desperate path, have prepared them to re-enact on a global scale ceremonies of collective crucifixion and rituals of mass rebirth." (p. 220)

Nevertheless, at the heart of Wright's poetics, inherent in the notion of the juxtaposition of disparate elements and in the ensuing problem of how they are linked in other than a mechanical way and just how the mutual molding is to take place, is a Nietszchean disregard for communication. In its place is what appears to be the "big bang" theory of creation of new forms, whether political or literary. More will be said about this aspect of Wright's poetics in the chapter on Kenneth Burke and his stimulation of Wright's thought.

It is, however, to Wright's fiction that we must turn to get the fullest view of the results of his poetics. Whatever fields he may have wandered during his writing career, he has achieved his place in the world of Western culture primarily as a short story writer and novelist. In these genres, his poetics, only roughly developed in theory, was most richly exemplified in the various instances in which he took the "fluid lore of a great people" and molded it with, or molded to it, dynamic issues of our era.

2

FOLKLORIC
TRANSFORMULATIONS

Wright's poetics, however unemphatically he dwelled on it in its theoretic mode, exerted a definite influence on his fiction. In *The Man Who Lived Underground*, which will be discussed fully in a later chapter, Wright was explicitly concerned with codifying in a literary performance that fluid reality-giving "something" that he had sensed most strongly in Afro-American folk expression. Other examples of his fiction, however, contain evidence that he did not always go back so far—he did not always try to create ex nihilo a new form that contoured this folk impulse. Following the bent of his poetics, he took what was somewhat less fluid, given its oral nature, the lore folk created as expressive containers of their sense of the ultimately real, and attempted to keep its "inner processes" but not its outer shape. The outer skeleton or template was his twentieth-century conception of black American life, molding his tale into an authentic Afro-American literary work.

"The Man Who Killed a Shadow" and the first part of *Native Son*, with their vestiges of the folklore that he had absorbed almost osmotically as a child, provide examples of the manner in which, and the degree to which, Wright's blueprint for Negro writing shaped this lore and utilized for his own purposes the ambience it retained from its original association with the folk impulse.

Written in France in 1946, "The Man Who Killed a Shadow"

is a strange little story that seems, from a traditional Euro-American literary viewpoint, barely to bother with the conventions of fiction. More to the point of this study is that Wright's account of his story's origin would seem to rule out any discussion of its relation to folklore. In 1960, as part of a never completed preface to *Eight Men*, ("Roots and Branches,") that traces the origins of the stories in the collection, Wright wrote five pages recounting a 1945 meeting with Charles Houston, a Washington NAACP attorney. Houston told of a strange murder case that he was involved with, strange not because a black man, Julius Fisher, had killed a white woman in broad daylight in a church, but because of the black man's undemonstrative, abstract way of explaining what he had done.

Wright's immediate explanation for the man's attitude was that, psychologically, he had not killed the woman; like the white world in general, she simply had not existed for him as a real person. The story's strange tone is partially accounted for, then, as Wright's attempt to convey the mental/emotional reference frame of his protagonist.

The story thus seems to have no connection whatever with folklore. Furthermore, as Fabre has pointed out, Wright utilized a court transcript of the case from which he drew the details of the crime. Yet the particular details that he chose to emphasize in his story—the National Cathedral setting; the various weapons; the repeated assaults; the age of the victim; above all, the effect that the sound of her screams had on Julius Fisher—lead us to see the ghost of a folk form. The details and the emphases he chose to add, particularly those of the victim's eyes and the pull they exerted, the reverberation of the screams through the room and corridors and his protagonist's brain, and the sexual overtones of the case, indicate that the case and its actual details appealed to more than just Wright's desire for realism. They fit a pattern that would have been imprinted in his psyche by his unreflecting childhood absorption of Afro-American folklore.

This work contains shades of images and themes of a certain folktale, a Negro version of what Sterling Brown described: "A favorite object of lampooning, familiar in general folklore, was the old maid, the master's sister. One of the fanciful plots has her turning into a squinch [screech] owl, her long drawn wails voicing her yearning for a husband." ("Negro Folk Expression," p. 11)

Versions of this tale seem to have been fairly widely known. Richard M. Dorson has published at least two, one gathered in Michigan from a woman who was raised in Tennessee and Mississippi. ("Young Man in the Morning," in *Negro Folk Tales in Michigan,* p. 1931) He refers also to a version gathered by Elsie Parson in North Carolina and indicates that he himself had collected three other variants of the tale in Michigan. (p. 231) Another one that he published was told him by a man in Bolivar County, Mississippi, ("Negro Tales from Bolivar County, Mississippi," p. 113), across and down the river from Elaine and West Helena, Arkansas, areas in which Wright spent two or three years in his childhood, surrounded by "a wealth of legends, surviving ancestral beliefs, proverbs, folk sayings, tales and superstitions ranging from voodoo to Christianity. (Fabre, *Unfinished Quest,* p. 26) The more elaborate version alluded to by Brown is found in Zora Hurston's *Mules and Men,* purportedly collected by her in central Florida.

Only in Hurston's version is there an overt racial slant, in that the old maid, Miss Pheenie, is explicitly the master's sister. In this version, the old maid is smitten by her young niece's suitors. One of them, observing her "stand around and peer at 'em . . . wishin' she could git courted and married" (p. 181), impishly flirts with her, and when he leaves he tells her that if she will sit on the roof of the house all night, he will marry her in the morning. Taking up his offer, she spends a bitter cold night on the roof, crying out, "C-o-o-o-l-d on de house top, but a young man in de mawnin' " until 4 A.M., when she tumbles from the roof frozen to death. (pp. 181-82) Only in this version is the story connected with the creation of the screech owl. Hurston's narrator finishes his tale by pointing out that the very next night after Miss Pheenie's funeral, she reappeared on the roof top "shiverin' and crying" in the form of an owl. (p. 182)

The tale comes at the end of several characters' conversation concerning the owl's cry in its folk role as a harbinger of evil and how the owl must be silenced before the evil can befall. Two of the ways recorded by Hurston—putting salt in the fire and turning an article of clothing inside out (p. 181)—are also among those listed by Newbell Niles Puckett. (*Folk Beliefs of the Southern Negro*, p. 483) In summarizing the owl lore, Puckett also provided a brief summary of (or speculation concerning) its origin: "Many of the characteristics of Hel were transferred to the Germanic Frigg, and, as such, the owl is her messenger, and the hooting of an owl . . . in Europe and in Africa . . . is indicative of death. . . . Thus coming from a double source, it is no wonder that the hooting of an owl is regarded by the Negro as a death omen." (pp. 481-82)

The tone of Wright's story is far more serious than Hurston's or any of the other versions of the folk tale. Wright knew Hurston's work; at least he reviewed *Their Eyes Were Watching God* for *New Masses* in 1937. He thoroughly disparaged the book because he felt Hurston presented only a "quaint" picture of Negro life, depicting only pathetic or humorous characters, the types a white audience likes to see. In Wright's tale, the fact of Maybelle Eva Houseman's maidenhood is underlined by the doctor's testimony, postscripted to the Grand Jury's indictment of Saul at the end of the story. That she is forty would qualify her as an "old" maid, according to attitudes of the 1940s. Like Miss Pheenie, she desires a young man, though she is considerably more aggressive in seeking one, drawing up her skirt, spreading her legs, and then calling Saul to look under her desk. As in the folktale, the man has no intention of mating with the old maid, and this is highlighted by the "un-wedding" detail of Saul's pulling (as he attempts to drag her body to a hiding place) a thin gold ring from her finger, a detail otherwise inexplicable, although there seems to be a half-suggestion near the end that its theft is the preposterously alleged motive for the murder. While no owl is specifically present, the woman is characterized by a repeated image that suggests an owl: "A strange little shadow woman . . . who stared at him all the time in a most peculiar way . . . he would turn around and find her staring at him . . . he paused and turned and saw her staring at him . . . the woman always stared at him . . . she was sitting in her chair at her desk, staring at him with unblinking eyes." ("The Man Who Killed a Shadow," pp. 161-62)

Earlier in the story, Saul, new to the ways of Washington, is informed by one of his street-wise friends that "if you were alone with a white woman and she screamed, it was as good as hearing your death sentence, for though you had done nothing, you would be killed." (p. 159) The very phrasing of this passage is that of the folk "magic" recorded by anthropologists and by Wright himself in *Black Boy*, e.g., "If I kissed my elbow, I would turn into a girl" (p. 81), with the same illogic existing between the two events. Consequently, when Saul attempts to walk away from the advances of this woman and she commences to scream, uppermost in his mind is "to stop that shadow from screaming a scream that meant death." (pp. 164-65) He resorts to tactics similar to those listed by Puckett as ways to "shut the owl's mouth," "to avoid the ill luck or to make the owl hush up." (*Folk Beliefs*, p. 482) Saul first beats the woman's head with a piece of fire wood, conveniently available in this library, and after it breaks in two, Wright has him take the time to fit the pieces carefully together and replace the stick on the pile before the fireplace. Puckett lists as one variant to stopping the owl's screeching: "cross two sticks and put them in back of the chimney to break the owl's neck." (p. 483) Saul next attempts to choke the cries off; Puckett has recorded, "squeeze your wrist (this will choke the owl to death); . . . put salt or a shovel (or a horseshoe) in the fire to burn his tongue (or strangle him); or tie a hard knot in the (righthand) corner of your bed sheet, handkerchief or apron to choke him to death." (pp. 482-83) Saul then recalls a knife in his pocket, opens it, and plunges it into the woman's throat. Puckett's sources give the advice: "Stick a knife in wood" and "open your pocket knife." (pp. 482-83) Both Puckett (p. 483) and Hurston (p. 181) give the counteraction of removing an article of clothing and turning it inside out. Saul strips the woman of her underpants, using them to wipe up the blood dripping from her head and throat as he drags and carries her to a place where he hopes her screams will not be heard.

Wright's story, in addition to these details evocative of folk beliefs, also has several qualities reminiscent of broader folklore characteristics: "Folklore . . . provides American literature with belief in the supernatural, a source both of mystery and of metaphoric criticism of established rationalistic values and Christian institutions. . . . Folk belief depends upon communally sanctioned practice of allegory as a cultural cast of mind. And the fragmented annals of our folk heroes comprise a set of rituals peculiarly adapted to our preconceptions of the fate of the American character in a universe both unpredictable and benign." (Hoffman, *Form and Fable*, pp. 13-14)

Such a passage suggests a way that Wright might have found to connect his concern about the lack of "metaphysical meanings" in American (actually, all of Western) culture expressed in *How Bigger Was Born* with his conviction, as expressed in "The Literature of the Negro in the United States," (*White Man, Listen!*) that indigenous black folklore—"The Forms of Things Unknown"—contained not-yet-realized depths of subject matter and themes for black writers.

The setting for the story's central action, the National Cathedral, and furthermore its library, surely implies a "metaphoric criticism of established rationalistic values and Christian institution," just as does Saul Sanders's universe. While not benign, it is extremely folkloric in its dense permeation with intangible but strong forces, and in its singular unpredictability, filling Saul with "a sense of the transitory quality of life, which always made him feel that some invisible, unexplainable event was about to descend upon him . . . as long as he could stifle the feeling of being hemmed in, as long as he could conquer the anxiety about the unexpected happening, life was bearable." ("The Man Who Killed a Shadow," pp. 157, 160)

While Wright's voice in the story suggests psychological explanations for this feeling and for Saul's dominant characteristic of thought (his viewing of the entire social world outside himself as comprised of insubstantial shadows), Saul's mind is characterized by two qualities commonly considered to be "folk." Not stupid, he is uneducated: "None of the people who came and went in Saul's life had ever prized learning and Saul did likewise." (p. 158) Uneducated, he views and comes to accept external, objective reality as a "vast shadow-world that came and went, pulled by forces which he nor nobody he knew understood." (p. 158) In place of understanding, he develops a kind of ritual that enables him to cope with and placate this "object that stood between him and a hidden and powerful sun." (p. 158) First, even though his early deprivation of parents, siblings, and eventually of his seemingly stable grandmother had given him a sense of the world's unreality, "he projected his misery out of himself and upon the one thing that made him most consciously anxious" (p. 158), upon the white world. Then as he grows older, he resorts to a communally recommended routine of Saturday-night drinking: "[Whiskey] helped to banish the shadows. . . . He felt that whiskey made life complete . . . whiskey really depressed him, numbed him somewhat, reduced the force and number of the shadows that made him tight inside." (p. 159) He is told by other blacks with whom he drinks that anger at the shadows (police), who drop into their lives and claim them without warning or explanation, is dangerous: "the best thing to do was to take a drink." (p. 159)

The folk quality of the story also exists in its folkloric mode. This mode concerns the architecture of fiction, of written literary works as opposed to oral, verbal expressions. It is a subdivision of what Barre Toelken, borrowing from Northrop Frye's notion of mode, calls a "traditional mode"—"a conventionalized ordering of literary design according not to the demands of verisimilitude but to the expectations of tradition." (*Dynamics of Folklore*, p. 338) For Toelken, the nature of such a structure is related to the principles that Axel Olrik observed and set forth in his 1909 essay "Epic Laws of Folk Narrative." Wright's story—and in fact the structure of a number of his stories—while coming from sources that appear on the surface far different from Olrik's, nevertheless shows modalities of the structural characteristics that Olrik delineated.

Olrik framed his description of folkloric structures within the contexts of the "Sage" and the "Sagenwelt"—the former an all-inclusive term referring to "such forms as folktale, myth, legend, and folksong," and the latter indicating "an independent domain, a realm of reality separate from the real world, subject to its own rules and regulations [which] take precedence over the everyday rules of objective reality." ("Epic Laws of Folk Narrative," p. 129) The words that summarize Olrik's notion of the "Sagenwelt" also describe Wright's view of the Negro folk mind, which he witnessed in his grandmother and which he created in his character Saul: an independent domain, a realm of reality separate from the real world, subject to its own rules and regulations. While such a description might also apply to a psychotic state, Wright saw such an outlook as essentially creative; his grandmother and the singers of the blues and other folk expressions were very strong people, capable of surviving excruciating difficulties. Even their violent reactions, as Max says of Bigger's murders, are acts of creation.

Wright indicated in the intended preface to *Eight Men* his awareness of the unsubtle terseness of both the language and the structure of this story, and he suggested that these were perhaps the results of attempting to write for a foreign audience. But the concise, undemonstrative statements and direct, flat-out unsubtle presentation of events are also obviously equivalent to Saul's state of mind, and they also parallel two of the less obvious "formula" that Olrik found controlling the essential structure of folk narrative. He speaks of the single-strandedness and the strict patterning of these tales in "Epic Laws of Folk Narrative." (p. 138) They focus on a single plot, concentrating on moving forward to the outcome of the single line of action, without great regard for any more detail than is absolutely necessary. The result is a rigid stylization that "has its own peculiar aesthetic value. Everything superfluous is suppressed and only the essential stands out salient and striking." (p. 138)

Because of this severe economy, the folk narrative has a flatness to it. According to Olrik, "It does not know the perspective of painting; it knows only the progressive series of bas-reliefs." (p. 137) The "Sage" thus "rises to peaks in the form of one or more major *tableaux scenes* . . . sculptured situations . . . based more on fantasy than on reality" that "frequently convey not a sense of the ephemeral but rather a certain quality of persistence in time . . . lingering actions . . . [which] possess the singular power of being able to etch themselves in one's memory." (p. 138) In "The Man Who Killed a Shadow," the images of Maybelle Eva Houseman's bright, unblinking staring eyes and of her pink panties as she sits rigidly still at her desk have this quality. Realisticaly, the latter image is implausable; if "her dress was drawn halfway up her legs" as she sat at her desk, it does not seem likely that Saul could see that her "thighs thickened as they went to a V clothed in tight, sheer pink panties" ("The Man Who Killed a Shadow," p. 163), even if

41

he approached near enough to look at the alleged dirt left under her desk. Omitted from the image also is such a realistic detail as stockings, which a woman in her occupation and in that time period would logicaly be expected to wear. Instead, we read of her "naked thighs." All is pared to reinforce an image central to the tale: that of the black man/white woman sexual encounter, which has the status of myth in United States culture.

Her screams also take on this sculptured quality. In the logic of the spatio-temporal world, they are fleeting disturbances of air; in the story they become solid, block-like entities. No precise adjectives alter or qualify them; they are simply unadorned, forthright screams that crushingly avalanche into Saul's life long after Maybelle is unable to produce them.

Other laws that Olrik found shaping folk narrative that can be observed in Wright's story are related to number: the Law of Contrast and the Law of Repetition. The "Sage" is limited to two characters per scene, and these characters are always polarized. According to Olrik, "this very basic opposition is a major rule of epic composition" and requires that the characteristics and actions of other characters be antithetical to those of the protagonist. (p. 135) The relevance of this law to "The Man Who Killed a Shadow" needs no elaboration, but the Law of Repetition, related to the number three that "reigns supreme" (p. 133) in purely oral tales, does call for comment. Olrik says, "Every time that a striking scene occurs in a folk narrative, and continuity permits, the scene is repeated. This is necessary not only to build tension but to fill out the body of the narrative. There is intensifying repetition and simple repetition, but the important point is that without repetition, the *Sage* cannot attain its fullest form. The repetition is almost always tied to the number three." . . . (p. 133)

Beyond the fact that the vivid scene that climaxes this story contains within it three brutal attempts by Saul to silence Maybelle's screams—clubbing her, strangling her, and finally stabbing her in the throat with a conveniently remembered pocket knife—repetition is a frequent characteristic of Wright's work. For example, his earliest story, "Superstition," is structured as a repeated visit to a family by the narrator on two successive Christmases; in "Big Boy Leaves Home," the central action is dramatized, then repeated twice by Big Boy to his parents and then to the church elders; *Native Son* and *Savage Holiday* are divided into three alliteratively titled parts.

As Negro spirituals in the twentieth century have come to be seen as veiled expressions of the desire for freedom from the political condition of slavery in this life, the modern, driving concept of racism with which Wright shaped, in this story, the original lore of the owl moves that basal legend from the realm of the mystical, and even from the "quaint" or poetic, to the midst of contemporary society and modern psychology. It offers one rational explanation for the original lore's continuation or existence, at least in the United States; it is a disguised, underground expression of a social reality that the slaves were not allowed to discuss openly—the sexual problem that slaves posed for whites. Such a rationale for the owl lore, probably never fully articulated but understood, would be gradually lost or submerged even further as Afro-Americans gained more freedom and privacy in which to express their views, but it would still add a potential dimension to the significance the palimpsest-like lore.

On the other hand, such significance could have been lost or, for many, have been nonexistent because of the Afro-American folk ability to give reality to the owl lore in its literal sense, apart from any view these folk had of reality as inherent in objective social conditions. Such a treatment would place the lore within the province of religious belief, something Wright would see only as erroneous, however much appeal it might have for readers, and in need of updating. Insofar as Saul's is a naive folk mind that Wright was patently seeking to manifest, the use of images and a pattern relative to the world of Afro-American folklore was remarkably fitting.

The form of racism that Wright molded to the Afro-American owl lore was itself a kind of folklore. In one sense, racism is a rational concept, something Wright could grasp and understand, derived from an objectively existing attitude that caused much of what was happening in the modern world, a concept that offered, unlike a god, a demonstrable explanation for actions and events. In itself, however, it is an irrational projection, a subjective response to fear of chaos, onto an inappropriate, erroneously perceived cause; it is a lunatic creation of "the other," the fear-bringer, in the image of the black person. In this latter sense, it is something within the domain of folklore. The particular sexual aspect of this racism which Wright used is a folk motif that he saw more characteristic of white folklore than of black.

The nature of the relation of this white lore to Wright's poetics is brought out in *Pagan Spain*. During a visit to Seville, he witnessed a Holy Week festival that included a procession in honor of the Blessed Virgin. As in Ghana, he was struck by similarities between what he saw in this ritual and things he had seen back in the United States, except this time the similarities existed between Old World practices and the behavior of white Americans of the Old South. Attending the statue of the Virgin were marchers dressed in long robes and tall, pointed hoods that suggested the garb adopted by the Ku Klux Klan. The function of these marchers also suggested the Klan to him:

> These hooded penitents had been protecting the Virgin, and in the Old American South hooded Ku Kluxers had been protecting "the purity of white womanhood." Even if the White South . . . had copied their tactics and costumes from here, it did not explain why men loved to march in defense of what they felt was female purity. Some underlying reality more powerful than the glittering Virgin or southern white women had gripped these undeniably primitive minds. They were following some ancient pattern of behavior and were justifying their actions in terms that had nothing whatever to do with that pattern. (p. 237)

This "ancient pattern of behavior" and the illogical terms of racist American sexual taboos that were used to justify it are the source of the modern concept that Wright used to reshape not only the owl lore in "The Man Who Killed a Shadow" but also the more unequivocally religious Afro-American lore that undergirds much of the crucial action in the first part of *Native Son* in which he was also articulating the frame of mind of a segment of the black American underclass. As he later felt he was attempting in *The Man Who Lived Underground*, he was, in *Native Son*, also contouring the essential quality of his grandmother's religious outlook, the viewpoint he saw as typically that of Afro-American folk, in secular—very secular—twentieth-century terms. Thus the language of Mary Dalton's murder contains within it another narrative. Wright tips us into this other narrative by certain discontinuities or references within the sociopsychosexual narrative that are terms proper only to a religious context. These terms create breaks in the surface narrative, doorways through which the reader can enter into another realm of discourse, that of myth and that of myth of a particular kind.

The brief description he gives of Afro-American folk religious behavior and psychology in *Twelve Million Black Voices* can be read as a summary of the rising emotional pitch in Bigger as he becomes increasingly involved with Mary and his ultimate reaction at the end of this section of the novel:

> The preacher's voice is sweet to us, caressing and lashing, conveying to us a heightening of consciousness. . . . As the sermon progresses, the preacher's voice increases in emotional intensity, and we, in time and sympathy with his sweeping story, sway in our seats until we have lost all notion of time and have begun to float on a tide of passion. The preacher begins to punctuate his words with sharp rhythms and we are lifted far beyond the boundaries of our daily lives and upward and outward, until drunk with our enchanted vision, our senses lifted to the burning skies, we do not know who we are, what we are, or where we are.
>
> We go home pleasantly tired and sleep easily for we know that we hold somewhere within our hearts a possibility of inexhaustible happiness; we know that if we could get our feet planted firmly upon this earth, we could laugh and live and build. (p. 73)

The mythic quality of this Afro-American religion is not totally visible in its ritual, the ritual that Wright more or less worked with consciously, and that had been ingrained in him by repeated exposure in his uncritical childhood. But mythic forms or meanings are inherent, nimbus-like, in the verbal images he consciously structured along other, even secular, lines. They were thus invented by Wright in the basic sense of that word. As he observes in "Roots and Branches," writers are not always fully aware of everything that the word patterns they spin might signify; they do not always see what is right in front of their eyes, even though they have created these patterns and been stimulated by them to the shaping of still further images.

The mythology that blooms in this section of *Native Son* is that of voodoo, and it is virtually present in the religious form that Wright knew, especially in its most pronounced trait, the phenomenon of possession. This trait marks the continuity, however tenuous, between the varieties of Afro-American and Afro-Caribbean folk religions, as studies such as the Reverend Henry H. Mitchell's reveal:

> A much more obvious "instinct" among Black American slaves was probably that of possession by deities. . . . How this African tradition or "instinct" evolved into a firm Black Protestant doctrine and practice raises some interesting questions. . . . Haitian psychiatrist Emerson Douyon found some of the voodoo devotees he tested complaining that they could not get rid of the loas . . . which occasionally possessed them. They were making the effort in order to climb the social ladder and be identified with a "higher class" culture. . . . However, their complaint continued, "if they joined Protestant churches to get away from voodoo they would then be possessed by the Holy Spirit."
>
> The power and tenacity of the cultural conditioning related to possession is clearly manifested here. It is not the sort of thing that one can shed with ease, and voluntarily. It is rather, deeply imbedded in the human psyche by subtle and powerfully influential hypnotic other folk means. It is transmitted and maintained in ways most of which are not planned or conscious, and it is therefore retained involuntarily. In the city where Douyon did his tests, these supposedly primitive possession rites were actually in the process of cultural deemphasis. People were attempting to exercise what is called upward mobility, and to shed "less sophisticated" customs. But the conditioning was irresistible; and it was reinforced by the healing, life-supporting values of the possession tradition. (*Black Belief,* pp. 136-37)

Thus it is that, as if in a process not unlike the "coming though" of John Grimes so powerfully described by Baldwin in *Go Tell It On The Mountain,* the tapping more or less consciously into one religious form in order to reshape it by means of his secular forces gave Wright an uncanny perception, the power to speak in a version of tongues. He released a panoply of forms in one sense unknown to him, forms that nevertheless bespeak the fluid lore that he was seeking to contour, revealing a dimension that is not visible in its Afro-American Christian folk form.

The series of forms or images at issue here consists of doors, the color blue, Mary's bedroom, the trunk, the knife and axe, the blazing iron furnace and, very importantly, Mary and Mrs. Dalton.

Doors figure prominently in the latter part of the first section of *Native Son* from the time Bigger arrives at the Dalton house until his decision to leave the car door open as he prepares to return home. Wright calls attention to the image by repeating it frequently and by the momentous tone of passages in which doors are the focus of Bigger's attention. When Bigger first approaches the Dalton house, he is conscious of doors because of an implicitly realistic consideration: how is he to enter this "world of white secrets carefully guarded"? Through the front door or by the more traditional rear entrance dictated by his southern, Jim Crow upbringing? Wright not only devotes two paragraphs to this matter of doors and entranceways but he heightens the sense of the fatefulness of the door's opening by the rhythm of the prose. Bigger walks from the front gate to the locked driveway and back again; he hesitates; then

> timidly, he lifted the latch on the gate and walked to the steps. He paused, waiting for someone to challenge him. Nothing happened. Maybe nobody was home? He went to the door and saw a dim light burning in a shaded niche above the doorbell. He pushed it and was startled to hear a soft gong sound within. Maybe he had pushed it too hard? Aw, what the hell! He had to do better than this; he relaxed his taut muscles and stood at ease, waiting. The doorknob turned. The door opened. He saw a white face. It was a woman. (*Native Son*, p. 46)

Once in the house, Bigger passes through, and is introduced to, other doors, more incidentally treated by Wright but notable because of their number: doors to his room, to the kitchen, to the basement, to the furnace, to the garage, to the car.

When Mary Dalton is unable to enter the house under her own power, and after Bigger carries her upstairs, the momentousness of doors is again stressed:

> He got her as far as the door and stopped. Was this really her room? . . . Suppose he opened the door to Mr. and Mrs. Dalton's room. . . . He felt strange, possessed, or as if he were acting upon a

stage in front of a crowd of people. Carefully, he freed one hand and turned the knob of the door. He waited; nothing happened. He pushed the door in quietly . . . he lifted her and brought her into the room and closed the door. (p. 83)

In this passage, the specific mention of possession and of a behavior in front of a crowd, as well as the altering of cadences, metaphorically relates the action to an Afro-American folk religious ceremony. The emphasis on doors suggest symbolically that Bigger's possession is not by the Holy Spirit—no tongues of flame or whirlwind here—but by Papa Legba, the loa invoked first in voodoo ceremonies, the force, the gatekeeper, that opens barriers separating humans from inspiration by other loas.

The notion of what loas are has relevance to Wright's creativity here, his poetics in practice, and hence to account for this section's impact on the reader, for its power to strike the reader with a sense of reality. The loas are Haitian versions of African orishas—once humans, ancestors of the now-living, repositories and transmitters of physical and cultural life. Passed beyond merely temporal existence, they nevertheless remain in contact with it and, in fact, need that contact to thrive. They remain repositories of life in its most primal sense and are channelers of that life to any individual who serves them and allows them to incarnate themselves in him. According to Zora Neale Hurston, they are myriad and their mythological expression more than abundant: "No one knows the name of every loa because every major section of Haiti has its own local variation. It has gods and goddesses of places and forces that are unknown fifty miles away. The heads of "families" of gods are known all over the country, but there are endless variations of the demigods even in some localities. . . . Hence the long list of Ogouns, Erzulies . . . Legbas." (*Tell My Horse* pp. 138-39)

Janheinz Jahn, synthesizer of voodoo studies by Herskovits, Metraux, one-time Surrealist Michel Leiris, and others (studies that themselves systematize and homogenize voodoo beliefs and practices far more than they are found in situ), points out the Wordsworthian reciprocity of this possession: primal life force is intensified in the human participant who heeds the ceremonial rhythm signifying the presence of a particular loa and surrenders his movement to its control; the orisha-loa itself is strengthened by the willing consent (or suspension of disbelief, perhaps) of the possessed. (*Muntu*, p. 63)

In voodoo's mythic expression of its theology, the initiating life force to which the initiate must willing give himself is not only the guardian and opener of doors but also the protector of roads and streets, all paths and conduits. Legba is also deemed present where such roads cross, and voodoo iconography has readily recognized and taken over the Christian cross, with its signification of the *axis mundi*. Legba is the genius of the crux, the intersection of the "street of the loas," the vertical bar rooted in the "waters of the deep" (an expression for the permanent locus of the loas) along which they ascend to make contact with the horizontal bar, the human, earthly world. (p. 42) Legba is therefore also the life force presiding over decisions; or, rather, it is the spiritual form of decisions such as Bigger's to enter the Dalton home in the first place and his later choices of action regarding Mary, or in Wright's decision to use the image of doors, the genius that led him to fix so naturally on it in order to express that genius.

As in the voodoo ritual, the presence of Legba in Wright's creative process marks only the beginning of his possession, of his inspiration, as it does of Bigger's. Once the door is open to the renewed influx of primal life, energy can flood the possessed, depending on his cooperation with its varigated currents. Relatively undifferentiated in Afro-American Christian folk ceremonies, the richness of this contact with the initiate's ultimate reality is expresed in voodoo by a number of nuances imaged as other loas, which in turn are also represented often by tangible symbols. These same nuances show up in *Native Son* as Bigger's initial decisions to enter the Dalton house and, especially, Mary's bedroom, unleash emotions to which he surrenders control of his physical and mental movements.

When, for example, Bigger is inspired to build a defensive case for himself against charges of Mary's death, his plan is triggered by the presence of a trunk. In the subtext of Haitian voodoo that Wright's language has potentially created, the trunk is a sign of the possessive presence of a primal life nuance sometimes called Zaka. This loa is the particular friend of peasants and farmers, of rural outlanders in general, with something of an animus toward urbanites. It seems to be a figuration of that pattern of primal energy or rhythm often referred to in other mythologies as "nature," the productive power responsible for the vegetable and animal forms needed to sustain human life, as fertility. This nuance is symbolized by (among other things such as thunder, lightning, and life-giving rain) baskets and hampers—containers that hold the harvest produced by nature (Jahn, *Muntu,* p. 44), a function that Wright's trunk fulfills:

> They could prove that he had been inside her room! But suppose he told them that he had come to get the trunk? That was it! The *trunk!* . . . He could take the trunk to the basement and put the car into the garage and then go home. *No!* There was a better way. . . .
>
> He went to the trunk and eased the top down and dragged it over the rug to the middle of the floor. He lifted the top and felt inside; it was half-empty. . . . He . . . *Yes!* He could, he could put her *in* the trunk! . . .
>
> Yes, put her in the trunk. (*Native Son,* p. 87)

Other nuances of this signified primal life force in Bigger's possession or in possession of him are revealed in the language of his inspired recognition and acceptance of the fiery furnace and the knife and ax, his allowance of them to control his actions. As Wright's language images the scene, the blazing furnace and its song first mesmerize Bigger; then, a metaphoric fire enters his body, which shakes as his mind is invaded by an idea the furnace, filled with a "quivering" fire, seems to instill:

> He stood in the darkened basement with the trunk upon his back and listened to the roaring draft of the furnace and saw the coals burning red through the cracks. . . . His hand, seared with fire, slipped from the strap and the trunk hit the floor with a loud clatter. He bent forward and squeezed his right hand to still the fiery pain.
>
> He stared at the furnace. He trembled with another idea. He—he could, he—he could put her, he could put her *in* the furnace. He would *burn* her! . . . He went to the furnace and opened the door. A huge red bed of coals blazed and quivered with molten fury. (p. 89)

When Mary's decapitation is dictated by the furnace, Bigger is described standing before it, thinking about incinerating the observant white cat. His thoughts of the cat trail off, and the next paragraph begins abruptly with his taking out his pocket knife. When Bigger applies it to Mary's throat, Wright describes the knife in a manner that implies it too has been possessed by the fire in the furnace: "He touched the sharp blade to the throat, just touched it, as if expecting the knife to cut the white flesh of itself, as if he did not have to put pressure behind it. Wistfully, he gazed at the edge of the blade resting on the white skin; the gleaming metal reflected the tremulous fury of the coals." (p. 90)

When the knife is unable to complete the beheading, Bigger becomes "hysterical"; he wants to run away but he is paralyzed, "with eyes glazed," although he is "tingling with excitement," obsessed with the sense that he "*had* to burn this girl." A hatchet first rivets his attention, then his will, and restores mobility: "He saw a hatchet. *Yes!* That would do it. He spread a neat layer of newspapers. . . . He got the hatchet, held the head at a slanting angle with his left hand and, after pausing in an attitude of prayer, sent the blade of the hatchet into the bone of the throat." (p. 91) The hatchet is also imagistically identified with the fire when Bigger tosses it into the furnace after Mary's body and covers all with a blaze of coals.

In a voodoo religious context, language describing and linking flaming furnace, knife and ax speaks in symbols indicative of the presence of a whole group of loas, or ogou, versions of the Yoruban divinity Ogun, the god of iron and fire. Major forms of these loas are variously associated with fire and war, with blacksmithing and iron, their icons decorated with sabers and machetes.

This whole key episode in *Native Son*, climaxing with the grisly severing of a head from a corpse and Bigger's shoving the bloody newspaper "wad" containing the disembodied head into the furnace, casts shadows of the closing of the voodoo ritual. The successful voodoo initiate is possessed finally by one or a number of loas considered obscene, grotesque—loas of death. Their presence at a ceremony celebrating renewed primal life seems inexplicable. Chief among them is one called, among other titles in various locales, Baron Samedi—Baron Saturday, the favored day for voodoo rituals. Wright's verbal forms conjure this loa in *Native Son* by specifying Saturday, conceived as beginning with the jangle of an alarm clock when the novel opens and ending when Bigger climbs into bed again in the dawn hours of the next morning, as the time of the action. Houngan-like, Wright invokes the presence of this nuance of primal energy, its riding of Bigger, by the seemingly gratuitous violence of the decapitation: the skull is one of Baron Samedi's representations. (Jahn, *Muntu*, p. 45)

Baron Samedi is also symbolized by the cross, usually black, and he is also referred to as Baron-la-Croix. This loa's association with the *axis mundi* indicates the connection between openings and closings, beginnings and endings. What ascends from "the deeps" under the form of Legba also descends along the same path. The manifestation of the life force has, among other figurations, a circular pattern, a pattern of the never-ending, the eternal. The ritual ends when the manifestation "dies," when the possessive energies depart the participant to return to the depths, or, rather, when he is possessed by the Baron. Death-like, he falls down, holds his breath, remains motionless. (Jahn, *Muntu*, p. 45) Bigger returns home after the completion of his horrible activities in the Dalton house, and "in five minutes he was sound asleep." (*Native Son*, p. 92) As in the case of the voodoo participant, the patterned series of images that Wright creates and that might be titled "Bigger's ritual" also ends with the image of someone who has achieved a mental condition in which inhibiting mental conflicts have been resolved, inner and outer environments have achieved a closer relationship.

The successful participant in a voodoo ceremony is "most refreshed after violent seizure" (Jahn, *Muntu*, p. 40), and Wright pictures Bigger at the beginning of the next section of the novel, after his sound sleep, as feeling that he "had created a new life for himself. . . . The hidden meaning of his life . . . had spilled out. . . . Elation filled him". (pp. 101-2)

The images of seizure, of trancelike possession and its resultant euphoria are, of course, all common to the often described Christian Afro-American church service in the United States, but the voodoo subtext of this climax to the first section of *Native Son* also brings out more fully the "ancient pattern of behavior" whose existence Wright speculated was behind the more reprehensible folklore of American racist sexual taboos. While this lore shapes the images depicting Bigger's and

Mary's interaction in the foreground of the section, in the voodoo subtext, the images of Mary and Mrs. Dalton have the rhythms of the one female loa in the voodoo pantheon, Erzulie-Freda-Dahomey.

These patterns make the characters' narrative actions eloquent with a complex of fears and aspirations long encoded in mythic expression. Mary Dalton's existence as symbol, even within the symbolic context of the novel, is underscored by Wright when he has Bigger think of her and the Dalton household in terms of the figurations he has witnessed in the movies. The images on the screen are more significant, more satisfying to him than the reality of the Daltons' existence; they retain, in Wright's telling phrase, "the mystery of the thing"; they give him a "sense of the life he has never seen." (p. 35) When Bigger enters Mary's bedroom with her, however, Wright establishes the merger of Mary's socioeconomic and sexual ideal existence with her physical reality. She ceases, for Bigger, to be the unpredicatable person he has had to reckon with and becomes a reality only in her illusory, or what Wright would call her "poetic," form. She is, as Grandmother Wilson's religion was, an objective existent, but with a reality projected by Bigger from some deep inner source of his own; she becomes a mediating form that has derived from outside himself, yet a mediating form that seems to call to his consciousness the name of something within himself, to call forth its allegiance.

Like "The Gay Woman" of the screen had been for Bigger, Mary Dalton and Mrs. Dalton become for the reader, as well as for Bigger, twentieth-century versions of an expressive pattern that has long manifested itself in folk and learned cultural forms involving female representations. In the mythic context of voodoo, both Haitian and Afro-American, the pattern involves the counterpoints of youth and age, of virgin and mother.

The mythic figure of Erzulie, evolved in part from an African sea-goddess, is manifested in seductive and sensual behavior, and her lore has her the amour of several male loas. One of her emblems, the color blue, is apparently associated with her not only as a mark of her sea-birth but because of her erstwhile consortium with the loa Agwe, the life spirit of the sea and its storms and, by extension, rebellions. In Afro-American conjuring lore, remnants of the emblematic blue possibly show up in such phenomenon as that reported by Zora Neale Hurston: "All up and down Florida one hears of the Blue Light" (the burning of a blue candle) that is part of several hexes, at least some of which are concerned with love matters. ("Voodoo in America," p. 395). In secular lore, *Dan Burley's Original Handbook of Harlem Jive*, a copy of which Wright sent to Gertrude Stein, records the expressions "lights a solid blue," meaning lights of the "right" color, and "house without chairs where the lights are a solid blue," meaning a "good time flat" or a "shady rendezvous." Related to these uses is the musical genre "the blues," often dealing with sexual behavior. Other signs associated with or representative of Erzulie are the heart, perfume, and other items considered luxuries, often gathered in a ritual bedroom or a shrine dedicated to her in voodoo churches.

Wright's language describing Mary's drunken behavior and the exhilaration it produces in Bigger reveal a pattern similar to that ascribed to Erzulie, both in terms of things sacred to her and as seen in those "ridden" by her in the voodoo ritual. Wright uses the phrases "hazy blue light" (three times) and "blue darkness" to describe the illumination surrounding the action between Bigger's entering the kitchen with Mary and the commencement of his plans to delay detection of the killing. Mary in a sense flirts with Bigger; even while in the car and coming into the house she repeatedly rests her head and body against him. Once they are in the bedroom, his actions take on a corresponding sensualness:

> His senses reeled from the scent of her hair and skin. . . . Her face was buried in his shoulder . . . Her face turned slowly. . . . Then her head leaned backward, slowly, gently; it was as though she had given up. Her lips, faintly moist in the hazy blue light, were parted. . . . Her eyes were closed . . . her face came toward him and her lips touched his. . . . He . . . laid her on the bed. . . . He tightened his fingers on her breasts, kissing her again, feeling her move toward him. (*Native Son*, pp. 83-84)

But the heart that is emblematic of Erzulie is as likely to be pierced by a sword as by an arrow. Erzulie is more than an Aphrodite: pictures originally intended to depict the Blessed Virgin, a white woman in a blue veil, often appear in her shrines. The significance of the Sorrowful Virgin Mother as well as that of the erotic Venus vibrates around the Erzulie pattern. Hurston points out in *Tell My Horse* that Erzulie is in some branches of voodoo imaged as an older woman, "red-eyed . . . and terrible to look upon." (p. 147) In the bedroom scene in *Native Son*, Bigger's actions, as his physical and imaginative life forces merge and gather toward a climax that is implicitly to be sexual, are under the sway of Mrs. Dalton as well as that of Mary. Mrs. Dalton, the white woman pictured as the heart-pierced sorrowful mother, strikes terror in Bigger. The narrative crisis this figure precipitates leads to a narrative solution far more elaborate than what a simple sexual denouemont would have accomplished.

Wright's language divides this mythic entity into two forms; in the voodoo context, contradictory as they are, the two forms are merged, as they are in Bigger's petrifaction, the image of their "possession" of him. The contradiction is compounded, and apparently with little problem for devotees, by the understanding that Erzulie is physically neither virgin nor mother. The paradoxical images of this are, however, more concerned with a subtle spiritual realization than with the mere bodily condition. This realization, which the voodoo myth of Erzulie struggles to express, is at once incarnate in the narrative of Mary Dalton and closer to, more clearly reflective of, the "ancient pattern of behavior" that Wright surmised lay deeply and murkily ingrained in what appear to be southern and Spanish sexual attitudes toward women. Maya Deren's explication of the Erzulie myth is apropos to Wright's narrative and also inches toward this ancient pattern:

> Voodoo has given women, in the figure of Erzulie, exclusive title to that which distinguishes humans from all other forms: their capacity to conceive beyond reality, to desire beyond adequacy, to create beyond need . . . woman as the divinity of the dream. . . . It has denied her emphasis as mother of life and of men in order to regard her (like Mary, with whom Erzulie is identified) as mother of man's myth of life—its meaning. In a sense, she is that very principle by which man conceives and creates divinity. . . . Even though (and perhaps precisely because) it is so difficult for the [Haitian] to acquire even those things which are requisite for daily life, he is almost obsessed with the vision of a life which would transcend these, a dream of luxury in which even the essentials of life are refined to appear as indulgences. The lady of that sublime luxury is

Erzulie. In her character is reflected all the elan, all the excessive pitch with which the dreams of men soar. . . .

As Lady of Luxury she is, above all, Goddess of Love, that human luxury of the heart which is not essential to the purely physical generation of the body. She is lavish with that love as she is generous with her gifts. She treats men with such overflowing, such demonstrative affection that it might seem, at times, embarrassing. . . . Nothing is meted out or budgeted, there is more than enough; this is her way of loving, this is the divine fecundity of the heart. A heart is, indeed, her symbol, most often the pierced heart identified with Mary. (*ivine Horsemen*, pp. 138; 141)

A case could be developed that, insofar as capitalism is based on the assumption of scarcity, the values expressed in Erzulie are as anticapitalistic as any Communist doctrine. The point to be stressed here is that through the voodoo subtext Wright's religion-tinted language opens, to the reader, the image of Mary Dalton to a significance beyond the Realistic mode of the narrative, as Wright has also indicated by connecting Mary and the Daltons with Bigger's dreams as embodied in the movie images he had experienced earlier. In the image of Mrs. Dalton, the connection between the Christian Sorrowful Mother and this lavish, luscious Erzulie finds one form of expression, a form that the following passages, also from Deren, help clarify:

It is upon this diminutive feminine figure that man has placed the burden of the most divine paradox. . . . Erzulie is the loa of the impossible perfection which must remain unattainable. Man demands that she demand of him beyond his capacity. The condition of her divinity is his failure. . . . Hence she must weep. . . .

So, Maitresse Erzulie, weeping, comes to that moment which has been called her paralysis. . . . [In the ceremony] her limbs, her neck, her back go limp. Her arms, stretching across the shoulders of the men who support her . . . her head tilting . . . the lids closing over eyes turned inward toward some infinite darkness, she presents . . . the . . . attitude of the Crucifixion. So she is carried . . . to some adjacent private chamber. Stretched on the bed, her arms outflung, she falls asleep. . . . she is the dream impaled eternally upon the crossroads where the world of men and the world of divinity meet, and it is through her pierced heart that "man ascends and the gods descend" (pp. 144-45).

Mary Dalton, of course, does not weep; that function of the

loa is conveyed in the image of Mrs. Dalton, but in the emotional spirit informing ths scene, Mary is undoubtedly for Bigger the impossible "dream" whose "impaling" or sacrifice accomplishes the modern and Western view of the incarnation, the descent of divinity into mankind. As Wright later in the novel states through Boris Max, Bigger's act of killing Mary was creative, and what was created was Bigger himself, not only as a man in control of his own life but as the divinity creating that man. When Bigger tells Max "Whatever I killed for, I am!" we are able to see just how fully Wright's depiction of the Dalton women provides a parallel to the role of the voodoo loa Erzulie. Insofar as Erzulie represents, as Deren puts it, "man's myth of life . . . that very principle by which man conceives and creates divinity," she and her modern versions, such as the Dalton women, are fit contours for that "something" that Wright's poetics was so concerned with.

Wright was undoubtedly no more aware of the mythic voodoo dimension he was giving this section of *Native Son* than he was of the source in his own experience of the emotion-laden images of the black male in the white woman's bedroom and the disapproving white mother. It took Dr. Wertham's persistent analysis to dredge the latter from Wright's psyche ("An Unconscious Determinant in *Native Son*," pp. 111-15), and even then Wright's memory of the incident was hazy. More deliberate was his giving to the language in which the action is expressed a religious and supernatural tone, derived in part from gothic "pop" fiction that was a staple of his youthful reading, but even more largely from his childhood experience of Afro-American religion and its ceremonies.

Wright's more or less conscious motivations for using such a language were multiple. In addition to his abiding fascination with the essence of his grandmother's folk religious orientation were more purely literary considerations. One of these, no doubt, was his own personal share of Afro-American artists' concern with naming his own terrain. Writing in the twentieth century, Wright nevertheless was facing the problem that confronted early nineteenth-century American writers. Like them, in writing of the American experience in a new environment, he had to use in his surface narrative the images of a thing considered diminished, ugly, by those not of that environment or experience. Like them, Wright, as an artist, had to make something of this desert, the uncharted wilderness of Afro-American life in the twentieth century. By means of certain images that are part of the representational, "realistic" narrative level, he, like those earlier writers, managed to forge a link between that level and myth. As with those earlier writers who had to deal with a seemingly ahistorical American landscape and a scrawny civilization, Wright was able to reveal that "the Great Mother" still lives there, even though the landscape remained unkempt.

Put another way and in a totally twentieth-century literary context, what Harry Levin has said of James Joyce regarding the modern use of myth is applicable to Wright's use of it in *Native Son:*

> The metaphoric impetus [revealed in] working experimental transformations into traditional continuities . . . provides . . . the transmutation of . . . citizens into mythical archetypes. . . . In the novel, as Naturalism had left it, the environment came dangerously close to swamping the personages. That was not the fault of the Naturalists, but of the situations with which they dealt. The dehumanization of art . . . mirrors the dehumanization of life. Joyce, by resorting to metamorphosis and even to mock-apotheosis, was trying to rehumanize his characters; and he succeeded in giving them contour, if not stature. Journalistic novelists like John Dos Passos and Jean-Paul Sartre, seeking a panoramic or kaleidescopic approach to the urban scene, have imitated Joyce's structural method. . . . [The result of that method is that] the apparent sordidness and purposelessness of our day . . . are transmuted into a symbolic reenactment. . . . Some of those cross-references seem far-fetched, and others grimly ironic; yet as a whole, they interpret for us data which would otherwise be meaningless. ("What Was Modernism?" pp. 624-26)

In Wright's novel, through the implicit images of voodoo ceremony (itself partially metamorphosed into Afro-American folk religion as well as into secular folk appropriations, just as prehistoric lore was altered by Homer's adaptation of it), fictive Chicago citizens acquire archetypal dimensions. Wright's apotheosis of Bigger is a mock only in the sense that it affronts the Christian doctrine of incarnation by inverting it: Bigger, entering into his human life by asserting his own reality against "the other," becomes God—the Old Testament God. The divine, in Wright's cosmos, does not descend from heaven but rather ascends from the waters of the deep.

Wright knew the technique of playing naturalistic details of individual life against a background of larger significance. As Margolies has said, Wright knew his Dos Passos and his Joyce, demonstrating his knowledge in his pre-*Native Son* apprentice novel *Lawd Today*, in which the antihero's quotidian routine is parasyntactically laminated over Lincoln's birthday radio speeches and other media pronouncements. In that novel, however, perhaps because of its close modeling to modernist writers, the antihero's actions, and perhaps the myths themselves, are patently and ironically rendered more inhuman and meaningless by playing the myth over them, as one could argue is also the case with Leopold Bloom. In *Native Son*, on the other hand, if one recognizes the mythic transparency in place, the imaged actions of manslaughter and dismemberment are given a humanity—although in a most disturbing form. It is a form Wright finds as reprehensible as the religion his grandmother seized upon and the movie shadows Bigger responds to; both are attempting to name the same reality, the same source. The additional layer of myth introduced by the voodoo subtext, a myth itself not seen as an adequate statement of the reality, nevertheless attempts to convey the presumed primal essence, an essence that is discovered in the very act of asserting it.

The presence of the folk forms in "The Man Who Killed a Shadow" and *Native Son* does not merely enhance, by universalizing or adding psychological force to, their socioeconomic historical dimensions. These were coded in Realistic or Naturalistic verbal and mythic structure that gives one meaning to the lives of all of the space-time Sauls and Biggers whom Wright had known or known of in a nonfictional context. Wright's poetics, welding these dimensions to folk paradigms, propels these works into a denser sphere of symbolic structure. The novel thus exists as myth (the author's complex consciousness) surrounding myth (the fluid lore) surrounding myth (twentieth-century forces), as the result of Wright's poetics.

Afro-American lore provided Wright with more than just the

voodoo and the owl paradigms. His blueprint or poetics, involving the structure of mythic overlay—projecting one set of events or constructs against another that is more or less implicit in such a way as to utilize the correspondence of both to attract the human sense of reality—was itself derived from the folk expression Wright had absorbed. It is another version of his reference to his grandmother's and the blues' penchant for yolking disparate things together in some overruling "mood" that gives these elements their meaning. It is probable that he responded to Joyce (and to Dos Passos, who was responding to Joyce) because of an awareness that there was in them a process corresponding to what he thought he perceived but had not fully grasped in Afro-American folk expression. That such was the case is supported by his statement in "Memories of My Grandmother" where he wrote explicitly about a connection he recognized between folk usage and Gertrude Stein's use of language and between the Surrealists' theory and practice of art and black American folk expression.

3

MODERN FORMS:
USES OF STEIN
AND SURREALISM

Wright frequently talked about what he called Gertrude Stein's "influence" on him. In print, his most elaborate references to this occur in *American Hunger* and in a 1945 review of Stein's *Wars I Have Seen*; a little less publicly, he was announcing this influence as early as 1937 to other delegates at the American Writers Congress. (Fabre, *Unfinished Quest*, p. 549, n. 4) Among his unpublished papers are two early 1940s references to Stein and to verbal practices he engaged in under her aegis when he was beginning his writing career. Exactly what Stein-at-a-distance did to or for him is not immediately clear. His best known works—*Uncle Tom's Children*, *Native Son*, and *Black Boy*—do not obviously or clearly suggest Steinian influence. As he is generally regarded, Wright seems antithetic to Stein rather than someone susceptable to her influence: she, so almost entirely concerned with pure art, with the poesis of expression; he, with racial and economic injustice, with the praxis of affecting sociopolitical change. She was a fairly identifiable example of art for art's sake; he was a prototypical "black power" writer to whom art for its own sake is a discredited, effete, bourgeois game. Wright's published and unpublished comments on the relationship are marked with inconsistencies and prima facie improbabilities that, left unexplored, encourage among Wright's students two views of this "influence": that a literary snobbishness, however defensively and unconsciously developed during his formative years, led him to claim a connection with Stein; or, the kinder attitude, that he did not know exactly what he was talking about. For example, he could condemn Zora Neal Hurston's *Their Eyes Were Watching God* because it presented "quaint" views of Afro-Americans, the way white Americans liked to see them, and yet call "Melanctha," with its stereotypical references to the "simple, promiscuous unmorality of the black people" and "the wide abandoned laughter that makes the warm broad glow of negro sunshine" (Stein, *Three Lives*, p. 86), "the first realistic treatment of Negro life I'd seen when I was trying to learn to write." (Wright, "Why I Chose 'Melanctha,'" p. 254) On the other hand, the frequency of his claims and his friendship, both epistolary and personal, which was eventually established with Stein in 1945-46, indicate that his professions of regard for her prose were not just bluff. In spite of all the incongruities, it would seem that Stein's prose did provide him with a kind of forest of Arden or Prospero's island, functioning for him as Paris had done for American expatriate writers and artists of the 1920s. He seems to have felt that her prose contained the deeply attractive "something," that he had found in his grandmother's outlook; the "something" that he could never fully explain but that led him to some valuable, speculative insights concerning Afro-American language and the nature of Afro-American folk imagination. Hence an investigation of his relationship with Stein's work provides a better understanding of his poetics.

Wright's discovery of Stein's work took place between 1925 and 1934. Some of his comments on this discovery suggest that the appeal of her prose had something to do with what has been perceived as her stylization, her emphatic exaggeration of certain linguistic features and practices that has called so much attention to her work. In *American Hunger*, the narrative indicates that Wright arrived in Chicago from Memphis in the winter of 1927 and held a series of menial jobs until June when his first temporary employment in the post office afforded him leisure for reading and attempts at writing: "Repeatedly I took stabs at writing, but the results were so poor I would tear up the sheets. I was striving for a level of expression that matched those of the novels I read. But I always somehow failed to get on the page what I thought and felt. Failing at sustained narrative, I compromised by playing with single sentences and phrases. Under the influence of Stein's *Three Lives*, I spent hours and days pounding out disconnected sentences for the sheer love of words." (p. 22)

While this passage presents some difficulties that we shall take up later, the implication that he attempted to use her prose as a superficial model for his own is reinforced by other evidence. Among his unpublished papers are notes for a lecture that he gave in early 1940 titled "What I Think Writing Is," (File 511) in which occurs the remark "experiment in words—Stein," followed by one of the same sentences he gives in *American Hunger* as an example of the kind of writing he had produced with Stein's prose in mind. Also, in two extant apprentice novels, traces of such stylization seem to be present. Margolies says, somewhat disparagingly, that *Cesspool*, a novel Wright worked on between 1931 and 1936, but which was not published until 1963 as *Lawd Today*, shows in its experimentation with techniques that "Wright had learned . . . his Gertrude Stein only too well." (*The Art of Richard Wright*, p. 90) Specifically, he believes Stein's example shows up in the way Wright revealed his protagonist's character" in circumscribed, repetitious phrases and expressions [which] he catches in fragments and snatches of Jake's conversation. (p. 100) Margolies also detects echoes of Stein in "certain cadences" in Wright's short story "Long Black Song," written in 1936, and opines that the pared-down quality of some of Wright's stories composed as late as the 1950s may be Wright's version of something he "fancied his idol, Gertrude Stein, had done." (pp. 67, 83)

Wright's other apprentice novel, "Tarbaby's Dawn," which exists only in an unpublished typescript, contains somewhat stronger evidence that Wright used Stein as a model for at least some of his writing between 1934 and 1936. For example, these passages expressing sexual passion and climax—

> All of him was feeling in her. . . . Gradually he began to see and feel it all and he felt her helping him to feel her and then he had her, feeling him and her coming to a dark red point of hotness and blazing red and red and red. . . .
> . . . the fleeting sense of that hot wet dark red bath that was leaving

63

him. He kissed her hard again, trying to make the old fleeting feeling stay, yet feeling it leaving knowing it was leaving and would leave. (File 906)

—are comparable to passages from "Melanctha'"

Things began to be very strong between them

. . . Everyday now, Jeff seemed to be coming nearer, to be really loving. Everyday now, they seemed to be having more and more, both together, of this strong, right feeling. More and more every day now they seemed to know more really, what each other one was always feeling. More and more now every day Jeff found in himself, he felt more trusting. More and more every day now, he did not think anything in words about what he was always doing. Every day now more and more Melanctha would let out to Jeff her real, strong feeling. (Stein, *Three Lives*, pp. 154-55, 168)

In addition, while Wright mentions only *Three Lives* and "Melanctha" (his favorite in this collection) in particular as Stein works he had read by 1934, portions of "Tarbaby's Dawn" evoke other pieces by Stein. In or between several chapters of this novel, Wright included lengthy, poetic passages that represent dreams of Tarbaby's actual experiences, which the reader has read in the preceding section of the novel:

Water
Water below
Water below wide brown deep
Wide brown deep water
Water wide brown deep . . .
Something will happen Tarbaby
Water will happen Tarbaby
A tree will happen Tarbaby
Tree sways in water wide brown deep below around a tree

Something will happen
Something will have to happen
Something will have to happen soon. . . .

Although much more consecutively narrative and fitted into a traditional narrative structure, these interchapters resemble parts of Stein's "rose" poem, "Sacred Emily":

Next to barber
Next to barber bury

64

Next to barber bury china
Next to barber bury china glass . . .
Put something down
Put something down someday in
Put something down someday in my
In my hand
In my hand right
In my hand writing
Put something down someday in my hand writing.
(Geography and Plays, pp. 181, 185)

But the extent to which Wright seems to have focused on the stylization of Stein's prose and used it as a model for his own is at best limited. The sentences he gave in *American Hunger* as examples of those he churned out by the pageful under her "influence" do not sound like Stein's: "The soft melting hunk of butter trickled in gold down the stringy grooves of the split yam"; "the child's clumsy fingers fumbled in sleep, feeling vainly for the wish of its dream"; "the old man huddled in the dark doorway, his bony face lit by the burning yellow in the windows of distant skyscrapers." (p. 22) Moreover, Fabre cites (*Unfinished Quest*, p. 578, n. 7) a version of the yam sentence that occurs in other unpublished fragments of Wright's papers in a context that indicates it was written in Memphis in 1925 or 1926, and makes no mention of Stein. If Wright were trying to imitate what he thought of as Stein's style in the period between 1925 and 1927, such efforts left few traces. His earliest story, "Superstition," published in 1931 and probably written in 1929 or 1930, contains nothing suggestive of Stein's sentence structure. The sentences are, however, on a par with those allegedly inspired in him by *Three Lives*. Regarding the poemlike passages in "Tarbaby's Dawn," an anonymous note filed with the typescript indicates that at least one reader saw Dos Passos rather than Stein behind the device. What is certain is that Wright, showing his typical independence, abandoned this technique half way through the novel. If it were Stein-inspired, its abandonment seems to indicate that he did not feel that the element in her writing that had appealed to him was capturable by so patently mimicking her. Insofar as style is superficially conceived as a particular way with words and sentence structure, his use of Stein's work as a model was neither pervasive nor permanent and does not, therefore, totally account for the importance he attributed to her work in his development as a writer.

If, however, style is thought of not merely as external and decorative but as interior and integral, or, as Sontag puts it, as "the signature of the artist's will"—as the form chosen to make the work perceivable, the coequal convex of content's concave—then Wright was "influenced" by Stein's style.

In 1955, in "Writers and Their Art," his unpublished reply to aspiring young Indonesian authors, Wright commented that "subject matter is simply the outer dress of the emotions which [the artist] seeks to convey," a remark that prefigures Sontag's belief that "the matter, the subject, is on the outside; the style is on the inside." (*Against Interpretation*, p. 17) Thirteen years earlier, in *American Hunger*, Wright also referred in passing to a similar idea as a cause of the appeal of "Melanctha" to him, one that goes deeper than the surface notion of style. His purpose in writing the sentences quoted above was "to capture a physical state or movement that carried a strong subjective impression." (p. 22) He recognized in Stein's prose, and was trying to achieve in his own writing, the mythic quality of language—the essence of imaginative literature. A short passage in *American Hunger* indicates his awareness of the problem he faced as a novice litterateur: how to give his fiction the ring of truth; how to create illusions that were or seemed real: "I strove to master words, to make them disappear, to make them important by making them new, to make them melt into a rising spiral of emotional stimuli, each greater than the other, each feeding and reinforcing the other, and all ending in an emotional climax that would drench the reader with a sense of a new world." (p. 22)

Such a purpose can be seen behind the sexual passage quoted above from "Tarbaby's Dawn." But the emotional response Wright most consistently wanted to elicit in his readers was much more in the line of actual rather than aesthetic emotions, which Stein's work is more likely to arouse. It is not easy, therefore, to see how Stein's work fed such a purpose in him, how her prose, so marked by artifice, could strike him as having the kind of genuineness he was looking for.

Wright's first published testament of his affinity for Stein's writing, although it refers to what is usually seen as her style, to her "repetitive rhythms" and "grammarless prose," gives an account of its appeal that is, on the surface, quite different from and less believable than that presented in *American Hunger*. In the 1945 *P.M.* review of *Wars I Have Seen*, he said that "random curiosity' while he was browsing in a Chicago public library led him to Stein: "I took from the open shelves a tiny volume call *Three Lives* and looked at a story in it, entitled *Melanctha*. The style was so insistent and original and sang so quaintly that I took the book home. ("Gertrude Stein's Story Is Drenched in Hitler's Horrors," p. M15)

What is most difficult to accept about this account but important to his poetics is his claim that, as he continued reading *Three Lives* his "ears were opened for the first time to the magic of the spoken word. I began to hear the speech of my grandmother, who spoke a deep, pure Negro dialect and with whom I had lived for years. All my life I had been only half hearing, but Miss Stein's struggling words made the speech of the people around me vivid. From that moment on, in my attempts at writing, I was able to tap at will the vast pool of living words that swirled around me." (p. m15)

This account, although describing an effect that is definitely significant for a writer, flies somewhat in the face of what he had written four years earlier in *American Hunger* regarding the inspiration of Stein. If the sentences he describes as producing by the pageful do not sound like Stein, they sound even less like "living words" drawn, as the *P.M.* account implies, from the verbal atmosphere of Afro-American language.

Claude McKay's opinion of Stein's Negroes typifies that of many Afro-Americans. Although not dealing specifically with Stein's language, it seems applicable. In Stein's story, he "found nothing striking and informative about Negro life. Melanctha, the mulattress, might have been a Jewess. And the mulatto, Jeff Campbell—he is not typical of mulattoes I have known everywhere. . . . Melanctha seemed more like a brief American paraphrase of *Esther Waters* than a story of Negro life. (Brinnin, *The Third Rose*, p. 121) Since that novel by the Edwardian George Moore was a favorite of Wright's, his fondness for it might have merely, if exaggeratedly, carried over to the similarities he perceived in "Melanctha."

Wright did have some doubts himself, but they were triggered, according to what he said in *P.M.*, not by a sense of any inherent ontological gulf between the two languages but by political considerations. A "sharply-worded newspaper article" by "a left-wing literary critic" whose opinions Wright respected condemned Stein's prose as reactionary and led Wright to wonder if he "had . . . been duped into worshipping decadence." To settle his misgivings, he conducted an "experiment in words," but different from what he had described in *American Hunger:* "Desirous of ascertaining the degree to which Miss Stein's prose was tainted with the spirit of counter-revolution, I gathered a group of semi-literate Negro stockyard workers . . . into a Black Belt basement and read *Melanctha* aloud to them. They understood every word. Enthralled, they slapped their thighs, howled, laughed, stomped and interrupted me constantly to comment on the character." (p. m15) A kind of response Stein herself might have appreciated, but one that might lead most literary critics to wonder about the depth of these workers' understanding of Stein's work. Wright, with his knowledge of Negro folk audiences, took the reaction as approbative and confirming his own opinion.

His sense of correlation between Stein's prose and the Afro-American use of language was not a totally unique phenomenon. In addition to the stockyard workers' response (as he interpreted it), Wright's view of the general realism of the story has also been expressed by other notable Afro-American writers: "James Weldon Johnson felt in *Melanctha* that Gertrude Stein was 'the first . . . white writer to write a story of life between a Negro man and woman and deal with them as normal members of the human family,' and the novelist Nella Larsen wrote a letter to Gertrude in which she said 'I never cease to wonder how you came to write it and just why you and not some one of us should so accurately have caught the spirit of this race of mine.'" (Brinnin, *The Third Rose*, p. 121)

While neither black nor a writer, Virgil Thomson, Stein's friend who collaborated with her on the opera "Four Saints in Three Acts," used an all-black cast for the original 1934 production because, in addition to black singers' better diction, carriage, and movement, he felt they have "an intuitive, culturally conditioned ability to understand Stein's text." (Rockwell, "Virgil Thomson's 'Saints' Goes Marching On")

Regarding "Melanctha," because Stein's story did not treat Afro-Americans as either buffoons or as completely exotic primitives (although there is something of that in Melanctha's "feeling" approach to "wisdom" and its erotic undercurrent), and since it did not resort to the "broken jingle" convention of her time—depicting Negro speech by means of odd spellings and misuse of big words—Stein's story would undoubtedly have seemed relatively realistic. But Wright, directly, and Stein herself, indirectly, have furnished other explanations, some very brief and circumstantial and others more detailed and philosophical, as to how Wright's imagination could intuit a link between Stein's avant-garde prose and the language of his black Mississippi background.

No doubt one cause was that his imagination, however moved by formal, professional literary artists, had been shaped early, as he indicates in *Black Boy* and "Memories of My Grandmother," by the folktales and other lore, religious and secular, conveyed to him by his mother, grandmother, and undoubtedly nearly everyone he knew during his formative years in Mississippi. Stein's prose is certainly folklike in its most famous characteristic, its repetition.

In "Portraits and Repetition," she revealed that this characteristic was related, as is much folk expression, to oral tradition: "When I first really realized the inevitable repetition in human expression that was not repetition but insistence . . . was when . . . I . . . lived . . . principally with a whole group of very lively little aunts who had to know anything . . . as there were ten or eleven of them they did have to say and hear said whatever was said and any one not hearing what it was they said had to come in to hear what had been said . . . I began consciously listening . . . You listen as you know." (*Lectures In America*, pp. 168-69)

Emitting this particular wave of folk sound to one who knew what to hear, her language could have provided a "shock of recognition." Wright mentions in the "Memories of My Grandmother," for example, his awareness of folk blues, characterized in both lyrics and music by a repetition that is yet not exactly a repetition but an incrementation.

Among Wright's revelations concerning the connection is a brief interchange between several characters in his early novel, *Lawd Today*. One character mentions having heard of a famous white American woman living in Paris who writes sentences like "a rose is a rose is a rose." Another makes the intriguing comment that this sounds like Cab Calloway, and still another character objects that even Calloway never said anything so crazy. (p. 150) The perception touched on here is of similarity between Stein's language and "scat" or "jive" talk. But since this use of language is largely an urban and very secular sub-dialect of black language, a perception of a connection between it and Stein's prose does not explain fully how Stein's language could lead Wright to hearing the language of his less urbane and more religiously oriented grandmother. The most complete explanation of the connection which Wright ever attempted is found in "Memories of My Grandmother."

Wright's great sense of totality, of unity, while drafting *The Man Who Lived Underground*, was the result of a number of previous experiences coalescing in him during the act of composition. In addition to the central experience of his grandmother were those of Freud, Surrealism, and of "Melanctha." Faced with the multiplicity of experiences, he began the memoir with a disclaimer concerning the strict chronology of his memories, thus disarming criticism concerning discrepancies in the essay. Like a Wordsworth or a Frost, Wright did not, perhaps could not, always attend fully to certain conscious experiences, which then later threw their shadows across his psychic path, affording him experiences of his earlier experiences. He may thus have encountered "Melanctha" a number of times, at first "stylistically" and then at a later date in an entirely different way.

The dominance of his grandmother's mind-set, which he puzzled over but did not accept because he had rejected the religious form it had found in expressing itself, also led him to an incipient view of language, which he later in the memoir relates most explicitly to his reading of "Melanctha." Overhearing, when he was a youth, his elders discussing Leopold and Loeb, then much in the news, and commenting on the pair's linguistic abilities, Wright recounts his having been possessed by a quirky wish: to be able to stand outside the English language, to defamiliarize it so that he might experience it as pure sound. His family thought this a weird, unpropitious wish, not realizing any more than he did that it was their religious teaching of living beyond this world that lay, ultimately, behind such an idea.

"Melanctha" was, among other effects, to gratify this impulsive desire. In the memoir, unlike his account in *P.M.*, he implies that his discovery of the story was only indirectly fortuitous. His introduction to Stein, according to this version, was prompted by a newspaper account that referred to Stein as an oddity and mentioned her "a rose is a rose is a rose' line. The account assured him that the woman was decidedly out of her head and that all her work was condemnable, with the exception of "Melanctha," which, though somewhat balmy, was nevertheless a worthwhile novella. He also states that he read the story while his grandmother was living with him in Chicago. Since she died in 1934, such statements, if reliable, indicate that he came within Stein's orbit sometime between 1930 and 1934.

Like the *P.M.* version, this memoir also indicates his experimentations to verify the validity of his perceived connection between Stein's prose and Negro speech. He reversed, he says, his previous practice of avoiding his grandmother as much as possible; instead, he involved her in conversations so he could delight in her manner of speech, the folk speech that Stein's story had made it possible for him to hear for the first time. This activity also seems similar to one Fabre reports in his biography: Wright engaged, in 1930, in recording the speech of his black co-workers at the Chicago post office, in preparation for an intended novel about South Side Chicago (p. 86), but the story of the stockyard workers as it appears in the memoir differs from the *P.M.* version in one significant detail. Wright, prompted by a labor journal critic's put-down of Stein as to how he could have discovered Afro-American folk vernacular in such an unlikely source, reads "Melanctha" to these workers, and they respond with outbursts highly indicative of amused acknowledgement of Melanctha's behavior. They began spontaneously to compose extensions of Melanctha's thought and her way of speaking. Attributing this power to produce spontaneously Stein-like expressions of their own indicates even more strongly than the *P.M.* account the similarity Wright perceived between Stein's written esoteric language and the speech and thought patterns of Negro folk expression.

The memoir is more extravagant than the account in *P.M.* concerning the reaction "Melanctha" prompted and more indicative of what Wright heard that was "Negro" in Stein's use of language. The story not only recalled his adolescent wish to hear English, but caused him to hear his grandmother's speech for the first time, to hear the tonal quality and the beat of her uncomplicated, resonant sentences. This incongruous association gave him a marvelous sense of Afro-American folk language in general as unadorned, musical, unpolished, joyous, and very much a product of the Negro personality. Even more significantly, with regard to Stein's relationship to his poetics, Stein's prose enabled him to hear not just the sensory linguistic aspects of Negro speech but, for all its unembellishment, a convoluted physical arrangement behind this language.

What the memoir suggests is that what he heard was not what Stein's characters were saying but rather Stein's attitude toward language. He tells us that, while in school, he had been made to study correct, standard English. Such a language is fine, he says, if one aimed at a bourgeois career in education or business, but it was near-fatal to one of a more philosophic cast of mind, to one who sought the meaning of what was happening around him, for it diverted his attention from a very important sign of the immense realm of emotion that surrounded him. Stein, a famous white literary personage, was using language in a way that made this familiar, standard English seem odd. The adjectives he uses to describe what her language had opened his ears to in Negro speech indicate that she made him aware of a validity in language that was not in the scientific mode, not presenting clear, concise, exact, discrete concepts or logical discourse. She made him aware of the validity of prose perceived not, as he had perceived Mencken's, as a weapon but, in its sensory qualities, as music or incantation. This was language, recognized, however controversially, as literary; it was expressive of psychic powers, not so much cognitive or semantically communicative as affective or, more bluntly, voluntaristic.

Stein's own expressed intention regarding her experimentation with language in "Melanctha" encourages such a reading of Wright's response. She was not attempting to use "words . . . as the authentic dialect of Baltimore . . . Negroes." Any dialectic elements that seem to be present were used as "a pretext for liberating the language from literary conventions." (Sutherland, *Gertrude Stein*, p. 41) In *Wars I Have Seen*, Stein was to comment that as a child she was always disturbed by Negro dialect encountered in her reading. By the time she wrote "Melanctha," she was beginning her attempt to turn language into a paint-like medium, into a material exactly malleable, as Flaubert once called for, to a sense—her sense, in this case—of facts, rather than to facts themselves. Taking her cue, as she has said, from Cezanne, who she understood was occupied with "the idea that in composition one thing was as important as another. . . . I was obsessed by this idea of composition, and the Negro story . . . was the quintessence of it . . . it was not solely the realism of the characters but the realism of the composition of my thoughts. . . . I was not interested in making the people real but in the essence or, as a painter would call it, value." (Haas, *A Primer for the Gradual Understanding of Gertrude Stein*, pp. 15-16)

At the end of *Wars I Have Seen*, indirectly but along the same line, she attributed the conversational differences between World War I and World War II American troops to a linguistic behavior that seems clearly to reflect her own practices:

> The only way the Americans could change their language was by choosing words which they liked better than other words, by putting words next to each other in a different way than the English way . . . we use the same words as the English do but the words say an entirely different thing . . . the Americans of the last war, they had their language but they were not yet in possession of it . . . that generation . . . was beginning to possess its language but it was still struggling but now the job is done, the G. I. Joes . . . dominate their language and in dominating their language which is now all theirs they have ceased to be adolescents and have become men. (p. 259)

Echoing and amplifying the "dominate" note of such a Stein utterance, Marianne DeKoven, in her book *A Different Lan-*

guage, a study of Stein's experimental writing, concludes that Stein's avant-garde prose both

> concealed and encoded . . . troublesome feelings about herself as a woman. . . . But Stein did not merely stifle or deny her anger, her sense that she did not fit and that the deficiency was not hers but rather that of the structure which excluded her. In effect, Stein's rebellion was channelled from content to linguistic structure itself. A rebellion in language is much easier to ignore or misconstrue, but its attack, particularly in literature, penetrates far deeper, to the very structures which determine, within a particular culture, what can be thought. (p. 36)

She also points out Stein's place

> very squarely within what Richard Poirer has identified as the American literary tradition in which rebellious imaginers use style to create an alternative "world somewhere." Writers in this tradition resist
>> within their pages the forces of environment that otherwise dominate the world. Their styles have an eccentricity of defiance . . . they try to create an environment of "freedom," though as writers their efforts must be wholly in language. American books are often written as if historical forces cannot possibly provide such an environment, as if history can give no life to "freedom," and as if only language can create the liberated place . . .
> Within *Three Lives,* . . . the detachment of writing from coherent thematic content is the beginning of leaving such content behind altogether, of attempting to create "the liberated place" entirely through language. (p. 37)

A few transpositions and substitution of racial for sexual terms make clear how relevant Stein's prose is to black American folk expression in general, to Grandmother Wilson in particular and definitely to what in Stein's prose led Wright to sense a connection between it and Negro speech.

Parallel to Stein's conscious, intentional bending of English to conform as exactly as possible to the way her subjective mental processes constructed her emotional/ideational world was Wright's grandmother's bending of it to conform to a subjective mental world conditioned to a degree by a religious conviction. The absence of the religious in Stein's prose removed one block to his seeing and hearing what was being done with language in his own environment. The idyo-syncratic appearance and sound of Stein's printed language, a bit bizarre even in as early a work as "Melanctha," removed other blocks. He had already been impressed with the power of language as used by certain "classic" white authors whose works he was devouring, without quite understanding how to achieve this power in his own writing. He had also been impressed by the force achieved by folk blues composers. Stein and her use of language bridged these categories. Her obviously will-full way with English, the way of a recognized if not well understood grande dame of Euro-American belles lettres, seemed to sanction the language practices he had known all his life. The black folk of Mississippi and his grandmother approached language in an "abstract" manner, similar to Stein's, giving meaning not according to objective facts but from an inner "something"—a vision, attitude, conception—more genuine than anything exterior. What Stein's prose catalyzed in Wright was a realization and above all an appreciation of the strength of what for a better word has to be called personality, a strength of personality that such an attitude toward language objectified, however deplorable or illogical the external conditions or subject matter that clothed it.

That such a view of Stein's prose was in Wright's mind is also suggested by the two Afro-American publications he sent to her in 1946. One was *Dan Burley's Original Handbook of Harlem Jive*, referred to in chapter 2, in which Burley states that "Jive, like cussing, is a language of emotion; a means of describing how one is affected by certain experiences or situations. . . . The twisting of language to suit the user has been one of the things that brought Jive to its highest development." (p. 73) Burley also refers to Zora Neale Hurston's comments that "the Negro's reaction to language is an emotional one, not an intellectual one. It is the sound of words, their flexibility, and the way in which they may be combined with other similar words that impress him—not their meaning." (p. 74)

The reality of such language, like the reality of Gabriel Prosser's hopes and of Grandmother Wilson's religious views, came from within, from a version of what is called faith, the unflagging will to affirm, from irrepressible *life*, that inexplicable "something" that literary critics often fall back on when confronted with a work that, in spite of multiferious flaws, is nevertheless incontestably good.

Coleridge, in his attempt to define imagination, resorted to the theological doctrine of the Trinity. However abstruse and incomplete Coleridge's remarks may be, insofar as they bring together the mental power called will, a religious focus, and a notion of personality, they provide a precedent to what Wright's experience of Stein's prose affectively revealed to him about imagination—the reality sense. Rooted in the ulterior consciousness of self-identity, of the perpetual, primal, obscure, and literally ex-static terror of self-unweaving and the simultaneous willed rush to reintegrate—whereby the human self, like the trinitarian deity it images, repeatedly actuates and enacts its undeniable "I AM"—the secondary imagination bodies forth in the fancies of rhythms, cadences, incantations, the self's own sense of its unweaving and reweaving, its real being in existence.

In a cloudy way (although possibly not much cloudier than Coleridge's), Wright, partly through the agency of Stein's prose, came to a similar awareness of what gave verbal art (and other forms, although they were not, except for black American music, a concern for him in his memoir) its power. That he never polished "Memories of My Grandmother" or attempted to have it published would suggest that he recognized it did not include all that he meant. Possibly, too, negative reactions to the original drafts of *The Man Who Lived Underground*, which had inspired the essay, caused him to doubt the feelings he had while writing it. A question also remains as to why, given the early probable dates of his encountering Stein's work, he did not attempt to meet her when she visited Chicago in 1935. Whatever the cause, when he later wrote the version of his encounter with her prose which appeared in *American Hunger*, he seems to have forgotten what he had written in this memoir, or else his awareness of the similarity of Stein's prose to his grandmother's language did not occur to him until later in the writing of the autobiography. On the other hand, he seems to have remembered more of the memoir just a year or two after finishing the autobiography when he wrote his *P.M.* review. In January 1945, perhaps preparing for his review of her book or semi-consciously preparing for his trip to France, Wright

could still say "Am reading Stein's *Narration* and find it fascinating. . . . How odd that this woman who is distrusted by
everyone can remind me of the most basic things in my life. . . .
Yes, she's got something, but I'd say that one could live and
write like that only if one . . . could claim one's own soul."
(Fabre, *Unfinished Quest*, p. 587, n. 17)

However incompletely articulated, Wright certainly sensed
that if he were to write "Afro-American" well, which meant
with power and reality, he would have to claim his own subjectivity, for "subjectivity, when [it is] thrown forth in art and
moves others, proves the oneness of mankind." ("Writers and
Their Art," File 811) In "Memories of My Grandmother," he
indicates that the wonders of this "representative I" were
brought to his conceptual awareness not only by the link
between Stein's prose and his grandmother's language but
also by his discovery of Surrealism and his perception of black
American folk expression as its modality.

On the surface, Wright's claim of an enlightening connection
between Surrealism and Afro-American folk expression seems
as suspect as his linking of Stein to folk. In the 1930s, Surrealism was definitely an "in" art movement, and Wright's
adoption of it in 1941 initially suggests the same trendy snobbishness in him that his professions for Stein do and/or the
same doubt that he knew what he was talking about. However,
his comments revealing his understanding of Surrealism and
its relation to Afro-American folk expression and its viability
in twentieth-century American art provide another lode of
exploration into the thought behind his "blueprint" for Negro
writing, his poetics.

Remote indications that Wright's observations may not have
been completely off course or entirely opportunistic are found
in such phenomena as the Surrealists' interest in "primitive"
artifacts and folklore. And Alex Olrik's definition of the
"Sagenwelt" makes it sound very much like a surreal world.
Furthermore, given the implications of Wright's attraction to
Stein's plasticistic language—and to anyone cognizant of
twentieth-century pronouncements about a general Afro-
American outlook, such as the "Black Aesthetic" promulgated
in the 1960s and 1970s by Afro-American writers trying to
produce a literature for and of "the people"—Michel Car-

rouges's summation of Surrealism, written in 1950, will sound familiar:

> [It] is not a philosophy . . . it takes no stock in demonstrating theses by setting up a framework of abstract reasoning. It is plunged into life itself and not into the twilight zone of abstractions . . . it is both *praxis* and *weltan-schaung*. . . . It is . . . the result . . . of a tragic conflict between the powers of the spirit and the conditions of life. It is born of an enormous despair prompted by the condition to which man is reduced on earth, and of a boundless hope in human metamorphosis. . . . [Its] violence comes from the unbearable tension between the two poles of immediate life and that other existence that lies within our power. . . . [Its practitioners] unleash the spirit of negation like a corrosive acid that will dissolve social and cultural prejudices, and even the most natural feelings. They try to dynamite structures of thought and, if possible, even behavior, so as to enter into a new and flaming cloud of unknowing. Yet at the same time, they are the demiurge of new worlds in perpetual expansion. They preach revolt against the human condition and proclaim hope for the transfiguration of life through poetical magic . . . a desperate effort of the spirit to affirm unconditionally its immediate supremacy over the machine of death. (*Andre Breton and the Basic Concepts of Surrealism*, pp. 1- 3]

Somewhat more immediately, Wright's own openness to Surrealism would certainly not have been hampered, as was his early affinity for Stein's prose, by political considerations. He was much impressed with sometime Surrealist Louis Aragon's not obviously Surrealistic poem "Red Front," which he read in translation in 1933. Wright's long 1935 poem "Transcontinental" was modeled on it, and dedicated to Aragon. Whether he knew of Surrealism as early as 1933 is uncertain, but in some manuscript passages excised from the published version of *American Hunger*, he surmised that, had he known of Dada in 1929-30, he might have followed its inspirations. In "Personalism," apparently written between 1935 and 1937, he advocated the use of any and all techniques, including those of Dada and Surrealism, in order to express a writer's deepest subjective feelings. In "Memories of My Grandmother," where his fullest references to Surrealism and its role in revealing the strengths of Afro-American folk expression to him occur, specific items suggest that his attention was directed to Surrealism by the MOMA exhibition of Surrealist and Dada art and by Dali's publicity-grabbing behavior in the United States in 1936. Particularly interesting, in light of Wright's linking of Surrealism and Afro-American folk expression, is Kenneth Burke's mention of *Native Son* in "Surrealism" in the 1940 edition of *New Directions in Prose and Poetry*. About the same time that Wright was working on "Memories of My Grandmother," Burke was expressing the opinion that the different levels of consciousness that structure *Native Son*, from the image of the cornered rat at the very beginning to Max's cerebral courtroom speeches in the last section, establish Wright's novel as surrealistic. (p. 564)

In Wright's memoir, which has nothing to say about communism (although its spirit is present in alternative versions of the dialectic), Surrealism is ranked as the second significant force, just after Stein's prose, that he remembered encountering after arriving in Chicago and that helped him clarify the mystery of his grandmother's and the blues lyricists' way with language and composition.

Using seven verses from "Dink's Blues" as he found them in the Lomaxes' collection, *American Ballads and Folk Songs*, he elaborated on their characteristic that Surrealism was to illuminate:

Some folks say dat de worry blues ain' bad
It's de wors' ol' feeling I ever had

Git you two three men, so one won' worry you min';
Don' they keep you worried and bothered all de time?

I wish to God eas'-boun' train would wreck,
Kill the engineer, break de fireman's neck.

I'm gwine to de river, set down on de groun'.
Ef de blues overtake me, I'll jump overboard and drown.

Ef trouble was money, I'd be a millioneer,
Ef trouble was money, I'd be a millioneer.

My chuck grindin' every hole but mine,
My chuck grindin' every hole but mine.

Come de big Kate Adam wid headlight turn down de stream,
An' her sidewheel knockin' "Great-God-I-been-redeemed."
(American Ballads and Folk Songs, p. 193)

He also undoubtedly had in mind myriad folk utterances of the type he was to list in *Black Boy:* "If I pulled a hair from a horse's tail and sealed it in a jar of my own urine, the hair would turn overnight into a snake. . . . If I kissed my elbow, I would turn into a girl. . . . If I stepped over a broom that was lying on the floor, I would have bad luck." (pp. 63-64)

Very much like the lore that had some objective validity and was referred to in the preceding chapter (that if a black man were standing next to a white woman and she screamed, it meant his death), these sayings juxtaposed elements that had no rational connection; the grammatical condition had no logical or actually causal connection with the result; the conditioning, the connection, exists only in, and grows out of, the verbal construct alone. In the blues song as a whole, as well as in its parts, he points out the lack of narrative sequence, of any reason for one verse to occur where it does rather than elsewhere. The whole composition, if it could be called that, is so loose and open-ended that verses could be made up and added ad infinitum. The material of each of the couplets is likewise disparate, drawn from quite different geographical locales, and they are, to put it mildly, not possessed of any great intellectual interest. What consistency the song as a whole has is a vague sadness, but Wright indicates that it is something other than that particular emotion that ties the verses together and makes the song a unit. The "blue" feeling is mentioned twice, but Wright states that the significance is not in the verses but is rather something imposed on them from without. His comments on the blues lyrics indicate that Wright was clearly aware of Surrealism's celebrated and characteristic mode of expression—the formation of images and meaning by putting together items that do not normally or conventionally occur in conjunction, such as "exquisite" and "corpse" or fur as the material for teacups and saucers.

What lay behind this practice, Wright felt, was first of all an attitude of separation from the kind of mind-set that the "real" world demands from occupation with day-to-day issues such as one's job, food, clothing and shelter, what brand of cigarettes to smoke, and how to fix the plumbing. Surrealism shows up, he says, when a society develops a particular kind of relationship between its members, a relationship that separates people from the means of purposeful, rewarding productivity. This cultural socioindividual schizophrenic attitude could be found both at the upper as well as at the lower reaches of the social scale. Sufficient wealth allows a man to be removed from such mundane matters and so, strangely enough, does its opposite, especially if the person is forcefully kept from participation in the meaningful activities intrinsic to his society. Superficially, such statements suggest the hold that Marxian economic determinism still had on Wright's thought, as well as, perhaps, a naivete regarding the financial status of the Surrealists. His idea that Surrealism arises when people are not totally preoccupied with mundane matters and his reiterated statement that Surrealism is a stage of creativity, would imply his awareness that the distance from society that makes Surrealism possible, whether in its European or Afro-American manifestation, is more than merely a matter of economics. In his 1940 essay, *How Bigger Was Born*, Wright attributed to Afro-American folk a cultural insight that European Surrealists also possessed: modern Western culture lacked a "metaphysical" dimension. This lack, which leaves an unfulfilled deep human need, is partly responsible for the alienation of Afro-Americans such as Bigger although, as Wright tried to show through Bigger, they do not necessarily consciously think in terms of such lacunae. A stronger, more conscious sense of a like void was behind the Surrealists' disgust with the sheer materialism pervading Western civilization and was the very hunger they sought to satisfy.

It is important in attempting to identify those traits in Afro-American expression that Surrealism helped Wright to recognize that this "distance" was not only from, but also a result of being toward something. When a Surrealist poet (and an Afro-American folk blues singer, as such recent studies as Stephen Henderson's "Blues for the Young Black Man" have shown) juxtaposes verbal statements or resultant images that are not related by logic, requirements of verisimilitude, or any of the links conventionally sanctioned as real, he is trying to bridge this distance or alienation, paradoxically utilizing it in his attempt but not merely in order to reenter that normal world. Surrealism is, for Wright as well as for more recent, philosophical commentators, a movement, a "creative process," a "road."

81

While the Surrealist is alienated from the conventional bric-a-brac reality of the world, he has not fully entered the real or sur-real world, which remains therefore at a distance. The Surrealist, like the folk narrator with his "Sagenwelt," is thus between two environment. Although these environments differ, they are coincident, concurrent. The Surrealist does not seek to enter some mystical state or supernatural heaven; he struggles to attain the surreality of this world.

This characteristic of Surrealism is consistent with Wright's observation in "Memories" that, along with the condition of distance or alienation, there exists among the surrealistic characteristics of black American folk expression a robustness that urges the individual to come to grips in some way with the society from which he is disengaged. Wright insists on the sanity and wholesomeness of Surrealism (especially if one spells it with a lower-case "s") and the Afro-American folk outlook while anticipating the objection that Negroes are too unsophisticated, too intellectually innocent, to be mixed with, or to be capable of, anything as complex, esoteric, and decadent as Surrealism. The dream states, delirium, and paranoia—deliberately simulated by the Surrealists, to more intensely derealize the habitual reality of the conventionally apprehended world they were already rejecting—were far from being merely the lunatic games that popular notion labeled them. They would very likely correspond, in Wright's view of the matter, to what forced exclusion from this conventional world has led black Americans to: the production of an obliqueness of vision, of a different way of looking at the world, of conceiving and feeling it, a different means of relating entities. He comments, too, on his grandmother, whose behavior was made meaningful to him by Surrealism, saying that, in spite of the exasperation her actions and judgments caused him and others, no one ever considered her demented. In spite of his rejection of the extreme religious form her visible method of coping took, he acknowledged that she was a very strong person, capable of surviving with considerable dignity some of the most difficult times for black Americans. She was, says Wright, able to be in the world but not of the world. In the realm of Wright's published fiction, Bigger Thomas also appears interpretable in terms of psychosis; but Wright conspicuously violated the principle of realism, as some critics have complained, by not having Max consider insanity as a defense. Wright did not want Bigger considered "crazy," even though he depicted Bigger's grappling with his environment by means of actions, thoughts, and feelings that were ostensibly paranoid, schizoid, delirious. However, these states, although induced in Bigger involuntarily rather than willfully, are stressed by Wright as leading Bigger to a sense of an existence more real than that provided by his external, quotidian world. He, too, is very much in this world, but he is not of it. He struggles with two environments, creatively trying to invent—discover—the intense meaning of his life, using each of these antithetic environments to do so.

Whether we consider the fictional character or the actual "bad niggers" that Wright said he had in mind when he created his novel's protagonist, Bigger's means of grappling with these environments appear rebellious but wanton, reminiscent of Breton's remark to the effect that the essential Surrealist act consists of grabbing a gun, running into the street, and shooting wildly. If the fictional Bigger's behavior gradually becomes more purposive, it is only relatively so, and through a rather random sequence of events in which Bigger sees a possible pattern for his behavior. Just as Breton realized that the Surrealist's search for the sur-real could be manifested other than with a gun—with a pen or paintbrush, for example—so Wright recognized other forms. His grandmother used the external apparatus of religion; the blues singer and the jazz performer, a musical format.

Since Surrealism involves an effort to overcome alienation, isolation of the self from the other, it can, as Wright says, be seen as coming about operatively, if not theoretically, when people are intellectually and emotionally concerned with communicating something completely, in the sense, of Keats's desire to hand over experience bodily. It is this entirety of what an artist like Dali means, not scientific anatomy, that establishes what limbs of a human figure he will include in his painting and where he will place them in relation to each other. Similarly, the wholeness of what a writer presents is not determined by the formal, rationally ordered arrangement of the parts he includes, nor is it the photographic exactitude or plentitude of the realistic images that go into his work. The wholeness is established by the discernible emotion with which he holds these details and projects them into his work. These remarks tie his view of Surrealism to the internal "something" he had first observed in his grandmother and lead him into a rather detailed discussion of specific techniques found in Afro-American expression which are used to achieve this wholeness from a melange of disparate parts. Apparently because jazz has been repeatedly remarked as surrealistic by many critics, Wright devoted more attention to it than to the blues in this section of "Memories." In answering the question as to why Stravinsky, whom along with Dali he explicitly mentions as a Surrealist, is attracted to jazz, Wright revealed in more technical terms his view of how Surrealist movements function.

Among the characteristics of jazz that Wright considered surreal is that it is a definite, precise expressional arrangement, yet developed without any broad technical knowledge of what should be done to achieve most effective expression. On the one hand, such a remark suggests that he was thinking of folk jazz, jazz as it sprang up from self-taught performers in the backwaters of the early twentieth-century urban and rural South. On the other hand, his remark points to his awareness of a parallel between this lack of formal musical education and the European Surrealists' cultivated ignorance of techniques of expression—their development of automatic writing and collage, for instance. Both of these practices were intended to free the artist from his knowledge of past, conventional styles, and modes of expression and from rational, fully conscious control of what he produced. The Surrealist cultivates a dream state that will allow an uninhibited flow of images in an unpremeditated, new, dis-order; the folk Negro jazz musician, never having learned or submitted to the rigidities of socially condoned and therefore "real" music, spontaneously allows the sounds to emerge. Futhermore, as Alquié comments (*The Philosophy of Surrealism*, p. 99), "surrealist dialogues, games . . . collages tend to engender the masterpiece without an author, result of chance and of encounter," which is, in addition to being another form of instrumental alienation, also a move toward a form that resembles anonymous, spontaneous folk expression.

The creation that emerges, whether from a folk musician or from a poet like Breton, is not, however, an absolute chaos. Wright says that Surrealism displays a passion for a regulated recurrence of contrasting elements that function as a structural framework, but this, Wright seems to be saying, is only a functional device, a contribution of the intellect, to hold the elements together while the real meaning of the whole is obtruded on them. The recurring bass line provides the point of departure and return for the multiplicity of spontaneously developed, tonally shaded riffs, which, of course, when first heard, strikes the uninitiated ear as cacophonous noise rather than as music. Yet these sounds, shifting around among even various keys, are a fast, compressed string of sound images and moods that, for all their diversity, come to fit into an ingenious and ingenuous fabrication, a clarification of life.

The description that Wright gives, a description by no means novel, of jazz as a music combining a steady beat overlaid with personal, lyrical, intuitive riffs makes it a good symbol of Surrealism as a process that seeks to unify the subjective and the objective, the dream state and wakefulness, the real with the surreal. The "steady beat" suggests also the comfortable, semiconscious state Breton recommends so that automatic writing may take place. Breton also spoke of the "rhythmic unity" automatic writing produced, reflecting "the non-distinction more and more established of the functioning of the senses and of the intellect." (Balakian, *Surrealism*, p. 129). Wright's description of jazz has certain correspondences to Breton's description of his intent in *Nadja:* to relate his life as spontaneously as possible, according to its "most notable episodes," to produce "a world . . . of things suddenly brought together, of petrifying coincidences, of reflexes excelling every other mental flight, of harmonies struck out as if on a piano, of lightning flashes which would make us see, but really *see*, if they were not still more rapid than the others." (pp. 18-19; my translation) Then there is the rhythm of the flow of images that constitutes a Surrealist film such as "Un Chien Andalou," an unusual rhythm that seems none at all in conventional terms.

While much emphasis is placed on them, these rhythms provide, as Wright said of jazz, an ongoing mechanism that allows the development, the expression of the real motion of the work—its "e-motion." What Wright is more concerned with, what comes closer to the essential something behind Afro-American folk expression that links it with Surrealism, is more than just the recurrent arrangement of seemingly inharmonious elements; it is the power that emanates from a jazz piece as from Surrealistic literary and visual art.

While Wright's references to rhythmic order are compatible with Surrealism, his choice of words—sometimes suggesting that meaning is foisted on elements arranged in a deliberate scheme—suggests a limitation of his understanding of Surrealism. What Balakian points out as the Surrealist approach to poetry can be taken as applicable to all genuinely Surrealist art: it was "no longer to be an expression of ideas or emotions but the creation of a series of images, which would not necessarily owe their existence to an a priori subject." (*Surrealism*, p. 143) The recourse to automatic writing and altered states of consciousness was undertaken to escape from the kind of logical procedure inherent in having a preconceived pattern of reality that one then imposed on images or words. Wright's phrases seem to say that what is being expressed comes first, whereas the European Surrealists called for the supremacy of expression, in which something was then found as being expressed.

Carrouges points out that for the European Surrealists

spontaneous generation exists no more in the realm of the mind than in the physical world. Every word, every image used by our consciousness comes from an immense reservoir. . . . The consciousness does not create them, but only recognizes their projection onto its luminous screen, for they are pre-existent to this perception . . . these words flow from a source. Before the consciousness grasps them, they raise themselves to its surface. In the deep shadows of the unconscious, there are mental inclines along which the words tumble in marvelous torrents, shimmering with the reflections of their images, revealing the vast orographic and hydrographic system existing on the dark side of the mind. (pp. 103, 105)

His use of the concepts of preexistence and system highlights the Surrealist conviction that the surreal has an order of its own, into which such practices as automatic writing can tap. Since it is not the order of logic or of the conventional world, it appears to be disorder, nonsense, or madness. The jazz musician, to the extent that he enters a kind of intense revery or concentration on his music, would be producing spontaneous sounds, but there would be combined in a pattern or rhythm that is dictated by something objective within his subjective psyche, a "something" that makes itself known in an undefined feeling or mood.

Ultimately, in Wright's view, what imposes this new reality, what ties together the improvised varieties of sound and rhythm in jazz, the unrelated blues lyrics, or the logically disconnected items in his grandmother's world view or the images, is a profoundly experienced feeling with the great urgency to be vented. This "something" thus comes to be equated with the detectable intensity he finds in Surrealist works.

This deep feeling or intensity that Wright writes of corresponds to Breton's intent when he spoke, in the *Second Manifesto of Surrealism*, of "a certain point of the spirit from which life and death, the communicable and incommunicable, the high and low cease to be perceived as contradictories," a "supreme point" whose discovery or determination is the sole impetus of Surrealist activity, since it is the *axis mundi*, the real-surreal interface from which and to which all Surrealist behavior leads. It is the experience—however fleeting, dark, or anguished—of the solution of self with "the other," of crossing over the "enigmatic threshold separating the ordinary self from the deeper self." It is also the experience in which the singular, whether of self or of an external object, merges itself totally in the universal, "where lucidity is completely one with the sense of cosmic mystery . . . an instant of ecstasy and illumination" (Carrouges, *Andre Breton and the Basic Concepts of Surrealism*, p. 22), and moves about in a world of the unknown. While scholars may disagree on the esoteric roots of such a view, of this point toward which Surrealism inspires, they all agree that it is neither supernatural nor mystical. It is located in the human psyche, is contacted with and by means of immediacy, yet it is something to be expected, sought for, hoped for. According to Surrealism, modern man is alienated from self, which is as unknown to him as any aspect of the surreal, and when he attains self—the supreme point—Surrealism as a movement will come to an end. In the meantime, even the intuitions and revelations that come to the Surrealists are only approximations, foreshadowings, and sensuous images of the point, but not the point itself.

Further understanding of what Wright meant by the deep feeling behind Afro-American folk expression and its parallels to the Surrealists' "supreme point" is gained through Wright's crucial comments in *How Bigger Was Born,* his comments concerning the "primal fear and dread" that is also "a reflex urge toward ecstasy." His words call attention to angst as characteristic of that "dark part" of psychic life, yet he mentions the concomitant positive qualities of ecstasy and trust. This passage, usually cited as evidence of Wright's inchoate existentialism, could as plausibly have sprung, as French Existentialism itself owed a debt to Surrealism, from Wright's experience of a surrealist anguish, a deep feeling that he found prevalent in the Afro-American outlook and behind much of Afro-American expression.

As Carrouges explains it, Surrealist anguish comes not, as it does for an existentialist, "from a kind of dizziness in the face of an emptiness that suddenly opens underfoot" but rather "from a sort of terrible fascination: just as the traveler in a forest perceives in the very act of reaching for it, that what he took to be a stick is really a serpent, so the surrealist sometimes discerns in a banal, everyday object an unexpected sign of terror. It is not emptiness, but rather an excess of being, which causes his anguish." (*André Breton and the Basic Concepts of Surrealism,* p. 43)

This awareness of fullness, even excess, of being is inherent in the goal that Surrealist activity both seeks and springs from. To see from the "supreme point" is to realize that arid distinctions, such as the verbalizing (categorizing) that is devised by logical reason and the senses under its sway, are not the real limitations of reality. While the existentialist may be nauseated by the fullness of being possessed by a stick or a serpent but not by a self-conscious being, Breton says that

Surrealism will not rest as long as humans are able to see a difference between an animal, a flame, and a stone. Reality—the surreal—overflows such boundaries. Awareness, realization, however dim, of such a condition, makes one perceive a unity existing between even the most unrelated entities. It also provides the basis for an incorrigible and apparently inexplicable optimism, no matter how feebly expressed, that all opposition will be overcome.

The obverse of this is that seeing from such a point or "forbidden zone," as Breton refers to it, produces a universe that is unpredictable to consciousness because of its fluidity, and hence it is a cause of anxiety to a consciousness that is not fully into this point of view. While it is—as Wright said of Surrealism and the way of seeing he discerned behind Afro-American expression—a way of seeing things whole, because wholeness eludes clear and distinct conceptualization, it is also a way of seeing the universe as hazardous and chancy, of not knowing what to expect, of being in the unknown. Such a description applies also, of course, to a view of the universe found in the folk mentality in general. The sophisticated Surrealists had deliberately to seek to leave themselves open to chance, to *hazard objectif*—the surreal—which possesses structure unrecognizable to rational, conventional consciousness.

Life lived by one with such a viewpoint becomes a labyrinthine journey of invention, of discovery. Balakian elaborates on this journey in terms that can easily apply to Bigger, if not to Wright himself:

> the poet has long been represented as a captive trying to tear down his prison walls. . . . But the walls have gradually taken on a more dreary aspect and, for Surrealists, encompass the whole range of human experience. They mark the limits of the dream rather than those of reality. It is beyond those barriers that reality lies. . . . The surrealist movement opens with a grim realization that these walls that block the artist's vision are unshakable . . . the basic note is . . . despair. . . . Breton [is] unable even to *breathe* in a world that has lost all life for [him.] And there is no physical flight.

Such a condition leads to an "insatiable quest for the unknown;" using Baudelaire's words, to a "plunge to the bottom of the abyss, Hell or Heaven . . . to the bottom of the Unknown in order to find the new!" (*Surrealism*, pp. 7-8) This passage recalls Wright's use of the Shakespearian "forms of things unknown" to describe the folk utterances he found appearing in Afro-American art about the turn of the century. The phrase has a considerable degree of the same obscure clarity that Surrealists prized in the phrases and sentences that automatic writing helped them produce. It also suggests phantoms, specters, concepts that Breton was fond of using when trying to express his experience of his hidden self, his deeper reality, and that of other entities.

It also implies that these folk utterances are sibyline, giving highly oblique expression, like the works of the Surrealists, to something with which they were in contact but did not fully understand or that could not, perhaps, be fully grasped.

The extent of Wright's formal study or knowledge of Surrealism is not clear. No records seem to exist of his reading anything of Breton's, for example, or any of the Surrealist literary works. In spite of its importance to him, as stated in the memoir, he never sought the occasion to meet with Breton or Dali, although both of them spent considerable time in the United States during the 1940s. Fabre mentions that in 1941 Wright actually lived in an apartment at "Seven Middagh" in Brooklyn where Dali had once lived. When he traveled to France, unlike his interest in Stein's prose and its relationship to Afro-American speech, which led to personal contacts and exchanges of ideas, his regard for Surrealism seems not to have urged him to seek out any of the surviving French Surrealists. He did, according to Fabre, at least meet Michel Leiris, one of Breton's long-time confreres and author of several Surrealist works, including a "glossary" of Surrealist word formation, but that meeting occurred only at a "huge reception" in honor of Wright's arrival in Paris. He had, of course, indicated in the memoir that he did not espouse what might be called orthodox Surrealism for its own sake. As with communism, the techniques of Dreiser, Dos Passos, Stein, or the existentialism of Camus, Sartre, and Beauvoir, Wright's interest in Surrealism was apparently selective, the movement of use to him only insofar as it helped to amplify intellectually something he already knew experientially.

However far he cared to take his own formal knowledge of

Surrealism, his observations on the surrealistic characteristics of Afro-American folk expression—characteristics
which thus indicate that expression's qualifications for use in a
twentieth-century way—are not without value and validity. A
more thorough look at Surrealism's leading tenets reveals how
his interest in the movement increases understanding of that
pattern of thought called his poetics. His comments also seem
to have some relevance to more recent Afro-American works
noted for their "magical realism." Toni Morrison's novels, for
example, have been called surrealistic, a quality she seems to
acknowledge as picked up from Gabriel Garcia Marquez's
works. Marquez, on the other hand, admits to being influenced
by folklore; the fact that Morrison is responding to Marquez's
work because she hears in it something from her own Afro-
American folk culture is not totally impossible. Ishmael Reed's
novels and poems, clearly drawing on forms from black (and
white) popular culture, have also been recognized as surreal
from the time of their first appearance. Most recently, the
poetry of Michael S. Harper, heir to the aesthetic of the 1960s
and 1970s that called for literature of and from the people, has
been cited for its collage form of composition.

In terms of his own techniques, what of Surrealism that
seems most obviously to have impressed Wright was the
"wakeful dream," a state cultivated in artistic production by
Surrealists and an aura that pervades many of their works,
which employ realistic details or technique but in overall
contexts that give them a quality associated with dreams.

This condition is very evident in the *Native Son* scenes depicting Bigger's initiation into the Dalton's world:

He would see in a few moments if the Daltons . . . were like the
people he had seen and heard in the movie. But while walking
through the quiet and spacious white neighborhood, he did not feel
the pull and mystery of the thing as he had in the movies. . . . The
houses he passed were huge; lights glowed softly in the windows.
The streets were empty, save for an occasional car that zoomed past
on swift rubber tires. This was a cold and distant world; a world of
white secrets carefully guarded. (p. 37)

He looked around the room; it was lit by dim lights glowing from
a hidden source. He tried to find them by roving his eyes, but could
not. . . . On the smooth walls were several paintings whose nature
he tried to make out, but failed . . . a faint sound of piano music

floated to him from somewhere. He was sitting in a white house; dim lights burned around him; strange objects challenged him. (p. 39)

Bigger listened, blinking and bewildered. The long strange words they used made no sense to him. . . . He felt from the tone of their voices that they were having a difference of opinion about him, but he could not determine what it was about. It made him uneasy, tense, as though there were influences and presences about him which he could feel but not see. (p. 40)

The eerie disquietude that eminates from these scenes is not unlike the spirit that irradiates many Surrealist paintings. In the first excerpt cited above, the absence of people, the deserted streets suggesting empty distances of planes converging to a vanishing point, the oversized buildings, the "zoom" that stresses the silence, the phrase "swift rubber tires" suggesting free-roaming circles—all disembodied from the usual components—recall the Surrealist work of Chirico. All of these scenes suggest a world of indeterminacy, an untethering of ordinary objects—the houses, the piano music, the lights, the language, Bigger himself—by stripping away their usual significations and placing them in a foreign context. This practice gives rise to an emotional equivalent of what the Surrealists often spoke of as their objective—a conscious, awake-dream state of perception.

All of *Native Son*, in addition to depicting Bigger's descent into and movement through an unknown, the terrifying yet exhilarating exterior white world that is so rich and full of significance (value, meaning) that it is also not what it appears and hence is unpredictable, filled with chance—with opportunity and hazard—also depicts Bigger's journey through the depths of his unknown self, through a maelstrom into a sense of self that offers to cancel out the antinomies that conventional modes of apprehending reality have told him exist between himself and the rest of the world. While he has only a glimmer of this kind of unification, he has approached it, and there is a sufficient unification of self, within himself and in his relationship with the outside world, that Wright can have him exclaim, "What I killed for, *I am!*" By having Bigger utter and apply to himself the biblical name that God gave to Himself, Wright makes us see Bigger as a deified human; as deified, he is a being who somehow encompasses all, however deformed his external image may appear. In Surrealism, this all is achieved when one approaches the "supreme point." Wright, like Breton, has not only secularized the "point of origin for the Creation, and the point of action at which God created the world and at which all is contained *ab ovo*" (Carrouges, *André Breton and the Basic Concepts of Surrealism*, p. 14), but, as Alquié says Breton also did, Wright has psychologized it, placing it with the subjective, cognitive emotions and developing the consciousness of Bigger. The metaphysical dimension, so emaciated in modern Western civilization, is thus supplied by the very mind that requires it.

Wright's own sense of the novel's surrealistic quality is particularly revealed in the film he made of the book in 1949-50. He may not have sought the acquaintance of French Surrealists, but he is credited with having introduced into the film version one of its more successful features, one that shows the claim Surrealism still had on his imagination. Near the end of the film, in many ways its high point, Bigger's emotional state is recapitulated not through the rather static device of Max's courtroom oral presentation but by means of a dream sequence. Set designs include the Dalton basement that is transformed into something definitely out of the Surrealist paintings by Chirico and Dali. During the action, Bigger does not reach for a stick that becomes a serpent; he does reach out for a figure that appears to be his father but turns into the menacing police chief, and Mary Dalton's severed head (blond in the black and white movie) is merged with bolls of cotton in a huge field. The surrealist quality of the novel is perhaps further attested by the most recent film version. While not so obviously, it too preserves visual effects reminiscent of Surrealist paintings: wide-angle shots, scenes of sparsely furnished rooms with open foregrounds, suggestive of isolated individuals moving about in a dream-like environment.

However, it was, Wright says in the memoir, the composition of the original versions *The Man Who Lived Underground*, not *Native Son*, that brought together and incorporated most successfully in "contour" his grandmother's and the Afro-American folk's mentality, a pattern of thought parallel to the essence of what Stein's prose and Surrealism helped him realize was capturable in a secular, artistic, modern aesthetic form. That story, then, never published in its original length, needs to be investigated in order to see just what Wright had produced that he felt best fulfilled, up to that time, his own poetics. That story, even more pronouncedly than Burke had observed of *Native Son*, employs the Surrealist technique of juxtaposing disparate items.

4

"UNDERGROUND"
FORMULATIONS

Wright's poetics began with his experience of a "something" that he felt was essentially characteristic of Afro-Americanism. First sensed in his grandmother, he then discerned it in all Afro-American folk utterances: in the blues lyrics; in the black Americans' celebration of Joe Louis' 1935 victory over Max Baer; in Bontemps's fictionalized folk hero, Gabriel Prosser; in the politically jubilant Ghanaians; and even in the religious fervor of Spanish peasants. He wanted to harness this vital "something" to folk and forceful modern literary forms, which would then be altered by the "something" and by each other to create a "Negro writing" that would be distinctively expressive, as close as possible to the felt reality of Afro-American experience and at the same time identical to his own individualistic view of reality.

Modern forms, such as the techniques developed by Stein and the Surrealists, were close enough to features in traditional Afro-American folk expression to give him a conscious, germinal insight into how to develop this truth in his own works. Most critics might agree that Wright came as close as he ever would to achieving such a goal in his three most acclaimed works: *Native Son, Black Boy,* and some of the stories in *Uncle Tom's Children,* but Wright, at least at one time, felt that the original manuscript of his eventually much abused novella, *The Man Who Lived Underground,* best captured this "something"—the quintessential element in Afro-Americans that so characterized their sense of what is real—and best expressed in the story's "contour" his most successful rendering of his own blueprint. In addition to Stein's prose and Surrealism, other experiences—his discovery of Freudian dream theory (closely connected in time as well as in content with his discovery of Surrealism), of Twain's iconoclastic "What Is Man?", and childhood viewings of movies based on Wells's *The Invisible Man*—also have bearing on the novella's construction and content. Wright's own special emphasis on the story as symbolic enactment of the action of his grandmother's and all Afro-American folks' psychosis (Kenneth Burke's sense of the word, not exactly meaning a disease) focuses primary attention on the center and shape of his novella. Looking at it in Wright's own terms, it furthers an understanding and appreciation of Wright's abiding interest in the problems of literary creation.

That Wright encountered the factual germ of the novelette in *True Detective* in the early summer of 1941 is well known. He also was familiar with the works of Poe and Russian writers whom he knew had treated some of the same themes that emerge in his novella. Less well remembered is that, according to Margaret Walker Alexander ("Richard Wright," p. 202), he had also by that time read *The Road to Xanadu* and *Alice in Wonderland;* and, according to Fabre, he had some familiarity with Kenneth Burke's *Permanence and Change*. In the spirit of the first of these books, what he made of the factual germ must be considered in the work as he wrote it, not just in the truncated pieces eventually published. Most critical comments have been based on the version that appeared first in 1944 in *Cross Section* and then became widely available in *Eight Men*, the 1961 collection of his stories Wright gathered just before his death.

This published version consists at best of only about half of the first full-length manuscript that Wright drafted. Since what is being sought in this study is what he thought of as a dynamism that the novella expressed—the way a vapor trail expresses the movement of an atom through a cloud chamber—the complete version has to be considered. That Wright left some five drafts of the longer version makes looking for or at such a fluid aspect difficult, as does the length of the work.

Another problem is that such an aspect of the work is highly abstract, and attempts to describe it can quickly become not only tedious but confusing. Wright's references in his literary theory manifesto, "Personalism," to the need of a "ruling symbol" in a literary work, a symbol that is "the unity, emotional and philosophical," of all the images that constitute the work, need to be recalled here. They must be recalled in light of Burke's 1931 remarks that "the Symbol," which he describes as a complex attitude that permeates all of the critically standard aspects of a work (plot, character, and setting), is like a "word invented by the artist," of which the entire work is the definition. (*Counter-Statement*, p. 153). Like the hole of a donut or the information contained on those old IBM cards, this Symbol, the "verbal parallel to a pattern of experience" (p. 152) being sought in Wright's work may be discernible only by what surrounds or accompanies it. The hazards of trying to separate form and content need no comment, but the fact that Wright felt he had achieved in this story the shape of his grandmother's mental-emotional processes, excluding the religious matter she dealt with, requires that such an analysis be attempted.

Wright has provided a number of important clues as to how to read the novelette in terms of his own poetics. Some of these clues are observations about what might be called his precompositional syndrome. In 1960, as he prepared to include the shortened "The Man Who Lived Underground" in *Eight Men*, he worked on yet another preface intended to explain the genesis of each of these stories, the unfinished and unpublished "Roots and Branches." It reiterates explicit principles of his poetics which were first expressed a quarter-century earlier, statements that offer a guide to all of his works but especially to what is involved in this novella.

He starts with a deep bow to the role of the unplanned in the creation of literature, those features that are the result of nonmystical yet mysterious unconscious dynamisms moving the writer to produce inexplicable, wondrous combinations of personally and objectively derived phenomena into what comes to be seen as "story." Becoming more explicit concerning the nature of these forces, he speaks in terms of a well-known folk image that vividly recalls what he had written years before in "Memories of My Grandmother" about his fascination with her attitude; it also recalls passages from *Underground* itself. Before he wrote any fiction or nonfiction, he had been gripped by an indefinable attitude, as if he were "vainly seeking to recall something long . . . forgotten." Trying to find words to express exactly what he means, he compares the sensation to looking down from a great height onto a railroad yard, observing the cars being shunted about until finally they form a completed train. Leaving that metaphor, he says that when these recurring attitudes or moods are upon him, they seem to expand, absorbing into themselves, as he attempts to flesh them out in concrete images, memories of events or things he had read or heard about which the moods call up in him, memories that, while his, seem foreign to him. Drawing these disjointed, fragmented remembrances into itself, this feeling gives them an organic unity.

In the end he has to give up attempting to describe what goes on at these creative times; it seems to derive from beyond even unconsciousness: "I cannot fathom this 'thing.' . . . I cannot . . . say that it is my unconscious; or that it stems from some associational, condensing process of over determination such as is found in dreams . . . in trying to grasp this process in me, I encounter a reality that recedes and hides itself in another reality, and, when hunted too openly, it alters its whole aspect . . ., thereby escaping introspectional observation." ("Roots and Branches" File 751)

The imagery of the last part of these remarks sets up echoes of Wright's article on Louis's win over Baer, which released a "something" in black American folk: "Out of the darkness it had leaped from its coil. And nobody could have said just what it was. . . . A something popped out of a dark hole, something like a hydra-head, and it was darting forth its tongue." It also evokes Carrouges's image of the surrealist as one who reaches for a stick and discovers a snake. This imagery also has undertones of Shelley's Cave of Poesie and suggests a context in which Wright dimly saw the novella, making it revelatory of his own creative processes, a story about such things, justifying such a reading of it. Fabre's article on *Underground* touches at its conclusion on just such a way of approaching the story.

More direct—even direct*ive*—clues are found in "Memories

of My Grandmother." In addition to those past experiences that came together for him in the story's composition, Wright also gives an extended description of his own psychological state as he wrote. He describes having a sense of his own writing and reaching a judgment that it had a quality he wanted in it, a quality that is reminiscent of the condition of the "petty bourgeoisie" as Wright had depicted him in "Personalism." Very like that condition, this quality also reflected a tendency in his writing that was later to make him so responsive to French existentialism, as it had to some degree to Surrealism. From the time he began writing, he always tried to reach a distinctive yet dimensionless, characterless psychic location that he felt marked the real beginning of his story. At this zero milestone, his main character would seem to be shattered, so routed by fracturing experiences from the moral, intellectual, and emotional points of reference that he is a liquid entity, a kind of tabula rasa, an infinity radiating in all directions. This radical newness makes him plausibily capable of any course of action that Wright would choose, each course an attempt to shape into human being the contextual moral, intellectual, and emotional chaos he has come to experience as the reality of his life, to realize what he indeed knows, believes, feels.

Wright also describes his creative state, and what he writes, as being like a train that starts out slowly but, as it goes faster and faster, creates a rushing that, after the train has gone past, whirls any and all roadbed detritus about, giving a shape to the invisible wind. Changing the figure, he describes it as coming to an intense, white-hot, welding-torch-flame-like emotional pitch that melts familiar items, ideas, events, enables them to run together, and gives them a new significance.

Both the train movement and the torch heat metaphors, the rush and the heat of writing, give way to an analogy of this process with the constant bass fiddle throb in jazz, an analogy he draws several times in the essay. Like Stein, who spoke of her use of repetition as a device for expressing her characters in terms of rhythms of personality, and like Breton, who sought a "rhythmic unity" that automatic writing could produce, Wright seems to have felt that he wrote into existence a basis that he could express in expository prose only in figurative terms—a kind of vacuum set up by the swift passage of a vehicle through a space, a concentrated blue-white heat, jazz music. Had he lived in the age of space exploration, he might have expressed it in terms of the gathering momentum that enables a rocket to break gravity's hold and "float" free in undetermined space. It is a "movement" so strong that, like light, it becomes a constant. Furthermore, as his early aesthetic formulation, "Personalism," had called for the use of artistic expression as a "weapon of defense, of attack" by a "people at bay," so the hurtling of oneself verbally on the free void—telescoping events and fusing and hence changing meanings—is a palpable aggression, an assault by the reality of a living person on the dullness and responsiveness of the human world.

Once achieved, this emotional velocity, this psychological context of a motionless yet intense e-motion, provided a stable, rhythm-like wave that allowed, even suggested, all kinds of variations. Like the kingdom of Heaven, it could be wantonly figured in any of his mental constructs, showering them with value and significance.

The movement that thus undergirds the novella is a symbolic equivalent of the process he had observed in his grandmother and Afro-American folk, something in himself that he at least imagines is similar. He says further that, like all rituals and like the quality he felt quite noticeable in his grandmother, *The Man Who Lived Underground* is inevitably an ideation. Given his earlier insistence in "Memories" on the intensity of emotion he strives to achieve so that his character can attain a certain gravity-free condition, his recognition of an abstractness in the story makes for an interesting contrast. It also complicates the question of whether the underlying rhythm can be understood conceptually or is something that can be apprehended only experientially and aesthetically, a critical question at the heart of study of his poetics.

More easily dealt with for the moment are the images he so freely made up, the disparate elements he invented in response to what he had imbedded in his emotional perspective. The crisis, the intense pitch of emotional consciousness that is the cause and the result of freedom, of imagistic invention, is marked in the novella by the sewer. The adventures that Fred Daniels, Wright's protagonist, has in this second part of the novella are prominent and fairly consistent in all the various manuscripts and in the published version: the black church service; the dead baby; the undertaker's establishment; the movie theater; the real estate office and its safe; the meat locker; the radio store; the jewelry store. These all came, Wright maintains, rather surrealistically, determined only by whether they had the right feel. If any preconceived aim guided their creation, it was to allow his protagonist, like that of *The Waste Land,* to record fragmented bits of his culture. Using a Robinson Crusoe-like analogy, Wright further indicates the randomness of these episodes and the role played by his creative emotion—the unifying Symbol—in giving them meaning. As though anticipating a psychological critique of such automatic imagistic writing, Wright insists that the episodes, the emotional logic of their randomly arrived at ordering, is without significance except in relationship to itself. Sounding as though he were seeing the novella as an art-for-art's-sake expressionistic piece, it is his intent to focus the reader on the particular "something" that the imaged episodes and events of the story clothe.

Wright's observations regarding how the images in the story are to be taken give clues as to what is and what is not the conceptually apprehensible material as distinguished from what is being contoured. They do not, however, and cannot, provide any clearer conceptual knowledge of just what the contoured process is. They do not clarify the nature of the wholeness, the unity of all these images, the very unifying that is itself the dominant symbol of the work, the deep symbolic name, of which the images are the letters, of the shaping emotion that emerged in his grandmother as being religious. Furthermore, when, in "Memories of My Grandmother," Wright discusses the themes of the unpublished *The Man Who Lived Underground,* he only seems to be giving explicit and exhaustive information as to exactly what is merging the images and subsymbols into a whole.

Extending his analogy between surrealistic jazz and his story, Wright unequivocally states that the charge of murder leveled against Fred Daniels by the police provided the bass-like beat upon which he could play. Guilt thus seems obviously to be the Symbol that broods over the whole, lending unity and meaning to all the images, symbols, and movements in the story. The significance and hence the reality of the images Fred Daniels encounters is, according to Wright, obsessively read through this lens of great intensity inflicted on him by the police beatings and other tortures as they attempt to "sweat" from him a confession of a murder he has not committed. The establishment of this steady beat seems to be the function of the entire first section of the novella, the portion that has never been published, the writing Wright felt he had to do until he arrived at just the correct creative emotional pitch necessary for authentic, genuine, imaginative composition. Its omission would thus wreak a certain havoc on the overall unity and meaning of the story and on any attempts to analyze Wright's achievement.

The note of guilt is definitely present, struck repeatedly in the first section, sometimes by implication and, more often, directly. In the earlier manuscripts, when in the second paragraph Daniels is stopped by the police, implicit guilt is the first thing that is given as shading his consciousness: "He was a negro; he was black; he was in a white neighborhood; these were white policemen . . . they were going to ask him what he was doing in this white neighborhood." (*The Man Who Lived Underground*, Files 205, 212-215)

Once in the police interrogation room, he is subjected to a repeated series of questions, which builds up the sense of his guilt, since the questions assume he is guilty—of what, he does not know. The physical descriptions also add to this sense: the six-foot, two-hundred-pound policemen's sheer physical presence intimidates the five-foot, seven-inch, one-hundred-thirty-pound Daniels, as does "their endless walking, their rubber heels sounding hollowly on the wooden floor, like a drum being beaten, echoing inside his aching head." More overt but still highly figurative tollings of the guilt theme come after Daniels has been slapped, kicked, blackjacked, punched in the stomach just as he is swallowing water, and hung upside down until he passes out. At this point, the police (in later manuscripts, the district attorney—"a man in a grey suit" to Daniels) shove a paper in front of him and begin shouting the refrain "Read the paper and sign it," "Read it and sign it," "Read that paper," "*Read that paper and sign it,*" "Sign it. . . . Just sign your name to the paper," which is punctuated with Daniels' dazedly repeated "I'm going to sign it; yessuh, I'm going to sign it . . .

yessuh, yessuh, yessuh." After he finally does actually sign, succumbing to the lure of permission to sleep and to return home to see his pregnant wife, he dreams of being in a land of hot rocks, each holding a piece of white paper with blurred print. With a huge fountain pen in hand, "like a person in a flower garden," he goes from hot rock to hot rock, signing his name with great deliberation on each piece of paper.

After Daniels returns to consciousness, more or less, "guilt" becomes more explicit. He is taken to the Peabody home, scene of the double gory murder he has allegedly committed and made to confront the bedroom where the crime occurred. The room is so grisly—in the various manuscripts: curtains torn from the windows, chairs and tables overturned, drawers pulled out, a desk and a dressing table smashed, with shards of glass from the mirror glinting among the dark blood pools on the rug, and blood staining the sheets heaped on the bed and streaked over the green walls—that Daniels recoils and has to be forced to enter. He is struck mute: "If he were being accused of a crime as horrible as this, he was in deep danger." He begins to realize that "he had admitted a guilt whose loathsomeness stifled his soul." The police stare at him, "their eyes . . . hard in accusation and implacable in judgment." Overwhelmed, he swoons and receives a kick so light he almost laughs, but then he realizes that no kick or blow really matters. What counts is "what these men said, what he said," which has produced the unalterable feeling that "he was condemned, lost, inescapably guilty of some nameless deed."

The sense of guilt then begins to crop up in less forceful situations. When he is taken home to visit his wife, who is expecting their child at any moment, Rachel, not knowing where he has been all night and not yet realizing he is in police custody, greets him with complaints about his leaving her all alone at such a time, and he is "overcome with guilt." Later at the hospital, where the onset of Rachel's labor has rushed them in the police car, Daniels, semistupified by all he has been through, has to be guided about by Murphy, his police guardian, and by the nurses. When Murphy, grossly callous to Daniels's condition, comments, " 'Boy . . . you sure can make a lot of trouble'," Daniels is "abashed, consumed with a sense of guilt."

The notion of guilt instilled aboveground continues to appear in the next two underground sections. When Daniels first experiences the black church service, he is assailed by a welter of emotional reactions that later, in some of the manuscripts, he characterizes as "guilt." In a third visit to the church, Daniels thinks through his feelings, incidently employing a comparison that reveals Wright's sense of the unity of his grandmother's religious outlook and the processes of blues and jazz:

> These people were pleading *guilty,* singing out their sense of guilt in drunken songs of sensual despair. . . . *Guilt.* That was it. They [were] guilty of something . . . they had to die. . . . What he felt was not logical . . . its logic was buried deep in feeling . . . their passionate search for a happiness that they could never find made them feel that they had committed some wrong, a wrong which they did not understand, a wrong committed somehow without their conscious knowledge and for which they had to seek forgiveness. To die without finding the happiness that their hearts told them was for them, was what made them feel guilty.

When he encounters the dead baby, Daniels feels "it condemned him as affectively as had the policemen. It made him feel guilty." He later has a dream that dramatizes this guilt. Daniels and a woman carrying a baby are walking over water; the woman starts to sink, holding the baby over her head; Daniels reaches to save the baby, then places it upon the water, where it floats; he dives in an unsuccessful attempt to find and save the woman, growing "hysterical, for . . . his mission was failing." Returning to the surface, he rushes about over the surface "looking for the baby. *Where is it?* he called. The surface of the water stretched as far as his eyes could see and the empty air threw back to his ears a thin, mocking echo: "*Where is it?*" . . . He began to doubt. . . . *He could not stand upon the water any longer!* What had he done wrong? Who had condemned him? What crime had he committed to be consigned to the sea? . . . A whirlpool caught him and washed him downward spinning dizzily forever in cold water. . . . And he opened his mouth to call for help and water rushed into his lungs and he choked." (*The Man Who Lived Underground,* Files 205, 212-215)

In the movie episode, the guilt theme is touched upon both explicitly and implicitly in the various manuscripts. Just as the ultimate interpretation that Daniels places on his experi-

ence of the black church and in the dream sequence concerning the baby, where guilt—and Daniels' participation—is
"defined" as a failure of some kind, so the movie house episode
places the sense of failure on the audience that Daniels observes and on Daniels himself and thus carries the guilt theme.
The audience, laughing and shouting at the shadows on the
screen, is viewed by Daniels as "obscene, foolish, blasphe-
mous," violating "the dignity of human life" by "laughing at
their *lives*," "allowing their lives to run out in futility and
meaningless." In his imagination, he walks out of the section
from which he is viewing the audience and "hovering just
above their heads, his arms outstretched compassionately, he
reached forward and touched each person . . . tried to wake
them out of their dream of living death, out of . . . an obscene
happiness." Like the white waitresses Wright had worked with
in Chicago and was later to write about in *American Hunger*,
this audience lives, at best, only on the surface of life, filling
with distractions the void of meaning. In this case, unlike the
church group, these people do not seem to be aware of the guilt,
let alone of any unknown crime they may have committed to
earn it.

The more conscious guilt, induced in Daniels by the policemen aboveground, is expressed more directly, albeit
through another dream sequence. In the theater, his imagined
walking out on the air to the audience is cut short by a thought
that "no, it could not be done. No one could do it for them." Not
only is there no person, but there is no tradition, heritage, or
ritual that can lead them to "a richness of living." They "have to
find the road alone." Wright has Daniels filled with an intensely weighty melancholy that seems to be the equivalent of guilt.
In a second dream, Daniels's sense of guilt, resulting from his
inability or failure to act, is brought out more explicitly. Walking in the air again, he looks at a huge crowd below him
"gazing expectantly" up at him. He becomes angry, commanding them not to look at him but at themselves. They begin to
clap their hands, shout, and whistle to him as they continue to
watch him expectantly, as if "demanding that he perform some
act that would make them happy." When he refuses to do so,
but tells them to "*look in yourselves*," they grow sullen, shout
threats at him, and finally seize and curse him while a white

man in a blue uniform comes walking through the air to him with a piece of white paper he must sign. When he refuses, the white man says "in final judgment *then sink*, and [Daniels] felt the air give beneath his feet and he was falling down from a gigantic height."

The guilt theme becomes intensely present as the ending of the story approaches. Seeking some conclusive sign that his time to return aboveground has come, Daniels's sense of failure becomes stronger. In early manuscripts, contemplating the underground room he has turned into a collage of money, jewelry, and other loot gathered in his subterranean travels, those "serious toys" of the world aboveground, he again has the sensation of "hovering in space, looking down upon the futility and helplessness and meaninglessness and reasonlessness of human life." It comes to him "that no compassion which the human heart could hold could express in any degree the compassion which that awful sight evoked." Not only are the human hopes of immortality or the yearning for love, tenderness, and joy futile and useless passions that are doomed to total unfulfillment, but the ability of anyone to commiserate with this dolorous human condition is also inherently incommenserate with the reality. Daniels is an inversion of Keats's sick eagle, aware of depths he cannot attain: "His failure to summon up feelings that could do justice to what he saw, his sense of utter inadequacy culminated in an all-powerful conviction of guilt. It was his own weakness in the face of this supreme challenge that made guilt consume him . . . he buried his face in his hands and wept softly . . . not the weeping of a man who was merely sorry for something, but a man who was helpless with a helplessness that he knew would never be overcome."

Guilt also shows up in these manuscripts in an almost diametrically opposed fashion. As Daniels revisits the locations from which he has taken items—a real estate/insurance office, a jewelry store, a radio shop—he witnesses three people being third-degreed as he had been, and by the same policemen, to confess the thefts that they have not committed. He is tempted to either restore the stolen articles or to shout out the innocence of the suspects. In each case, however, he decides against such an action, (although in one manuscript Wright does have him audibly proclaim the watchman's innocence). Like Grand-mother Wilson's, Daniels's mental processes are dominated by a form that permits a general, deeply felt, sincere compassion for humanity but that also permits a disregard for the individual. The young accountant in the real estate office has, after all, been stealing money, if not exactly the amounts he is now being accused of. In Daniels's underground view, the young man "was guilty; he had always been guilty. . . . This accusation was merely bringing to the man's attention, for the first time in his life, the secret condition of existence."

Daniels feels the emotional state of the young man so intensely that it seems the accused man is "standing in the darkness by his shoulder, weeping." Yet when the accountant shoots himself in the head, Daniels "did not feel in any way responsible," and the dead man almost immediately departs from his awareness. In a similar mood, as he progresses to the jewelry store, "he knew that some drama of guilt and death was transpiring" but that his theft of the rings, watches, and diamonds has nothing really to do with it. Looking at the battered body and tired face of the watchman listlessly repeating his innocence to the battering policeman, he feels that "the watchman's being wrongly accused might [serve] to lift him to a higher state of awareness, a higher tensity of living . . . that was his whole attitude toward the plight of the watchman; his fatalism excluded the possibility of remorse."

When he revisits the radio store and witnesses a young black boy being slapped around by Johnson, one of the policemen involved in his own grilling in the first part of the novella, his identification with the falsely accused is most strongly brought about. Daniels's impulse is not so much to save the boy from a false accusation as it is to leap in and tell him to confess, to say he is guilty, but Daniels also feels an urge to tell Johnson that *he* is guilty as well as the boy being accused.

Guilt certainly figures prominently in the very last segment of the novella. In one manuscript, as Daniels climbs out of the manhole, he has a certain feeling that "he was in death now." In other manuscripts, this becomes "his guilt was his mortality in the face of this awful reality of sunshine and movement," and "He knew his guilt. His guilt was his failure, his weakness in the face of this awful reality of sunshine and movement that spelled death." Yet his very motivation in reemerging in the aboveground is to tell the authorities what he has literally and figuratively seen. Wright has also made clear that integral to Daniels's vision is the validity of universal guilt. Earlier, in several of the manuscripts, Daniels has mused and marveled over this aspect of his feeling: "Why was this feeling of guilt so seemingly innate, so easy to think and feel, so verily physical? It was as though, when one felt this sense of guilt, one was but retracing in one's living an indelible pattern drawn long before in blueprint. This feeling of guilt seemed to be following a road already laid and paved; as though one's feet, as one walked through a forest were guided by the smooth, worn path of many who had gone before."

Yet when he tries to tell the police what he has seen, what he has experienced, and especially when he tries to confess his guilt for the Peabody murders, of which he had been unjustly accused in the beginning, he sounds like a madman. His attempts to explain are fragmented because the police do not possess the vision, the overall conceptualized emotion that goes far beyond the simple understanding of guilt and that Wright says forms the context that would tie his statements into a coherent whole. That concept-emotion, of course, is what Wright intended Daniels to be trying to communicate, as Wright himself seemed to feel he had communicated it in this book by means of the surface theme or symbol "guilt." The police refuse to accept his guilt, burning his confession, explaining that the real murderer has been caught, and they are inclined to send him home or at least to a psycho ward.

Undoubtedly, Wright has made the guilt theme loom large in the story from beginning to end. Yet, it is not the Symbol, the "something" that is the unity linking all the disparate elements he concocted. It is, like all the other images in the story, only an intellectually apprehensible bit that indicates the presence and the "shape" of something deeper. It is like the religion in his grandmother's life, a form that indicates the presence of a "something" but is not that "something" itself. If "guilt" is, in Burke's terminology, the word that is the Symbol of this work, the definition given it by the rest of the story is so peculiar to this story that it ceases to be "guilt" in the most accepted sense.

For one thing, the guilt theme itself is not a unity. Guilt is not, in a sense, guilt.

From the beginning, a strong antiguilt theme exists. Throughout the entire first section, dramatic tension is maintained because of Daniels's refusal to admit guilt, because of his rebellion against it and all that would impose it. Even after his resistance is physiologically and hence psychologically reduced to the point where he questions whether he might indeed have murdered, he signs the paper merely to gain a chance to sleep and to be allowed to go home, not because he is ready to acknowledge the crime as his. Wright never has him lose awareness of his innocence, that a "world . . . had branded him guilty without cause," that "he had signed a confession, had admitted a guilt he had not felt." He is "the enemy," in one manuscript, of things like the dead baby and the guilt it makes him feel, for, like the church singers, if he is incapable of doing anything about it, if there was "no answer" to their pleas and yearnings for tenderness, love, and acceptance, then one has no reason to feel guilty about not finding or receiving them. Further, like Freud's notion that everyone has masochistic, homosexual, and sadistic tendencies that in effect makes the abnormal the norm, the notion that everyone is "guilty" readily equates with everyone is innocent. In one of the early manuscripts, Daniels wants to scream to one of the policemen that the watchman is innocent,

> that no man could explain his innocent guilt. Yes, of course the night watchman was guilty, but the night watchman did not know why. . . . How could any man know what he was guilty of? He wanted to yell: *He is innocent! I'm innocent! Everybody's innocent!* . . . And again he was overwhelmed with that inescapable emotion that had always cut down to the foundations of his living, that emotion that told him that, though he were innocent, he was guilty; though blameless, he was accused; though living, he must die.

These last thoughts lead to other difficulties in that they point to another aureolating theme. In some of the manuscripts, Daniels has perceived that his first three experiences—the church, the baby, the embalming room—promote "an identity of feeling" that does not seem to be that of guilt. Rather, it is that of a "death-passion," or a profound sense of *le neant*. He has "heard songs of the delicate and doomed folk of the earth, sad songs of a love for life tolled in the midst of death." Later, looking at the dead baby,

> he felt now just as he had felt then, even though the feeling had been caused by different things. Why should anyone murder a baby and throw it away or why should the hearts of those people in that church reach out for that which was not? . . . In him were pity and terror for life that is always dying . . . dies . . . never to look or hear or feel again. . . . What the woman had done would not help her . . . she was still dying . . . everything must end like this . . . must end upon a cold white slab, all tenderness must be stretched out in shameful nakedness, in finality.

Daniels is as much possessed by this "death-passion" as he is by any sense of guilt and reads his further experiences in terms of it. The aboveground and the underground are both alluring yet repulsive because, in a Coleridgean-like description, one is "that terrifying world of life-that-was-death above him" and the other "this dark world that was death-in-life down here underground." In the movie theater, the deathlike quality of the people's lives is brought out in the image of what Daniels wants to do for them: "to awaken them from the dream of living death . . . and do some deed that would make them live . . . rip off the illusions and reveal the naked, quivering fact of life." The diamonds, money, gun, and meat cleaver he collects are "glinting baubles of death" because the people aboveground kill for them; the watches he has stolen are hateful to him because they measure time, "making men tense and taut with the sense of passing hours, telling tales of death." The novella begins with Daniels emerging into the falling light of a summer evening, and when he first attempts to reenter the aboveground world, it is from the fruit store into the "dying light" again. He is frightened by the headlines he sees in a newspaper about his being a hunted murderer and retreats into his underground cave "where he could escape death by an embrace and acceptance of death; back where he could elude death's baleful influence by renouncing life." In the same early drafts, at the very beginning, this death theme is brought up casually in a way that foreshadows what is to come at the end. Protesting his innocence at the Peabody house, Daniels says

"I h-h-hope to . . . d-d-die if I ain't . . . t-telling you the t-t-truth."
"Don't worry," Lawson said with a quiet, assured smile, "you'll
die all right. . . ."
He stared at Lawson; at once as the words had fallen from Lawson's lips, all feelings of anger and protest fled. He found himself
smiling at Lawson and nodding his head in agreement. "Yes, sir," he
found himself saying, "we'll all die. But I didn't do this."

And during the policemen's questioning of him at the end,
when he says he felt sorry for them and they ask why, he says it
is because they, too, are dying every minute.

Ultimately, the manuscripts make it clear that death is the
very force that finally ends Daniels' self-exile underground.
Contemplating the collage of money, watches, diamonds, meat
cleaver, and gun that he has created in his cave-room, and
recollecting all the episodes he has experienced underground,
he reaches such a pitch of unconceptualized feeling that he
realizes "he had to get out of here or be crushed by these
images of death; he had to get out into the open and wrestle
with them, fight them, spread the word of their menace. That
was the only way for him now . . . he was weary of running
from death, dodging death, hearing songs sung to death. . . . He
had to go and meet this thing."

The death theme is not, of course, entirely distinct from the
guilt theme and may be one of the impromptu variations on the
guilt theme Wright thought he had developed. A kind of causal
relationship seems to link them, although, significantly, which
is cause and which in effect is not clear. The crime one has
committed necessitates one's death; but the sense of mortality
leads to a sense that one has done something wrong to deserve
it. However, Daniels's descent into the underground removes
him from the burden of guilt and at a price he is willing to pay:

His wife, Rachel, had lied; Reverend [Peter Taylor/Davis, pastor
of Daniels's church] had lied; Mr. and Mrs. Wooten [the lawyer/
judge and his wife who had employed Daniels] had lied; only those
policemen spoke the truth in their cynical way, for they had tried to
brand him so that he would be burdened with a sense of guilt so
deep that he would never lift his head. They had to place the yoke on
him, but he had escaped. People were happy when they did what
their bodies accepted as good, even though that good meant death!
. . . For what greater death was there than those who died minute

by minute in the obscene sunshine of the streets aboveground, where policemen enforced the law of guilt?

Just as there is "guilt" and then there is guilt, so there is "death" and then there is death. Wright's concern with these categories might make them appear as the symbol of the matrix that bonds the various elements.

The complications concerning just what is constituting the unity—or symbolizing the unity—of these various episodes Wright so freely and audaciously improvised do not end with the question of whether it is "guilt" or "death." For one thing, the passages in which Daniels irrevocably decides he must go back to the aboveground because he must face "this thing," do more than place a stress on death rather than guilt as the dominating perspective that skewers everything he sees. They also raise the idea that, after all, the relationship between art—symbols—and reality, an aesthetic theme, also imposes a meaning on all these images and other themes. It is the images of death that Daniels has been facing, the images only.

The death theme, especially when joined with the guilt theme and with the note of compassion that Daniels comes to feel so strongly, inevitably leads to the idea of redemption, an additional element in the contour of the "something" behind the story. Even before he goes underground, in some of the manuscripts, Daniels feels sorry for the policemen searching for him and even wants to help them, because finding him would not be worth their trouble, merely another addition to the "fabric of death." Once underground, he feels a great peace at being released from freely undertaken responsibilities, such as those for his wife and aborning child, and those imposed, such as the charge of murder, that he almost immediately begins to feel a great pity for all people aboveground. This pity increases when he observes the church singers and feels the urge to "gather all . . . about him, wrap them protectively in his arms and comfort them." He comes to recognize that "there existed an unappeasable tenderness which he and all others possessed, and that there was nothing to answer that tenderness, nothing but the cold damp earth upon which he now walked." In addition to the "death-passion" that links his experiences of the church singers, the dead baby, the corpse in the embalming room, and the people in the movie theater, he is filled with "one immense compassion for all that lived." He is "overcome with compassion as he looked at the tired old man [night watchman] asleep with the picture of his wife and his children at his side," mainly because the man is wasting his life, risking it each night to protect tawdry, "sparkling bits of stone that looked for all the world like glass." As in Wright's grandmother, this compassion has an odd way of expressing itself: in the next sentence, Daniels realizes he could put a bullet through the man's head as he sleeps and so release him from time, which is only a reminder of the coming of death.

Eventually, in the various manuscripts, this compassion and pity seem generated by an identity with those he observes, even though he is aware of a great distance separating them, and it seems to arise in him mainly as a result of his experiences with the church group. In his first view of them, he is aware that "when he had sung and prayed with his brothers and sisters in a church, he had always felt what they felt, but here, distantly sundered from them, he saw a defenseless nakedness in their lives that make compassion rise and drench his soul."

Later, when he returns to this scene a second time, "a strange new knowledge overwhelmed him: he was *all people.* In some unutterable fashion he was all people and they were *he;* by the identity of their emotions they were one and he was one of them."

In part, this unifying emotion seems to be an awareness, at least in the church group, of what Hugo described as "les hommes sont tous condamnes a morte avec des susis indefinis." In Daniels's view, all are seeking something that he has more or less found, even though they are often unconsciously seeking it in the wrong places or through wrong activities—in a nonexistent god; by killing unwanted babies; in distracting amusements; in material goods, such as money or jewels; or, like the police and nations, in power and armed physical aggression.

So great is his emotional response to this pathetic human condition that it leads him to the sense of his own guilt-inducing failure of ability to respond adequately: "his feeling of hovering in space and looking down upon the reasonlessness of human life made him understand that no compassion of the human heart could ever respond to that awful sight." This inadequacy of human pity leads Daniels, in one version, to surmise that "only a god could respond . . . maybe man invented god to feel what he could not feel, for men were overwhelmed . . . when they looked upon the reality of themselves." Along with his identification with others in this shared decadence—this abysmal ignorance and general deplorableness (Daniels is implicitly identified in several imagistic passages as an insect, a rat, a dog, a sloth, or a possum)—along with this "obliteration of self, another knowledge swept through him: "the inexpressable value and importance of himself." This "assertion of personality," comes from his sense that he has seen more than most people, that he has something to give them or to tell them, something that will awaken them from their deathlike illusion of life to life itself. This sense of self gives him "the conviction that he would go forth and devise some means of action whereby and through which he could convince those people of the death-filled quality that ate and rotted their lives and urge them to believe in themselves." He would "touch them and . . . tell them to come back into the house of life, back within the spacious temple whose dome had no limitation, whose wide recesses were as yet unexplored." In several of the manuscripts, just what he is urged to tell others, just what he will say, is not at all clear: "he himself could barely get hold of it, for it was *him*, and he was *it*." Though he has an equally strong impulse that he should not return to the aboveground, that the individuals can only enlighten themselves, at the basis of his emotions, at what seems to be the novella's climactic moment, is "a sterner quality of compassion different from that which he had been feeling based upon the experiences that he had had since he was down here. . . . This emotion made him feel that he had to rush forth, somehow, by any means and save people from this spell of death." This guilt-death-compassion combination becomes another theme or contour-marking piece of literary timber, that of redemption or salvation, or as in Wright's explicit statement in "Memories of My Grandmother," the Christian myth.

The Christian theme surrounds the unpublished version of *The Man Who Lived Underground* both in the way that such literary works as "The Rime of the Ancient Mariner" embody it

(Wright has developed an archetypal form in this novelette, which will be discussed in the next chapter) and in more direct ways. Wright admits to conscious implications of this myth, but it can be perceived only in nuances. In what appear to be the two earliest manuscripts, the movie theater episode suggests a Christ-like Daniels by way of water images, although the connection is not with Daniels but with the audience:

> From behind the ballooning curtains, welling up [from] an unimaginable deep, came the ceaseless roar of voices . . . entreating him to come into their perilous domain and feel what made them leap and dance. There came shouts, screams, whistles, and laughter like white-capped waves, tall, black, glistening as they loomed forward and raced in from the sea to the sands where men lived above ground; but the waves never broke, never quite reached their destination: they raced on and on, rearing higher and higher, and even when they subsided, they did not join the undertow, but simply, with the white caps still foaming, rolled onward and forward.

Prior to this, Daniels has experienced a great sadness that is also expressed in somewhat confused images of water and fishing: "Deep down in him was a vast space in which sagged a heavy weight of melancholy wrapped in a net full of eager curiosity. This net was being lifted out of the briny waters of a sea that lay in the depths of him." This image is continued when he enters the theater box:

> The moment his eyes had lit upon the faces, a profound feeling of eager despair had seized hold of him, as though the net he felt in him, with its heavy weight, had now been lifted clear of the water and now hung there with intolerable suspense, each slender twisted strand of the net being strained to contain the sagging mass of melancholy. With panic he felt the tiny threads strain, break one by one, until the black mass of despair broke through in one swift vast movement and fell backward, splashing loudly into the sea. . . . Overwhelmed he began to weep in the silence.

These descriptions are juxtaposed with the "compassion fired" images of his walking "out on thin air" and touching "each person there, [trying] to wake them out of their dream of living death." These images seem held together by, or fuse into, a tangled series of New Testament scenes of a Jesus walking on a stormy Galilee, reaching out to save the faltering fisherman

Peter (who himself walked for a time on the troubled water), and of a fisherman made a fisher of men, hauling nets of humanity, metamorphosed here into "melancholy" by a kind of metonymic translation. These images are picked up again in the dream Daniels has in which he walks upon the water in his attempt to save the woman and her baby, before a sense of hopelessness sets in and he begins to drown.

The Judaeo-Christian motif is also suggested by Old Testament allusions in which, still in the theater episode, Wright shifts his metaphor: "The torrent of voices all around him was like a cloak of many colors; he was wearing the voices, feeling the grain and texture of their sounds, seeking for the meaning he knew was in them." The reference to Joseph, the favorite son retrieved from the underground well to be first sold into slavery and then become the eventual savior of his people, not only alludes to Christ but carries other overtones as well; even with regard to the Messiah it carries a certain Old Testament flavor.

Other manuscript passages reflecting the New Testament include Daniels's second dream, in which the audience in the theater becomes a crowd looking up at him, expecting him to do something that will make them happy. This is certainly similar to the multitudes that follow Jesus, expecting him to work miracles of healing, sustenance, or perhaps of political import, and who turn against him when he does not fulfill their expectations. Another is Daniels's identification of his intended message to the people aboveground with himself. He does not know what words to use in his message, but he knows that the experiences he has had and what he has learned from them have gone "into his blood and bones." He was the statement; he had seen and lived the statement; he is the Word and the way made flesh, and when he confronts the police at the end, he is concerned that they acknowledge his presence, the reality of himself, even though, as he recognizes, his garbled attempts to tell what he knows are only making them laugh or indifferent. Even more explicit are statements that, as Daniels becomes increasingly aware of the unredressable direness of the human condition and more compassionate toward the race, "a sacrificial impulse . . . dominated him"; he is driven by a "passion which he felt was catapulting him toward death."

There are also the images that seem to prefigure the 1950s Dali paintings of the crucifixion: "he knew that he was trapped, pinioned to [a] fixed point in space, as though nails had been driven in his palms and feet, fastening him to a quivering consciousness to endure the emptiness of living," or, as in a later manuscript, when he again hears the church singers at a crucial point in the novella, "an image of himself nailed by hands and feet to the cross of space and time, the cross of knowing that there was no answer, no meaning, no aid, no tenderness; the cross of knowing that the flowing, grey water swept all . . . hope to the sea."

In one of the late manuscripts, when Daniels returns to the policemen who had originally charged him with the murders, one of them says, "Where in hell have you been? You've been gone three days," using a common enough expletive but giving it new significance by altering the time Daniels had been underground from an original two weeks in the earliest manuscript and four days in an intermediate version.

The increasing obviousness with which Wright asserts the Christ motif in the story creates the sense that perhaps this is the major theme, providing the contour of a religious attitude but without his grandmother's explicit religious content. Wright presents the legend as it might have been told from the consciousness of a very human Jesus, one who may have been possessed of a divinity but who nevertheless has to cope with that divine nature as any human does—through faith. Daniels is aware of a definite action he is fated to carry out, and although the details are, at best, vague, he knows that the result can only lead him to death.

To convey the strength and, at the same time, the vagueness of the calling or force urging Daniels on to proclaim the message of the underground, Wright inserts at various times Daniels's feeling that an invisible presence is in the underground with him, goading him to preach the gospel of pity and mutual compassion but never giving him any specific terms with which to do it: "It seemed as though he were playing a game with some unseen person, a person whose intelligence outstripped his own, a person . . . who knew what he was going to encounter before he encountered it, who knew how he was going to react before he reacted. . . . what living presence was here in this dark underground, pouring all this mystery into him? 'Who are you?' he shouted."

In his indecision about returning aboveground in spite of the impulse to do so, "He . . . felt that somewhere in this under-ground was someone who could help him, if only he could find him. Why did that mysterious person always stand just out of his reach? Why did that voice always push him to do things, and then not help him? . . . he would leap through this wall, through this steel [manhole cover], through time, through space, and grab that mysterious person and demand an an-swer." At other times, Wright seems to have flirted with making this presence symbolically visible in the figure of an old or elderly man (which will be discussed in the next chapter).

This struggle in Daniels, the dramatic conflict of the story, between the irrefutable pressure to tell others what he has come to know and his loathness to surrender his own peace, security, and even life in what will clearly to him be a futile effort, recalls the messianically prefigurative Old Testament prophet Jonah and the New Testament Jesus who weeps over a Jerusalem that does not know the time of its visitation. This is the Jesus who refuses to act because his time has not yet come, who is subjected to temptations in the desert and the garden of Gethsemane, where he shrinks from the fate that awaits him. Wright's version of the myth also emphasizes the Jesus who feels foresaken by the Father. While keeping enough of the outer semblance of the ancient tradition to make it recogniz-able, Wright makes it into a story that ends, as it were, with the crucifixion; there is no resurrection to vindicate Daniels, no carrying on of his message. He is his statement, and when he is killed at the end, his message dies with him. His return aboveground is a necessity, even a kind of ultimate luxury, for him, but it ends in his death and that has no more meaning than any of the other deaths he has witnessed. The closing image of his body twisting and floating in the sewer water current implies the worthlessness of his death, and insofar as it repeats the image of the dead baby with its mouth gaping a speechless protest, it brings back Daniels's own judgment: such a death is senseless because it does not bring the hoped-for freedom to the perpetrator. What is achieved by Daniels's death is not the redemption of a society but, at best, the self-satisfaction of an individual who sincerely felt that he could conquer death only by facing and embracing it. Death retains its victory, although in a crazily ironic way, Daniels has es-caped it, need never fear it again.

The Christ story is, like the guilt theme and unlike the death theme, one specifically mentioned by Wright in "Memories of My Grandmother." Such shapes as these, picked up in some cases willy-nilly by the rush of his creative intuition and that he saw as symbolizing what is behind the improvised adventures, do not stop with these two. He lists four others that are also clearly themes, if of lesser force than those just discussed.

He was aware of a political dimension to the novella. That Wright worked on the novella between July and December in 1941 no doubt accounts for the presence of such a theme. In the early manuscripts, it shows up rather subliminally at the novel's beginning, in fleeting images and metaphors, becoming more pronounced later in the novella and in later versions. When Daniels is first picked up by the police, for example, and is protesting his innocence, he has in one manuscript a sense of his protestation's futility, a sense that he will never make "a breach in the wall of brutality." Despite its anticipation of Daniels's later burrowings into basements, one of Wright's editors/commentators objected to the use of such an unnatural metaphor and stated that its "military associations" were irrelevant. Yet it is related to a later simile used when Daniels arranges about his body the tools he has gathered to dig through the various walls: he fits them "about his body, like a soldier arming himself for battle." One of the more pointed, if equally capable of going unobserved, references contributing to this political coloring is the description of the butcher whom Daniels observes and whose meat cleaver he requisitions. Even in the published version, Wright retains a caricature of Adolph Hitler and his politico-military actions: "The man's face was hard, square, grim; a jet of mustache smudged his upper lip and a glistening cowlick of [black] hair fell over his left eye. Each time he lifted the cleaver and brought it down upon the meat, he let out a short, deepchested grunt. After he had cut the meat, he wiped blood off the wooden block with a sticky wad of gunny sack and hung the cleaver upon a hook. His face was proud as he placed the chunk of meat in the crook of his elbow and left." (*Eight Men*, p. 37)

Then, when Daniels goes to the police station and tries to tell about the underground, the officers he talks to first joke with him about being a spy or a Fifth Columnist. A more obvious indicator of this theme is the newscast Daniels hears on the radio in his cave-room and the vision it calls up of tanks, warships, and airplanes shelling, bombing, and strafing; of soldiers bayoneting, shooting, and gassing others; of cities burning. This mass inhumanity to man evokes Daniels's compassion and he feels some compelling responsibility to struggle against it. In two of the latest manuscripts, possibly written after Pearl Harbor, the most explicit indicators of this theme occur at the end. Just as Daniels begins to redescend into the underground, with the intention of showing the policemen what he has constructed and seen, a siren sounds, as one had the first time he made the descent. This time, however, rather than that of a police car, it

> "Sounds like an air raid alarm," Lawson mumbled.
> The three policemen seemed to have forgotten about him and he was annoyed.
> "I'm going down," he said loudly.
> Another siren sounded; then another. Soon the rain-swept air was full of screaming noises. The three policemen stood stock still, their faces lifted. A huge bright beam of light shot from the city and stabbed the wet sky; another rose and crossed it; within ten seconds the air was full of bright columns of light, roving, searching.

People flock into the streets, screaming and weeping, and explosions begin to shake the ground and redden the night sky. Daniels then tries to tell the policemen that there is no longer any of the original need to go in his cave. The aboveground is now the underground: "*this* is what he had seen."

Another of the contouring themes Wright lists is racial, the problems of the Negro. Contrary to the impression the published version gives and to studies based on that version which refer to the deracination of the story, Wright is concerned in the complete novella not only with Afro-Americans' religious emotion but with their social, political, and cultural condition as well. The whole concept of guilt grows out of and reflects on the psychology of Daniels's being a Negro. As indicated above, his misadventure begins when he is picked up by the police because he is a black person in a white neighborhood, and he knows the reason. He thinks that if he keeps repeating the name of his minister, "leader of the black folk in this area," a man who is "quite a figure in the Negro community," the police will come to know that "they were not dealing with a stray man

who had no family and no friends, no connections anywhere."
His references to the pastor and his church, far from giving
him any status in the policemen's eyes, only cause them to
laugh and comment that they "know all about that," clearly
implying that the clergyman's prominence carries no weight
with them. In several of the manuscripts, Lawson is afraid to
turn Daniels over to a psychiatric ward because word of his
hospitalization might get back to the minister, but he is worried only because it might also get back to the white judge/
lawyer Wooten who had been Daniels's employer at the Reverend's request. Throughout the first section Daniels answers
"Yessuh" to most of the questions he is asked, even though he
does not always understand them, merely because of a
seemingly built-in sense of strategy of wishing to please the
police in every way. He is consistently addressed as "boy," even
though he is statedly twenty-nine years old. Just as Daniels
sees all whites as either blue- or grey-eyed, with blond, red, or
white hair, at various times his own nonidentity as an individual is stressed: the police, on the basis of his race, label him as a
murderer and attempted rapist; as he stands in the apartment
vestibule just prior to his first descent to underground, he is
judged first by a tenant to be a new resident in the building,
and then by another tenant to be the janitor; in the movie
theater, an usher assumes he is a patron; in the fruit store he is
taken for a clerk; when he reemerges from the underground, he
is either ignored by all, except for a few children, in spite of his
bizarre appearance, or he is seen merely as a drunken or crazy
"nigger" who amuses the three policemen. As he is trying to
communicate with them about such matters as human guilt,
the inevitability of death, and of the need for mutual compassion, he tells them he ate pork chops while underground and
implies he would have eaten watermelon if he had seen any,
and the policemen rock with laughter. At another point, after
listening to a blues song on his radio, he muses on black
American musical and religious culture in a way that offers a
broad perspective of views held by black people:

> He jumped and snapped his fingers, not in tune [sic] with the
> music but in a spontaneous gesture of recognition. He had heard
> the blues a thousand times. He whispered: they sure can think up a

lot of things to keep from looking at the . . . he could not find a word
for it, but what he meant was: meaninglessness . . .

"Those black people . . . that's all they do, that's all they let them
do . . ." He once had gone to church and had sung spirituals; he had
not even liked the blues. But in his mind he now linked the two
forms of music . . . here in the underworld, cut off from workaday
life, he preferred the blues to spirituals, for the blues were the
complete possession of the people who made them, whereas spirituals had something of the borrowed life about them; they hinted
more of death.

Rather closely related to this "Negro" line of contour, but
pointing also in the direction of a more purely aesthetic consideration of the unity of the story, is the motif of Prometheus,
which Wright seems to connect with a theme of revolt. Daniels,
in spite of his great desire to please, in order to mollify the
police and so be allowed to go home, at various times exhibits a
tendency to assert himself against the treatment the aboveground world is affording him. When first apprehended by the
police, he attempts to pull away from their grasp and mo-
mentarily resists being pulled into the police car. His refusal to
give in to the demands of the policemen until physically and
mentally worn down has already been discussed. When he is
allowed to visit his wife, he is enraged by the attendant policeman's smirking intrusion into the bedroom: "he whirled
around and glanced at Murphy with eyes full of hate. Murphy
gazed back at him with a quiet steady smile. "Mister, you can
see I ain't done nothing. Why don't you go on and leave me
alone?" . . . He felt that he was now coming fully awake, shak-
ing off the terror, eluding the horror, wiping the last of the
confusing cobwebs from his brain and eyes. Yes, this man
stood between him and all that was best and dearest in life."

But when he seems about to brave the policeman physically,
his wife screams out at the onset of her labor pains, and in
response to her needs, he is distracted from his purpose: "his
heart was swollen with despair; he knew now that never again
would he summon enough courage to defy Murphy." Throughout his stay in the underground, Daniels is repeatedly outraged
by the ways of the aboveground world: how it treats people and
the values it espouses and propagates. The black people in the
church should not be groveling, as he perceives their actions,

pleading for a sign of tenderness, of forgiveness for offense they have never committed, but standing up proudly, defiantly, self-reliantly. His death at the hands of a representative of those in charge of the "obscene" world of sunshine—of "the sun of authority," as Wright puns on the name of Lawson—because "he knew too much" (in both the published and unpublished versions) and would wreck things, reflects the personal re-belliousness and revolutionary potential of Daniels's outlook and values, even though he is not really thinking in terms of rebellion and revolution. Just by seeing things differently he is a threat to the established society. The novella could thus be read as a symbolic account of the history of black American consciousness and its development, although it does not offer any very positive prognosis for its future. Unlike Ellison's later underground dweller, Wright's protagonist attempts to leave the world of symbols in order to convey what he has learned to the space/time world, and he is killed for his trouble.

The relationship of this "rebel" theme with the myth of Prometheus is established by Wright on the premise that Daniels has come into the possession of a different understand-ing and attempts to give mankind an unauthorized view of humanity and society. Wright does not mention, but certainly was aware of, the parallels between this myth and that of Christ. He does avow giving a very modest ironic twist to the Promethean story, however, and thus implicitly to its Christian form. Prometheus knows the value of the fire he gives to man-kind; Daniels will die for a knowledge he possesses only imper-fectly. In Wright's view, this is because the knowledge is held only on the affective, emotional level; Daniels does not have the training or language to conceptualize and express verbally what he has discovered. He has realized a commonly dissemi-nated knowledge, which makes it new for him, but he cannot make it new for others. Like Prometheus, he has to pay an extreme penalty for his "crime," but more pathetically than in the case of Prometheus, the crime and the penalty do not afford mankind any great benefit. They do not because "the world" cannot comprehend his words—the policemen are thinking only in terms of the trouble his babbling will bring on them for the way they have handled the Peabody case. They kill him to avoid that, not because of any explicit understanding of or disagreement with what Daniels feels is his real message, but they are no more locked into their own perspective than Daniels is into his. Wright's treatment of this Promethean/rebel theme thus touches on the cause of the failure of Daniels's mission as being his inability to come to symbolic, communicable terms with his experience. This theme or contouring element can also be seen as having something to say about a poetics. Furthermore, Daniels's own integrity, his conviction that he must do what he feels he must do, even though his "message" is not of the highest novelty, and his doing it, although it seems to yield no practical benefit to anyone, does establish a sense that he is not unlike an art-for-art's-sake entity. As Wright had seemed to realize in "Personalism," just being what one is, however different or separate from the surrounding context, one has a value and stands as a social statement, a "word," even though the context, the society, the darkness may not comprehend it.

Guilt and all of the other themes are images in the story, as are plot and character. The complex attitude that is the Symbol of the novella, that is its unity, is manifested through them, but it is not them. Wright's specification of a guilt theme as the steady rhythm upon which he could improvise all the incidents he could devise—the church singers, the dead baby, the corpse in the mortuary, the movie theater and its crowd, the insurance/real estate office, the jewelry store, the grocery store, meat market, and radio store—gives way to a half dozen other themes that he saw equally present, but at least one other, the death theme, he did not mention. What he alleges to be a molding of the multiplicity into a unity is itself only one of another multiplicity of disparate items. Then there are the multiple "memories" that Wright mentions as somehow working their way into the story-as-contour—invisible man movies, Stein's prose, Surrealism, Twain's "What Is Man?" and dream psychology—contributing to contour the subjective "something" that combines discrete phenomena.

The contributions of Twain and dream psychology bring even more conceptual light to what Wright was attempting to contour, reinforcing comprehension of the driving force behind his verbal creations.

5

ARCHETYPAL   FORMS

Wright was aware of the psychological dimension to *The Man Who Lived Underground*. As he wrote the novella, the similarity of Daniels's mental state to pathological psyches became apparent. By the time he was writing the work, Wright had not only discovered Freudian psychoanalytic theory some years before (and disclaimed an overweening interest in it in "Memories of My Grandmother") but was investigating the psychology of Afro-American juvenile delinquents. He was involved in the case of a pathological black man, Clinton Brewer, whose story was to form the basis of *Savage Holiday* years later. (Fabre, *Unfinished Quest*, p. 237) All of these no doubt influenced what he put into the novella. Wright mentions the parallels between Daniels's withdrawal from the world and that of a schizophrenic: his hazy relationship to an objective reality; the crumbling of his identity, presumably referring to Daniels's loss of ego, which leads to an identification with all he encounters.

Freudian psychology is perhaps able to deal with the psychology of schizophrenia which Wright says he saw as a parallel to the novella. Daniels may justifiably be seen as a bearded loon by the time he reaches the police station at the end of the story. Certainly, like "The Rime of The Ancient Mariner," the first part of the novella naturalistically depicts enough causes and that would disturb the brain waves. Supporting the view that the novella may be seen as the symbolic presentation of a traumatized individual retreating into the psychic depths of a protective autism is the fact that Wright did not see his central character, anymore than he saw his grandmother, in a completely admiring light. Suggesting a psychological imbalance in Daniels creates as ironic a view as that built into the story on the Promethean and the Christian levels.

But Wright states emphatically that Daniels's emotional state and mental processes only resemble schizophrenia. He also states that by no means was his grandmother ever, by him or others, considered insane. He does not hold the belief that the Freudian psychological view fosters: that works of art spring from psychically unhealthy personalities.

Wright's interest in and use of psychological theory extended beyond its explanation and treatment of pathological states. In the fall of 1941, his acquaintance with psychiatrist Frederick Wertham, who had an interest in the connection between literature and psychiatry, led him to cooperate in a limited analysis that enabled Wertham to uncover "an unconscious determinant" of some of the imagery and emotional tone of the Mary Dalton bedroom scene in *Native Son*. No doubt Wright was also intrigued by comments Wertham probably made concerning the influence of Ella Wright and Grandmother Wilson on Wright's psyche. These comments can be surmised from Wertham's *Dark Legend*, which dealt with matricide and was a critique of Freud's analysis of "Hamlet," as well as from Wertham's published account of his analysis of Wright. In this latter piece, Wertham enlarges on Wright's memory, hazy even after analysis clearly recalled it to Wright, of the mother of the incompletely dressed young white woman employer whom the youthful Wright had accidentally come upon. Speaking of the blind Mrs. Dalton, whose creation Wertham implies was prompted, at least in part, by this "'nebulous'" mother, he asks "who is the woman who is blind but not blind enough, who does not see but who watches the secret acts of the hero? In Wright's life it may be sufficient to say that the ego ideal was largely derived from the mother, and not from the father. And the very symbol of the seeing eye that is blind fits the mother image." ("An Unconscious Determinant in *Native Son*," p. 114)

The first specific aspect of Freud's theory referred to by Wright is Freud's dream analysis and his perception of a relationship between it, Afro-American music, and Surrealism. Wright's early interest in dream psychology is attested by the alternate title, "Tarbaby's Dream," of his unfinished 1930s apprentice novel and its interchapter dream sequences. Dreams also show up in the climactic scene of his 1950 film version of *Native Son* and in the title of his last published novel, *The Long Dream*. His last novel, which is incomplete, unpublished, and unavailable to scholarly inspection, is titled *Islands of Hallucination*.

Freud's comparison of "popular dream books" with his own code of dream symbols might easily have prompted Wright to see a connection between Freud's theory and Afro-American folk psychology, a fusion of a powerful twentieth-century force with the fluid lore of his own race. Rather than Freud's dream symbols, however, it is the description of the dream process that Wright mentions. As expounded by Freud, this process does provide a model of the Afro-American folk psyche that would have fit well with Wright's intuitions. In *The Interpretation of Dreams*, Freud summarizes the process: "a dream is . . . a *form of expression* of impulses which are under the pressure of resistance during the day but which have been able to find reinforcement during the night from deep-lying sources of excitation. The respect paid to dreams is . . . based on correct psychological insight and is the homage paid to the uncontrolled and indestructive forces in the human mind, to the 'daemonic' power which produces the dream-wish and which we find at work in our unconsciousness." (5:615)

The resisted or repressed "impulses" are, of course, part of the unconscious, which is "a function of two separate systems . . . in normal as well as in pathological life." These systems are the "*Ucs.*," which is totally "*inadmissible to consciousness,*" and "*Pcs.*" (preconsciousness), whose "excitations—after observing certain rules . . . and perhaps only after passing a fresh censorship, though nonetheless without regard to the *Ucs.*— are able to reach consciousness." The Pcs. system "stands like a screen between the system *Ucs.* and the consciousness. The system *Pcs.* not merely bars access to consciousness, it also controls access to the power of voluntary movement and has at its disposal for distribution a mobile cathetic energy, a part of which is familiar to us in the form of attention." (p. 615) Part of the power of Pcs. is its ability to encode the wishes of the Ucs. by what Freud calls condensation and distortion or dissimulation. This schema, analogous to Freud's later formulation of Id, Ego, and Superego, is also roughly analogous to Jim Crowism and Afro-Americans's response to it, an analogy that would have struck Wright immediately: the agency of censorship performed by the consciousness, the "daytime" power corresponding to the repression exercised by whites, preventing access of blacks to that level of realization; the Pcs. corresponding to the "masks" and other form blacks devised to permit expression of the inadmissible-to-whites impulses to freedom, to self-fulfillment in ways that outwitted whites; and the Ucs. standing for all the deep, immortal wishes that constitute humanness or, as perceived by whites, destroy ordered civilization.

In *The Interpretation of Dreams*, while not speaking in racial terms, Freud gives two examples of "a similar distortion of a psychical act in social life": a general situation in which two persons of unequal power are concerned and the weaker of the two must take the greater power of the other into account; and specific cases involving writers. Quoting Goethe's Mephistopheles, Freud makes the point that "the best of what [the poet] knows may not be told to boys," necessitating oblique expression. Freud then cites the political writer who must disguise the truth that is disagreeable to those in authority if he is to avoid the repressive censorship of the ruling power. Freud concludes his social examples with the statement that "the fact that the phenomena of censorship and of dream-distortion correspond down to their smallest details justifies us in presuming that they are similarly determined." (*The Interpretation of Dreams*, 4:141-43) Regarding the latter example, Wright would have heard cognate views from Kenneth Burke about the way anyone needs to act if he wishes to get his ideas accepted by a recalcitrant dominant society. The passage from Freud, of course, described precisely the kind of writer that Wright and black writers from the Harlem Renaissance sought not to be, as his *How Bigger Was Born* makes clear.

One ramification of this schema is that the normal, awake, conscious Afro-American folk mind can be seen as a "sleep mind," a "night mind," or a "dream mind." Wright would have had no trouble accepting such a designation, as his depiction of Saul in "The Man Who Killed a Shadow" and his assessment of African consciousness indicate. Freud's description of sleep and its mental life delineates a process very like what Wright has assigned to his grandmother. Sleep, in Freud's words, "is a state in which I want to know nothing of the external world, in which I have taken my interest away from it. I put myself to sleep by withdrawing from the external world and keeping its stimuli from me . . . its psychological characteristic [is] suspense of interest in the world." (*Introductory Lectures on Psychology*, 15:88)

Mental activity is not impared in this state; it is not "*reduced*," Freud says, "like that of a feeble-minded person as compared to that of genius." It is, however, an activity "*qualitatively* different" from that found in awake consciousness, although "it is hard to say where the difference lies." (p. 90) Stimuli are still impinging on the mind, on the consciousness, but they are not primarily stimuli from the outer world. They arise from the body or the psyche of the subject; consciousness thus becomes "*a sense organ for the perception of psychical qualities*" (5:615) rather than of phenomena external to the subject. External stimuli are allowed into consciousness only after they have been screened—distorted, condensed, like the stimuli from the Ucs. and the body—in order to prolong sleep. The dream state is one "intermediate . . . between sleeping and waking" says Freud. (*Introductory Lectures on Psychology*, 15:88), and, as such, it is the domain in which the Pcs., between unknown interior sources of psychical excitation and the outwardly directed consciousness, reigns supreme.

Modeled on such a description, the awake folk mind, as envisioned by Wright, is like a mirror image of the "normal" awake mind. In the latter, the Ucs. and the Pcs. are more or less excluded, while psychical attention, wielded by consciousness, is devoted to dealing with the external world; in the former, it is the external world and consciousness that are more or less shut off while attention is held on the activities of the Ucs. and the Pcs. With such a model, Wright could easily see a connection between Afro-American folk and Surrealist modes of perception and expression.

Wright realized that psychiatry shared ground with religion, art, and philosophy. His relating the psychological theme developing in the novella to these other areas opens a critical door to discussion of this contouring element of the story, not as psycopathology, but in the more appropriately literary psychological terms of Carl Jung. Jung's psychological approach to literary analysis has a particular emphasis on symbol, rather than on mere signs of psychological symptoms. This gives it an ability to view even sex as a symbol, so that all sexual overtones of symbols may point to the essence of which sex is but a manifestation, not of the psychic state of the artist or that of the fictional characters he creates. It emerges as a logical concept system that is apt as a rationalistic metaphor for what is involved in the literary work.

Its serviceability to this particular study of *The Man Who Lived Underground* as the contour of a unity becomes even more apparent in Jung's "On the Relation of Analytical Psychology to Poetry" (*The Spirit in Man, Art, and Literature*). Here Jung asks a question identical to the implicit concern of Wright in "Memories of My Grandmother" and "Roots and Branches": "What primordial image lies behind the imagery of art?" (p. 80) Jung is thinking of, among other things, archetypes—"figures," which also include processes; the human racial unconscious—when he asks such a question; Wright is thinking more specifically in terms of the image behind his grandmother's religious, emotional thought processes and folk expression.

Yet, even though never mentioned by Wright as works he had encountered or that came to mind as he wrote his novelette, Jung's theories correlate with Wright's fiction, his aesthetic concerns, and his explanatory remarks concerning literary creation. In passages that Wright's "A Blueprint for Negro Writing" seems to echo, Jung states that such primordial symbols provide the social significance of art, giving it its ability to educate "the spirit of the age," to conjure up "the forms . . . best fitted to compensate the inadequacy and one-sidedness of the present." (pp. 82-83) Passages in Jung's *Symbols of Transformation*, touching on the nature of archetypes, sound not only like some of Wright's introductory remarks in "Memories of My Grandmother" and his comments in "Roots and Branches," but they are also reminiscent of Daniels's thoughts concerning the way guilt seems to be an attitude with great accessibility to the human psyche. Jung says that

> the way in which our ideas are formed and the order in which they are arranged . . . can undoubtedly be acquired and afterward remembered. That need not always be the case, however, because the human mind possesses general and typical modes of functioning which correspond to the biological "pattern of behavior." These preexistent, innate patterns—the archetypes—can easily produce in the most widely differing individuals ideas or combinations of ideas that are practically identical, and for whose origin individual experience can not be made responsible. (p 313)

In addition to these general correspondences, Jung's theories provide an even more philosophical system than Wright has provided, theories that come closer to describing intellectually the more external contour-symbol images Wright created and, by extension, the essential "something" Wright thought he saw in the Afro-American way of holding a world together. A case in point is the relationship between Wright's dream sequence following Daniels's visit to the movie theater, in which Daniels finds himself standing in space looking down on a great crowd of people, and this passage in Jung:

> a swarm of people . . . symbolizes a secret, or rather, the unconscious. The possession of a secret cuts a person off from his fellow human beings. Since it is of the utmost importance for the economy of the libido that his rapport with the environment be as complete and as unimpeded as possible, the possession of subjectively important secrets usually has a very disturbing effect. . . . The symbol of the crowd, and particularly of a streaming mass of people in motion, expresses violent motions of the unconscious . . . the idea of the swarming thoughts now rushing in upon consciousness. (p. 207)

Jung's statements throw light not only on what is going on in Daniels's mind but perhaps also tell us, or reinforce what Wright himself has told us, about what was going on in the author's as he wrote. A large number of boxcars shuttling about is not unlike a milling crowd of people.

Another such concept is that of the animus, an archetype that Jung describes in terms that vividly recall the figure and vague function of the old man whom Wright had flitting

131

through the manuscript versions of his novella. According to Jung, such an old man is an archetype of the spirit, as opposed to the libido, and "symbolizes the preexistent meaning hidden in the chaos of life." (p. 37) He appears when the hero is in a very difficult situation that requires "profound reflection or a lucky idea" if he is to free himself; the old man is the personification of such a "thought" and seems to have to appear as coming from outside the hero. (p. 217) In Wright's story, this aid is most explicitly rendered in the version in which Daniels shakes hands in the theater box with an "old kindly white-haired man" who he thinks understands what he is feeling and is encouraging him, but it also shows up at the end in the elderly policeman who guides Daniels to the three policemen who are the controllers of his fate. The "illuminating quality" Jung sees in this archetype is particularly striking in Wright's story in the old man who tends the furnace in the theater basement. His lunch box, which Daniels steals, with its food and matches, contains crucially needed sustenance and light. This figure's occupation as firetender is also a common feature of the archetype, which in various fairy tales Jung finds bringing a firebrand—fire, too, being a recurring symbol of spirit. Jung also found that in many tales, since the old man frequently takes the firebrand away, mankind steals it from him. (p. 224) The elderly policeman at the end, insofar as he is a policeman, is identified with the aboveground, which is repeatedly referred to by Wright as the locale of "obscene sunshine." As a policeman, he would also, like Lawson, be considered a "sun of authority," as well as a guide to that outstanding fire.

Wright's equation of the aboveground with sunlight seems to be giving the usual associations with sunlight and this archetype a modern ironic twist, converting it to a darkness. Jung finds that the archetype of the "Wise Old Man" has also appeared elsewhere in association with darkness: "In one Balkan tale, the old man is handicapped by the loss of an eye. . . . The old man has therefore lost part of his eyesight—that is, his insight and enlightenment—to the daemonic world of darkness." (p. 226) Wright's old man, as he is able to stoke the furnace without turning on the overhead light, is identified with the darkness as well as with firelight. As night watchman, he is first discovered, his presence felt, in pitch darkness, his eyes closed in sleep. When Daniels next sees him, during his grilling by the police, his eyes are "red and puffy." Just before he shoots himself—in the published version this act seems to be the final sign to compel Daniels to return to the above-ground—he stares "vaguely" around.

This archetype in Jung's view is, of course, a father figure— the guide and mentor and sustainer at crucial turns in one's life. From a Freudian angle, these references might seem to be some kind of expression of Wright's feelings toward his own father. In Jung's psychology, the figure takes on a broader significance that fits it in more holistically with the other elements contouring Wright's novella. As a superior and help-ful old man, he tempts Jung "to connect him somehow or other with God" (p. 225), a connection not hard to imagine even when he appears in a suffering form. Such a temptation is also at work in Wright's story in ascribing to Daniels the impression of a someone, superior to him in intelligence, who is pushing him on to a prescribed destiny, even though that destiny can only involve his own death.

A number of other images in Wright's story are also quite susceptible to Jungian analysis. Water images, especially those in Daniels's dreams of seas or large expanses of water, are for Jung symbolic of the unconscious. Jungian theory is also helpful when one notices the curious connection between water and fire that Wright establishes in the movie theater basement scenes. When Daniels turns on the water spigot to wash his hands and drink, the "water flowed in a smooth silent stream that looked like blood." This "mad," even to Daniels, surrealistic image is the result, realistically speaking, of the water picking up the red glare emanating from the furnace, a glare that turns even the darkness red. When Daniels proceeds to urinate, he watches the "red stream strike the floor," giving off "acrid wisps of vapor." Given the stated warmth of the room, something other than realism is prompting Wright to produce such an image. It makes a kind of sense if read in light of Jung's discussion of urination as a recurring symbol of the psychic life force, combining spirit and libido—fire, from which urine takes its name (*urere*, to burn), and water.

The image of the underground, when looked at from Jung's

theories, moves the contour of the story closer to the heart of Wright's poetics. Unlike the other images just discussed— which are rather fleeting, even dead-ended, or, using Wright's music analogy, like the independent riffs of a folk jazz piece— the image of the underground is consistent enough through two-thirds of the story to suggest that it is the dominant "beat." In Jungian parlance, it is symbolic of the archetype of the anima as mother, and, if not as explicitly stated, even as grand-mother.

One feature of the maternal significance ascribed by Jung to "the city, the well, the cave, the Church" (*Symbols of Trans-formation*, p. 213), all figuring prominently and in that order in Wright's story, needs to be recalled and emphasized here. Water (the well), the source of life, is an important part of this archetypal symbol (which is really a system in itself), and the anima, even when expressed to the consciousness as the moth-er, can be not only a life nurturer but a life destroyer. In the folk tales of many lands, the sun is devoured by the sea even though it returns each morning. As Jung puts it in *Symbols of Trans-formation*, the "mother is not only the mother of all abomina-tions but the receptacle of all that is wicked and unclean. . . . Thus the mother becomes the underground, the city of the Damned." (p. 215) The relevance of all this to Daniels's sewer is clear enough, but to Wright's view of what motivated his grandmother, it is a bit more complicated.

This image of the underground reveals more of what is behind Wright's thought processes and those of his grand-mother than he gave it credit for. In his awareness, the under-ground was Daniels's equivalent, although inverted, of the psychic heaven his grandmother seemed to be inhabiting as she peered out into the world. Jung senses the underground as a kind of maternally oriented image of the libido, the un-differentiated, seemingly chaotic, and hence unintelligible psychic prime matter beyond, which was, even for Jung, the human racial unconscious that is constituted by the arche-types. His grasp of the significance of this negative form of the mother image relates the underground to the "incest tenden-cy." Incest for Jung does not mean a literal sexual urge to copulate with the mother any more than the underground is symbolic of the actual mother. Rather, "the libido of the Son, whose object was once the mother" (p. 222) is what is ultimately being expressed. From this perspective, Wright's story depicts the struggle of a human consciousness to revitalize itself by coming again into contact with, and entering again, the deepest womb of the mind. This is the womb of the unconscious itself, the instinctual psychic life force, and from there it can be born again, carrying a certain felt reality, an energy that carries over to its expression of itself. As such a struggle, it necessarily also involves the poetic effort to overcome the gap between experience and the verbal expression of that experience.

Revitalization and rebirth are not, of course, the only possible results of this retreat. Insofar as it is a return that brings the mind perilously close to an instinctive, even nonpsychic reality, it is a retreat to what can be most benignly imaged as a darkly grotesque parody of natural amoral childhood where one can live without responsibility in a kind of prehuman animal age "where there was as yet no 'thou shalt' and 'thou shalt not' and everything just happened by itself." (p. 235) Hence, even when resorted to in times of mental stress, it is a dangerous movement, potentially destructive of the full development of the completely human psyche.

This pattern is clear in the novella: Daniels, physically and psychologically hard pressed by his treatment at the hands of the police and overwhelmed with a sense of helplessness, first retreats into a kind of waking stupor, a dreamlike state, "his mind caught in a net of drifting images . . . fantasies . . . a screen that shielded him" from remembrance of his recent horrible experience. He longs for sleep and pleads to be allowed to go home, where he feels he will regain his grasp on what he has taken for reality and thus a potency for coping with these men, for establishing himself in their eyes with his own reality. In his semiautistic state, he is described by one of the policemen as being as easy to control as a baby. Once in the ironic version of sleep and home that is the underground (Daniels feels more at home upon entering the sewer than he ever felt in the aboveground), he experiences a deep sense of freedom, of being free of the policemen's charges of guilt, of no longer being responsible for his wife or his newborn son. This sense of freedom, of lack of obligation to do anything except give in to his impulse to roam and explore the sewer, is what lures him to stay in the sewer indefinitely, even though he recognizes that to do so is dangerous, "illogical," and that the sewer is actually repugnant to him.

Daniels is implicitly compared to various animals; he begins to show childlike or childish behavior, playing a number of "emotional games," some of which, like his thefts from the various shops, are performed only for their own sake, devoid of any motive that the aboveground would recognize or value. He laughs for no reason, or in response to scenes that would seem more likely to inspire tears or anger. In one manuscript, he explicitly compares himself to his newborn son, musing that he has gone back into the darkness just as his son was emerging from it, protesting, no doubt, as much as Daniels about returning to the aboveground. Daniels eventually reaches a point of moral freedom, retained by Wright in the published version, so free of any injunctions that he can entertain the possibility that "maybe *any*thing's right. . . . Yes, if the world as men had made it was right, then anything else was right, any act a man took to satisfy himself, murder, theft, torture." (*Eight Men*, p. 52) In the underground, distinctions and meanings blur, as in the womb distinction between self and environment is blurred and even, at times, the distinction between the distinctively human and other, more ancient forms.

Wright's image of the underground, it must be noted, consists of many compartments, even of several levels. Daniels is not always in the sewer but sometimes in unused portions of it, in basements, and even sometimes aboveground, although not really seen by anyone even then. In Jung's theory, the destructive anima is only one manifestation of and from the unconscious. The animus, both helpful or destructive, as mentioned above, is also a manifestation. So in Jung's theory, the incest tendency is matched by the incest taboo. The conflict in Wright's story—in the first part between Daniels and the policeman and, particularly in the second part, the conflict between Daniels's longing to remain in this world of darkness, a world of great emotional light and revelation, and his urge to return aboveground to tell others what he has come to know—is a form that resembles this Jungian dialectic. The incest taboo, Jung says, should be thought of as an "impulse [to] domestication"; "the separation of the son from the mother signifies man's leave-taking from animal unconsciousness." (p. 271) In further remarks that, applied to Wright's story, help demonstrate the unity of all of the themes and episodes that Wright devised, Jung equates this coming to self-consciousness with the myth of Adam's sin and guilt. Daniels comes to a higher level of consciousness partly as a result of the policemen's driving the sense of guilt into him, an action that he comes to applaud when he observes it being used on others during his underground adventures. However, the separation of one's self from the whole also involves awareness of individual death. As in Daniels's case, the fear of death is sufficient reason not to leave the mother; but to prolong or revert to this connection permanently produces, at best, the neurotic and all sorts of human monstrousness that is another form of death. Hence the incest taboo. The individual must move on to other "wholes," which, it would seem, must be provided by religion—Mother Church—the tribe, the city, or the nation as the conscious (what Jung calls "spiritual"), higher cultural organizations of humanity's instinctual forces. Daniels is both an "animal" consciousness—he lives underground, scurries through mud, slime, and dirt, increasingly shaggy and hairy, with clawlike nails—and, to a degree, a superior consciousness, seeing more and being more aware of what is going on in life than those actually involved in it. The image of his knowing what he knows only in lump sum, intuitively, emotionally, but intensely, conveys the import and lure of the incest tendency; his attempts to understand, to conceptualize, symbolize, and eventually verbalize what he knows embody the incest prohibition.

The ampler conceptual light of Jung's metaphors also catalyzes a view of the middle portion of Wright's story as an overall image of this conflict and as an attempt to image the very interface of such forces. This view, in turn, reveals the story's relationship not only to the "something" in Wright's grandmother and other Afro-American folk but also to Wright's more explicit statements concerning his poetics.

The mid-section of Wright's story in manuscript abounds in almost blatant images of the primordial. According to Jung, such material in "visionary" modes of writing "derives its

137

existence from the hinterland of man's mind, as if it had emerged from the abyss of prehuman ages, or from a super-human world of contrasting light and darkness." (*The Spirit in Man, Art, an Literature,* p. 90) Whether that is the source of these images in Wright's mind is a problem to be discussed later; there is no doubt that he meant Daniels's way of thinking and seeing to be involved with such a level.

Soon after entering the sewer, before he has had any of the encounters that dominate the narrative, Daniels wanders far enough from the main sewer to be beyond the sound of the rushing water. Absence of the sound releases him from the vestigial sense of water movement, a movement that had "measured things and made time." This timelessness, the merging or counterbalancing of differences necessary to mea-sure motion, is soon joined by a synesthetic experience of darkness so profound that it merges with the silence, and "he felt that somehow he remembered that this must have been the way it was before man came upon earth, before there was any living thing." This condition of "memory believes before know-ing remembers" is reiterated in a later image. Daniels is star-ing at a "stagnant pool of water covered with green slime," on which bubbles form and burst with soft sighs that sound to him like dying breaths. In addition to its synchronic features, this morbid image involves that of imminent human creation; Daniels compares his situation to "gazing into a swamp that existed millions of years before man came upon the earth" and feels that, if he looks long enough, "he would see human forms take shape and rise and slough off the sludge and yawn and begin to sing boastful songs of immortality." The material he regards is prehuman in itself yet, as the similies employed suggest, is capable of becoming human. Furthermore, Daniels's presence at this potential creation or evolution, even considering the rather heavy cynicism, suggests the super-human biblical Wisdom that sings of being present when the foundations of the earth were set. Still later in the novella, Wright indicates the interfacial quality of this primordial level of Daniels's condition so directly that calling it an image bor-ders on error. After hearing the church group singing again and accepting the inevitability of his eventual return aboveground with his message, Daniels falls into a deep sleep. Wright compares it to the autonomic physical function of breathing; more precisely, Daniels's psychic state has reached a point like that of the lungs at the moment of complete exhalation of old, stale air just before they inhale the new. He is on an inverted cusp; his emotional and, implicitly, because he is asleep, his conscious state are "suspended."

A persistent and pervasive imagistic indicator of the interface nature of the novella's entire mid-section is also highlighted by the application of Jung's passing remark that the psyche, rather than being considered merely as a "question-mark arbitrarily confined within the skull," be seen as "a door that opens to the human world from a world beyond, allowing unknown and mysterious powers to act upon man and carry him on the wings of night to a more than personal destiny." (*The Spirit in Man, Art, and Literature,* p. 95) Wright's story makes such extensive and seemingly "natural" use of the (Legba) image of the door that it is quite possible to overlook the relevance of its connotation as link, or barrier, between two worlds.

One manuscript of *The Man Who Lived Underground* begins with the innocent sounding, but eventually arresting, sentence "The white door closed behind him"; also, early in the manuscript, Daniels stands for a long time behind the condensation-covered glass of an apartment house vestibule door that hides him from the police and yet allows him to observe, without thinking about it, the backwash of water push open a manhole cover. This latter portal, charmlike, draws him, and once he is underground, a central concern is the opening or creation of doors between the underground (the sewer) and those parts of it more accessible to the aboveground. Invariably these doors cause Daniels to pause; they place him physically in one world while motivationally, attentionally, he is in another.

The interfacial significance of this image and its holomorphic relationship to the entire second part of the story is suggested by more than the recurrence of the door image. It is also conveyed by Wright's Chinese-box-like series of images that repeat the significance. Perhaps a more relevant comparison would be to Dali's painting "Nostalgic Echo," in which openings frame similar openings and shapes that themselves contain repetition of the openings and shapes. The most striking of the story's many mid-sectional instances of this image-within-an-image-within-an-image, all potent with the same import, occurs in the first three manuscripts of the story when Daniels is between the coalbin and the furnace room in the theater basement.

Daniels, like a slave who has run away to the dangerous safety of an unchartered swamp where potentially treacherous will-o'-the-wisps or jack-a-mah-lanterns lure him, is drawn by waves of unidentified sounds coming from beyond the door of the coalbin. He hesitates, weighing the possibilities of his being discovered against a great urge to know the source of those odd sounds. Daring to know, he flings the door open and drops to his knees in the opening, to avoid possible recognition or physical harm.

> But what his eyes beheld made him transfixed with terror and awe, and he stood again, involuntarily.
> . . . the loud roar of many voices coupled instantaneously with a lurid red glare that seared his eyes and entered the cells of his brain . . . no physical movement on his part or on the part of what he saw and heard . . . nothing but vision and sound, fused and heightened. . . . Terror was king . . . dictator . . . terror began to work its masterful strokes . . . he saw a huge, black dragon, crouching, roaring, rearing slowly to spring upon him, to devour him . . . deep in a nightmare . . . a black dragon with red gaping mouth and eyes, roaring a song of destruction, lay taut before him, warning him with its awful growl not to advance. . . . He was about to scream . . . but his throat could make no sound.

In the realistic framework of the story, this surrealistic vision soon fades, as surreal visions frequently do, into "innocent components": "A furnace, banked high with red coals that gleamed through cracks in the door, stood at the opposite end of a long basement; and through an open door to the right of the furnace came the roar . . . of human voices, almost hysterical and joyous in their chanting."

The opening of this door leads to two ranks of symbols: those created by Daniels which Wright intended as symbols of something in Daniels, and those more realistic symbols to which Wright reduces Daniels and which probably seemed so realistically right to him that what they express about and for himself would have been impossible for him to say otherwise.

Both ranks are understandable expressions of the in-between condition under consideration here. All symbols, given their nature as mental products groping to express what the mind does not completely grasp in its conceptual way, may exhibit such a characteristic, but Wright's images here are classic.

Opening the door has permitted Daniels to catch sight of something that expresses itself to him in what Jung calls the "figures that people the night world." (*The Spirit in Man, Art, and Literature*, p. 95). Like giants (Wright describes Daniels as feeling intimidated by the height and bulk of the policemen), dragons serve as guardians or defenders of "the treasure," are the monsters to be overcome if the prize is to be attained. The dragon, Jung says further, is a widely occurring figuration of the mother archetype, but in its negative aspects. It is therefore a meeting place, the confluence, of that which fascinates and lures and that which opposes or resists the allurement.

The realistic visual components of Daniels's particular dragon, fire and a furnace (or a container of that fire, both major images in several of Wright's works), also fit into this symbolism of the interface. The fire is associated elsewhere in Jung with a higher consciousness—the wise old man as fire-bringer, for example—while the womblike furnace is associated with the instinctual unconscious. Together, they might seem to be the prize itself: a superior consciousness contained within the instinctive unconsciousness or libido; again, a confluence. Like the dragon, the fiery furnace also suggests that which consumes and destroys, the possibility that development of consciousness will fatally repress the unconscious or vice versa. In most folklore, children who go into ovens are in deep trouble; in the book of Daniel, three young men manage to survive, blessed with an angelic visitation. Thus, the fiery furnace, like the door and the dragon, names in a realistic mode the surface between two forces.

Within this image of Daniels in the doorway confronting the image of dragon/furnace-fire, Wright has also created a Freudian-Kantian image of Daniels's emotional state: sublime terror. In wording especially significant vis-à-vis the emotion Wright emphasizes, Jung states that the dragon is a "symbolic representation of the fear of the consequences of breaking the taboo . . . to incest." (*Symbols of Transformation*, p. 261) It does not represent what happens if one gives in to the incest tendency, nor does it represent this tendency itself. Also it does not represent the impulse to domesticity, to take leave of the animal unconscious—the incest prohibition itself. Yet all three of these meanings are somehow communicated by the figure. What it seems to represent, then, is possibility of some sort. The interface of psychic forces is, conceptualized, possibility; the confluence of these forces—that is, the psychic entity itself, as well as the adequate symbol of it (and the psyche may not exist except in its symbols)—can "be" or "go" or "do" in a number of directions; it has not yet, as the saying goes, "made up" itself. It is between actualities. Morally speaking, in the area of guilt, it is a state of temptation; it has a sense of sin. If the mind can be spoken of in physical terms, and Wright would surely wish to do this, it has a sense of dying, of being between life and death. It is the condition expressed by Dali's surrealist "Invisible Man" and "The Endless Enigmas" in which represented objects become, without any alteration, other objects. It is a condition of considerable freedom, if not ultimate, radical freedom itself.

The whole underground section of this novella in manuscript is such an in-between. *The Man Who Lived Underground* starts aboveground and ends aboveground with change having been effected. Daniels is jolted from a relatively mindless identification with "the tribe"—normal, conventional daily life and its importance—to a seminally developed consciousness that involves a reidentification with the authority that calls, or should call, for responsibility and the marshaling of one's forces to establish the new and better whole that will nurture, protect, and support without swallowing. Such a change, like any change, is movement. Wright's story is movement, as he wanted it to be, symbolic movement, a merging or alteration of one symbol or symbolic construction into another. The entire middle section, considered as a symbol itself, is like motion in yet another sense, what might be called motion proper, as defined by Aristotelian and Thomistic philosophers: the act(uality) of a being in potency insofar as it is in potency. Daniels is neither where he was nor is he yet where he has the potential to be. He is in "the mother," though he is not yet of "the mother." As Wright says of Daniels, like Wright's grandmother, he is in but not of the world, because he has not yet willed or committed himself to staying in the underground. He is, but in the realm of the possible; he is an actuality, but is not totally actual. He is, in more modern terms, in that shadow that falls between the thought and the deed, in a kind of crisis or at a crossroad. Such a condition, and the more or less conscious psychic state that permeates it and that might be called its genius, is also, then, a locus of transformation. That is what the narration in this mid-section of *The Man Lived Underground* is about and what the narrative is: being in the realm of the fluid, of the alterable and altering.

This section was not the first that Wright had written concerning the condition of in-betweenness as characterizing a black person's mentality, nor was it the first time that dragon imagery and Jung-like terms had suggested themselves to him as expressive of a quite different, more specific "night world" than Jung probably had in mind. His article on Joe Louis's 1935 victory reads almost like an experimental version of this doorway/dragon episode with its use of images and similes to describe the "dynamite" uncovered in black folk:

> There was a religious feeling in the air. Well, it wasn't exactly a religious feeling, but it was *something*, and you could feel it. . . And it had come from deep down. Out of the darkness it had leaped from its coil. . . . Blacks and whites were afraid. But it was a sweet fear, at least for the blacks. It was a mingling of fear and fulfillment. Something dreaded and yet wanted . . . something like a hydrahead . . . darting forth its tongue.
> You started on the border-line, wondering what's beyond. Then you take one step and you feel a strange, sweet tingling. You take two steps and the feeling becomes keener. You want to feel some more. You break into a run. You know it's dangerous, but you're compelled in spite of yourself . . . here's the wild river that's got to be harnessed and directed. Here's that *something*, that pent-up folk consciousness. Here's a fleeting glimpse of the heart of the Negro, the heart that beats and suffers and hopes—for freedom. Here's that fluid something that's like iron. ("Joe Louis Uncovers Dynamite")

Jung labels this condition of possibility not only "dragon imago" but also with the word "fear;" Wright, in his Joe Louis article, associates the "something" in the air with feeling and then with the feeling of fear. In the manuscript *The Man Who*

Lived Underground, the emotion that symbolizes or signifies the awareness of the presence of this something is terror. This something is not fear or terror, but it gives those emotions their reality and hence their strength. Being fluid, changeable, transforming, and transformable does not sound like "iron," like a condition that could be behind the unyielding firmness exhibited by Wright's grandmother or could give rise to any kind of real, forceful feeling. Yet "potency" and "potential" come from the same root. In ancient and medieval philosophy, God or The One was considered as pure actuality, all that is and could be, with no possible existence; at the other extreme was pure material, a sheer infinite multitude of "may be" or potentiality, with no actual existence at all. Yet both were, in a sense, pure potency—God omnipotent, without limit, in being; matter omnipotent, without limit, to being. Both were considered ultimately unintelligible to the human *ratio.* Both, in whatever reality they have, are therefore unthinkable, since human consciousness (reason) seems to require a duality, a mixture of actual and potential, in order to operate in the dialectical way it does. Creation ("nature," physical reality) is such a mixture in motion, or it is itself a motion. This motion, this actual-in-potential, is reflected in the structure and feeling of the human psyche, but strangely enough, that aspect of psychic life called reason has trouble dealing with this mixture. It cannot handle it whole, even though it exists in that whole. In any case, what is unthinkable to the reason has, at one level of psychic life, the emotional equivalent of at least "disquieting." To some heretical minds, whether idealists or materialists, God and prime matter merge, like sides of the same nonexistent coin, but to be unthinkable is not, to other minds, exactly the same as to be unknowable. For romantic materialists, the ultimate that can be known can eventually be thought approximately; that is, symbolically—conceptually—as "possibility"; as "nothing, fixed"; or, more immediately, emotionally, but still only approximately, as, among other terms, "terror."

Wright makes it clear at the conclusion of the dragon/furnace episode that the terror Daniels feels is not what is most significant in his experience, nor is the chimera that terror has formulated out of the furnace and the disjunctive voices:

. . . as though in response to an imperious demand, he knelt . . . as though he were kneeling to render tribute, not to the vision before him which had deceived him . . . wrought by the vividness of his terrorized emotions, by the riot of his sensibilities, but in contrite awe before some monumental ideal stronger and greater than he, possessing some hold on life of which he knew not, but which dwelt somewhere within the vast, unexplored precincts of his own consciousness. The terror which had laid him low like a typhoon, had come from within, not from without . . . he felt as a man does . . . in a high-vaulted church, in an ancient cathedral paying tribute to the inner, terrifying majesty of human emotion, passion and feeling wrought in ponderous [piles] of delicate stone . . . he worshipped a part of his inner self which he had never known.

In the first three manuscripts of Wright's novella, this experience becomes central to all that follows. It constitutes the very message he feels he must take to the aboveground. His intention is not to be a terrorist but to spread the word of intensity, of being the conscious interface, the holding together of forces. This ability is not a static condition; it is more like a bridge or the medieval cathedral of Wright's simile, a structure of exerting, balancing multivectored energy. Earlier in the story, before Daniels has had his realizing experience in the theater basement and is wondering about the point of doing anything at all in the face of the inevitability of death that the underground has impressed on him, Wright uses another foreshadowing image. He has Daniels think, unaware of the implications of what is occurring to him, that "all a guy could do was to keep on moving. . . . There was something inside a man that made him want to move, even when he knew that his movement meant nothing." This "pure movement" is what Wright had called the essence of "the origin and source of folk values" in his review of Bontemps's *Black Thunder;* it also sounds very much like what lies behind the perceived Afro-American ability "to keep on keeping on." Even if eventually the physical nervous system's resources for manifesting this ability are exhausted and its perceptible form that is called "emotion"—or more specifically "terror"—fades, a sense of that emotion's "majesty," its "monumental ideal," remains and becomes the ruling passion. One can feel "blue," conscious that one's surface life is coming apart, yet know, not think, that tense interfacing is what one really is.

While Wright was not versed in the psychology of Carl Jung or in the ancient and medieval philosophical physics that offered an analogy for the discussion of psychic states, he had probably read Kenneth Burke's *Permanence and Change,* whose title suggests the kind of intensity described above as being the heart of Daniels's story and central to Wright's poetics. In chapter 7 of Part III of that work, "The Poetry of Action," Burke discusses a similar condition or state in mystics, for whom Wright held little sympathy, using physiological terms and socioeconomic parallels that would have been acceptable to Wright. The mystic trance is a condition of *"pure action,"* which can also be called *"complete passivity."* Since physical movement can be effected only by the repression of certain nervous stimuli and the indulgence of others upon muscles, an "assertion *in vacuo*" of all the conflicting nervous impulses at once, without accompanying muscular movement, may result, Burke speculates, in a "glow." Such a condition produces a "sense of attainment" that is both "complete and non-combative, suggesting a oneness with the universal texture as thorough as that which the organism must have experienced during its period of 'larval feeding' in the womb." Such a trance or "mystic 'revelation'" of unity with God or the universe, he says in further remarks germane to the behavior of Wright's character, "provided a man with a *categorical* dignity." Unfortunately, this "normal religious rationalization or virtue" was "consciously or unconsciously manipulated for all it was worth as a device for making man contented with his lot." Such a mystical condition does not inevitably bring about a permanent state of inaction; history is filled with examples of what Burke implies are baleful attempts "to establish in the practical realm the 'ideal city'." (pp. 248-49)

The intensity of feeling that has kept Daniels "prostrate before the invisible, magnificent throne of his own terror" is a defining experience to which Wright keeps referring in most of the manuscripts, and it assumes the nature of the vision that is the center of the conflict in Daniels. This experience is the core of Daniels's self; it gives him a sense of self, of his power and value, that raises him, in his own eyes at least, above the rest of mankind. Even as he stands in the theater basement, his fear of the underground and of being discovered are overcome by his sense that he is now "an invisible man, a man from another planet, from another level of consciousness," and this gives him a "right of actions which did not apply to the world aboveground." Yet, while the roots of a godlike superman or a megalomaniac are here, the sense of the fullness of his own reality also encourages an incipient centrifugal impulse, a kind of overflow that will carry that reality to others. He boldly ascends the circular stairs to the theater, where he gazes out on the crowd of laughing faces. They cause him to weep because these people are wasting their lives looking at shadows, illusions of their own lives;

> if, like him, they could have had an experience like his, then they would walk the streets with a deep faith, with the knowledge that somewhere within the walls of their blood and bones were vast edifices of meaning that were more important than any shadow they could devise! . . . He wanted to take those people by the hands and lead them into the vast, unscalable walls which formed the temple of consciousness, into the unlimited reaches of feeling and emotion that lay buried down in their bones, nerve, brains, and blood . . . knowing through his feeling that . . . there lay locked within each individual heart before him a reservoir of meaning and experience which could redeem and justify them.

Later, after he gets the idea that neither he nor anyone can give people this experience, he still prizes the primacy of emotions that come from this master passion, the intensity that constitutes a self. The separation from other people, given him first by the physical underground and then in this peak emotional experience, leads, at least temporarily, to his amoral game playing and to a kind of aesthetically motivated behavior. "The goal he sought was a multiplicity of a repetition of those many exalting experiences he had found since he [had] been underground . . . not their outward guise, but the magical impressions that they created in him . . . that crowned underground life with meaning and self-sufficiency. . . . He had reached a point in his consciousness where he stood . . . far removed from the claims of life. . . ."

He was free now to search for those queer experiences that

lifted him so high." (The Man Who Lived Underground, Files 205, 21, 213)

The experiences he has had so far, especially the one in the furnace room, have not been what could be called pleasant. On the surface painful, even depressing, the key to their value is in their intensity:

> . . . feeling the surge of terror that opened wide the deep caverns of his soul to a sweep of passion that he had never known any man possessed, was something that put the stamp of value upon breathing; was something worth searching for throughout the length and [breadth] of the dark underground . . . when he had lived aboveground he had never sought such experiences . . . had never dreamed that such experiences existed . . . he had deliberately shunned everything of an unpleasant character, all baffling aspects of life, any stress of emotion, all feeling that really hinted of deep passion. (Files 205, 212, 213)

This self-sufficiency, the fullness of being inherent in his newly acquired sense of self—that ocean of possibility, of indeterminate energy, which makes all emotion meaningful in its most direct, immediate expression—of necessity carries him over to other people. In the furnace room, Daniels experiences the throne, the majesty of his feeling, the reality of self that gives reality to consciousness, to the emotions that are expressive symbols devised by the consciousness; all this attests to the value of self and encourages the fostering of self. Wright, constrained in part by the linear nature of language and Daniels's consciousness to conceptualize ideationally only parts of that total self at a time, later gives Daniels another version of the furnace experience. This time Daniels is reconfronting the illusions of the black church group (or what he perceives to be their illusions) instead of those of a movie theater audience. Conditioned by the music, rather than the words of the hymns (as his dragon experience was conditioned by the facts of the furnace and the unintelligible sounds of the movie voices), Daniels feels

> Somewhere down in the depth of him . . . a vast . . . indescribable force trying to rise and break its way through into his . . . consciousness . . . It was as though he had forgotten something and in the act of trying to remember it, could not; but still it lingered,

taunting, teasing, on the tip of his tongue, just behind the wall of the next recollection . . . And he shrank with fear from this nameless feeling that was trying to capture him. . . . a strange power-knowledge . . . burst upward and . . . overwhelmed him with the conviction that he was organically identified with all people, that he was those people, that they were he, that in the identity of their emotions they were one, that this oneness was the only organic unity possible. . . . Concurrently with this profound emotional identification . . . swept through him . . . the conviction that he would have to go forth and devise some means of action by and through which he could convince those people of the death-filled quality that ate and rotted their lives and urge them to believe in themselves, to defy law and boundaries and act. . . . (The Man Who Lived Underground, File 205)

In a subsequent revision of this passage, the single source of Daniels's sense of the reality of self and of others is made more emphatic. In this manuscript, he has, prior to his theater experience, been puzzling over the various sights he has seen underground and has a vague sense that "*all* of those things meant one and any *one* of them meant all," but he does not know what that meaning is. After hearing the church group's music, he feels that

two impulses, opposed yet fused—like the positive and negative currents of an electric wire—struggled in him. One was like a strange power-knowledge overwhelming him with the conviction that he was organically with *all* people, that, in some symbolic fashion, he *was* all people and they were *he* . . . yet, con-currently with this profound emotional identification with others, with this obliteration of self, there swept through him . . . a heightened sense of the inexpressible value and importance of his own personality. (The Man Who Lived Underground, File 212)

"Conviction," "power-knowledge," and, at one point, "sterner compassion" are the manifestations to consciousness of the presence of the throne, the majesty; yet Daniels knows that while these manifestations are "altogether different" from the "sheer terror" experienced in the theater basement, "somewhere in him he knew that this present experience had been heralded by what had happened to him in that basement." Daniels's consciousness has encountered a point like the "representational I" that Coleridge mentions in one of his essays on Shakespeare, a point so deep or personal that it is transformed into other than itself, a point of forces and energies intensely holding together. Daniels is "in the very core of reality, in the tragic but somberly joyous heart of the world, a heart utterly self-sufficient and convincing." He is, "in some symbolic fashion," in that cauldron of undifferentiated forces—possibility—that symbols express, all people. In "saving" them from the nonrealization of their lives—from the surface actuality of lives lived much as Wright was later to describe the lives of the pleasant but shallow white waitresses he worked with in Chicago—by making them aware of their possibility, he will be "saving" himself, perhaps by bringing the symbol that is the unity that is the possibility to still another, qualitatively higher level of consciousness.

The intensity of the experience is also reflected in the bonding of Daniels's self and his consciousness of it in the symbolic expression that is emotion. Wright mentions several times that Daniels is not thinking these things but feeling them. After the experience of the "sterner compassion," of the feeling of "power-knowledge" that speak out the matrix, the "basic bedrock" that identifies self and all others, Daniels "did not question what he felt for *it* was he and *he* was it!" Even in later manuscripts, after Wright has toned down the furnace/dragon episode and eventually even dropped it altogether after noting to himself that the episode contained "bad writing," he kept this identification of the real signified and its real signifiers. Though his logical mind tells him not to, Daniels goes to the police station at the end, trying to tell what he knows because "his feelings now outweighed his mind. His *feelings* were reality: his passions were the only things in life that mattered; his *sensations* were the concrete items of existence." (The Man Who Lived Underground, Files 214-215)

This center, this "something," as a Jungian approach to the psychological contour suggests, was not only concretely expressed in the novella, but it also can be seen in the more abstract exposition of his essay on his grandmother and as motivating his ideas in "Personalism," his 1935-37 manifesto of literary theory. The starting point of his art, the "domain of the petty bourgeoisie" as he calls it there, becomes, in an interesting shift of metaphor, the "throne" or "majesty" that Daniels experiences. In its psychological fluidity and uncertainty, its "twilight" and dream-like quality, its lack of anything defined, it is yet the meeting place and source of "tendencies" that have no "hard/fast lines between them"—such as the "fascist tendency" that is infused with "religious ideology," lulling the individual and pulling him to the past, and the "proletarian tendency," with its more rational, scientific prompting to struggle for the fulfillment of the individual. The aim of such an approach to art is "the integration and resolution of discordant and conflicting impulses," not only those of the artist but the "warring, conflicting, paralyzed . . . defeated impulses of the collective individual consciousness." Like Daniels at his moments of realization in the novella, "a perfect personalist ceases to be a personalist, and becomes an artist writing for and speaking to mankind." The deep, complex consciousness is able to draw its strength from ancient and contemporary human sources and thus to address all mankind.

6

FREE WILL:
USES OF TWAIN

Wright's personalist starting point is marked positively by "one thing it has in abundance—emotional consciousness, intense emotional consciousness"; it is also described by Wright, mostly in negative terms, as a kind of void or lack. In "Roots and Branches," Wright was later to speak of the real starting point of his writing in similar terms: his characters reach a point of fluidity, of indeterminatness. His own feeling at this "breaking" point is compared to the void created in space by the movement of a speeding train, that pulls up and whirls about it all kinds of debris from along its track. In *The Man Who Lived Underground*, Daniels's contact with the invisible, "monumental ideal" is accompanied by a terror that is typhoonlike. Jung speaks of a wordless, imageless primal intuition as "a whirlwind that seizes everything within reach and assumes visible form as it swirls upward" (*The Spirit in Man, Art, and Literature*, p. 97); the Surrealists write of a "supreme point" within the psyche that is something hoped for, that liberates self, yet produces (or is produced by) a world of haphazard things that are unexpectedly brought together in revelatory lightning flashes.

Each of these descriptions indicates an experience of a psychic reality that is itself somehow intensely still—an eye or an I—not visible or nameable to the conscious mind yet full of a power that manifests itself in a first visible-to-consciousness

152

contour that is radically disordered and disordering—and is called emotion. Sometimes that emotion appears as "terror," as "sterner compassion," or any number of other terms. In every case it is an inclusive, intense, hard-to-name feeling; a passion in the sense of an undergoing, an enduring, so strong it has to be recognized and pondered, but so unnameable that, to the reason, it is dismissible as anything from "an undigested bit of beef" to a neurosis.

The problem for consciousness is to attempt to express this experience in its own terms, to symbolize it more overtly than is possible in the natural, spontaneous symbols—emotions. Here is the heart of Wright's problem of finding a nonreligious contour for Grandmother Wilson's religious emotion. Her master passion is religious because those are the intellectually apprehendible symbols she has contoured it with, the symbols that were faulty for Wright because they were based too heavily on the emotional and the disorderly. Philosophy and art, Wright felt in 1941, can also provide the matter that gets spun around by the force of this passion, making its shape visible. What Jung calls more obvious "psychological" material, the stuff of everyday, conscious, contemporary life (*True Detective* stories, Afro-American folklore, or Invisible Man movies) also lies along the railroad track. All of the images/themes discussed thus far are the material picked up by the whirlwind and indicate its contour. Wright's uses of Surrealism, Stein, and Twain have to be seen in the same way. They are also images that are pulled into the mental air around the passion and so reveal the vision, or, as Burke less grandly calls it, the "point of view" or "perspective."

Most of these themes show up in the contour of Wright's novella in the general way of their involving an outsider looking in, about having to gain a new perspective on a familiar scene or events. In addition to this general involvement in the story's contour, each influence shows up in other ways in the images that delineate in a nonreligious form the essence of Grandmother Wilson's outlook. Stein shows up, for example, in the way in which Wright seems to have written, not trying to censor his flow of words in the various manuscripts. They often read like the pages of sentences that Wright says he turned out in response to Stein's "Melanctha" when he could not write sustained narrative. Stein's remark that she wrote "Melanctha" while sitting in front of a Cezanne painting that made her realize one part was as important as another also seems to have some relevance to the concept of organicism that appears in Wright's novelette.

If sentences for their own sake, disconnected from any clear interest in narrative sequence are any indication of Stein's significance for Wright, she certainly shows up in the one clear sentence-for-sentence's-sake that Daniels types in the cave-room on the typewriter he has taken from the real estate office. After Daniels has carried all of his loot back to his cave-room, he turns into something of a symbol-making animal. Having liberated the items in his sack from their aboveground meaning, he proceeds literally to play games with them. On the typewriter, he writes a meaningless sentence: "It was a long hot day." Meaningless, that is, for him; but he keeps typing it until he gets it letter-perfect. No communication is intended; the object is solely the formal perfection of the words. As Fabre has pointed out ("Richard Wright: The Man Who Lived Underground," p. 219), the sentence repeats one that Wright had included in the first paragraph of the first section of the original manuscript. Such a device on Wright's part seems intended to emphasize the symbolic nature of the entire underground portion of the novelette. Like the sentence Daniels types, and like the sentences that Stein wrote, the section means only itself, is not concerned with, as Stein said of "Melanctha," the realism of the setting or people but with "essence," the "value."

Insofar as it does repeat the realistic, pseudo-referential sentence of the first paragraph, it functions again in a Steinian way; it says the same thing, but in a changed context that frees the words from their previous significance and enables them to express something else. Like Wright's grandmother's usage, it changes the meaning of the words even though the grammar and the arrangement of the words remain the same.

The sentence also functions holomorphically; taking the reader back to the beginning of the story, it ties the parts together. In doing so, it becomes a symbolic expression of what Wright is trying to get at in the whole story—the way his grandmother could tie together things that seemed to have no connection.

Wright's use of Surrealism functions in a similar manner. In the same section of the novella in which Daniels types the sentence, Daniels begins the construction of another symbolic expression of his life underground as he seems to be trying to come to grips with the meaning of all the events he has witnessed. This time, it is the creation of a literal collage: he glues to the cave walls the money he has taken from the real estate office. Having freed the money from its normal symbolic context, he prepares to give it a new meaning, turning it into wallpaper. Wright assigns Daniels no clear, preconceived idea of just what he intends. He acts on an impulse of "devilish" playfulness. Over a period of excursions out into the sewers and returns to the cave, he completes the collage by scattering diamonds and coins on the floor in front of the money-papered wall and then by hanging the gun, the bloody meat cleaver, the diamond rings and, most significantly, the pocket watches from nails driven into the wall. Described as "blobs of liquid gold," the watches seem unmistakably to make Daniels's entire creation an echo of Dali's "Persistence of Memory." Even the "yellow-green" color that hangs over the whole ensemble recalls that painting. Not only is this the best known of Dali's works, its title has special relevance to Wright's work. Daniels's collage "remembers" the aboveground in that its materials are taken from there. In a more particular manner, it recalls the opening part of the story. As Daniels's typed sentence had reverted to the opening paragraph, the collage carries the reader back to, or brings into the present scene, the Peabody bedroom that Daniels had been forced to view. That room's green, blood-smeared walls are reprised in the green money overlaid with the bloody cleaver, which itself repeats the idea of the hatchet that the police suggest was the murder weapon. The Peabody room is bathed in yellow sunshine as Daniels's room is bathed in the yellow light of an electric bulb. The glitter of the diamonds and coins matches the sparkle of the broken shards of glass on the Peabody rug. The money itself, which the police had badgered Daniels about as the motive for the killing, presides over the whole.

Whatever Wright understood of Dali's picture, he must have seen it as a symbol of his grandmother's outlook: in "Memories of My Grandmother," he compares her mind to a surrealist painting, with its melange of disconnected items. In light of his own experiences that were recapitulated in the writing of this story, the relevance of Dali's painting to his own mind and the story he produced is also suggested. Perhaps the most important thing this surrealist image reveals about his grandmother's mind-set, however, is that ability of mankind to create a reality that has the power to affect those who perceive them. Wright made no effort in "Memories of My Grandmother" to conceal his disdain of Surrealism as something in and for its own sake. What he did value was its potential for communication by refreshing the expressive quality of words or objects when they were taken out of normal contexts and rearranged. Like the characters in "Superstition," Daniels feels a power emanating, not just from himself or from some invisible force in the underground, but from this collage itself. The whole thing becomes for him the symbol of death, and it is a strong motivational force in his decision to return aboveground. While Daniels's collage is initially undertaken as a game, as something without serious purpose outside itself— like Ellison's view of a work of art-for-art's-sake and like Wright's grandmother's mentality, however seemingly unreflective of the way the actual world is put together—it comes to have an influence on its environment, thereby attesting to its reality. Yet the reality is paradoxical. Daniels feels he can no longer live with merely the images of death but must confront the actual thing. This reaction to a work of art is odd for a writer of fiction to assign to his character, and it may reveal something about Wright's attitude toward literature.

The invisible man image is also quite obvious in the contour. In addition to explicit statements of his invisibility, Daniels is not-seen in a variety of ways. He is, as Fabre has observed ("Richard Wright: The Man Who Lived Underground"), mistaken for what he is not—a store clerk, an apartment house resident, a drunk, a murderer, ghost, or a hallucination. The details concerning an invisible presence working on him may also be seen as variation of this image. Derived from H. G. Wells via Hollywood, the image is altered by the "something" that forms the vortex of the novella. The connection between the movie, a work of the devil in his grandmother's eyes, and her mode of seeing was fostered by the stress she and the whole of Wright's family put on the reality of unseen beings and forces. In Wright's own puzzlement over what motivated his grandmother, he knew her disposition was based on something invisible, or at least on something that was not clearly, rationally apprehendible; yet it undeniably made itself felt in a practical way. "Reality," as Burke defines it, "is *what things will do to us or for us*" (*Permanence and Change*, p. 22), and Grandmother Wilson's attitude certainly "did" to Wright. It was not until a symbolic expression, from a popular if not a folk cultural origin, greatly stirred his mind and emotions that the connection between the detested familial religious beliefs and imaginative forms revealed to him a new dimension of reality.

This invisible man image and that of Twain's in the essay "What Is Man?" were linked for Wright even before he involved them in the contour of his story. Twain's Socratic "Old Man," who is educating—or corrupting—the "Young Man" in this dialogue, has rationally convinced the youth that "Man" is an autonomous mind that functions quite without any help from the individual will. A supporting argument from dreams is introduced to show that, whether an individual is awake or asleep, the mind acts on its own, according to its own interests and laws. The Old Man asks, "We have wild and fantastic day-thoughts? Things that are dream-like?" to which the Young Man replies "Yes—like Mr. Wells' man who invented a drug that made him invisible; and like the Arabian tales of the Thousand Nights." (*What Is Man? and Other Essays*, p. 67) The mention of *Arabian Nights* also has some significance in light of the passage in *Black Boy* in which Wright recounts the brouhaha raised when his grandmother overheard a boarder telling those tales to the young Richard.

The genetic structures of Twain's own invisible man are more widely scattered and more subtly recombined in the contour of Wright's novella than this brief reference suggests. How Twain's essay molds, and is molded by, the "something" Wright is trying to make visible to critical intelligence involves a twofold complexity. First there is the relationship of Twain's ideas to Wright's story; then there is the relationship of that symbolic expression to Wright's grandmother's outlook.

Wright comments, in "Memories of My Grandmother" concerning the relationship of Twain's essay to *The Man Who Lived*

Underground, that he liked Twain's objective point of view on life. He links this quality to Twain's growing up in poverty in the Mississippi valley and he remarks that the starkness of such living must have sparked, even in many white people, a wistful questioning as to just what their lives meant or why they existed at all. This impressionistic response has little specifically to do with what is actually in Twain's essay. There is nothing wistful about it; its tone is more a rueful-to-borderline-bitter skepticism based on a view of humanness as a kind of perpetual motion, predetermined data processor. Since Twain's view of what constitutes humanness involves ideas about the origins of the mind and its function as a combiner of data, Wright surely saw, as he wrote his story, the further pertinence it had to his grandmother's mind-set. Also, Twain's answer to his title question is at some variance with what Wright seems to have tried to develop in Fred Daniels.

Twain's Old Man presents the argument that man's mind is merely a system of meshing mechanisms—feelings, intellect, physical sensation, will—for combining data derived solely from without; it is unable to originate anything. Only gods can do that. It is further determined, in how it can combine data, by individual temperament, the set of possibilities arranged by God. This temperament can be affected by training and by association with certain kinds of people, behavior, ideals; but it can respond to these trainings and associations only to the degree its given, unchangeable possibilities permit. "Borntemperament and an accumulation of multitudinous outside influences and trainings" (*What Is Man?* p. 98) produce what the Old Man calls "the Interior Master," "the independent Sovereign," "the insolent absolute Monarch," or the "Master Passion." Whatever individual differences exist, this Master Passion is always "a hunger for Self-Approval" (p. 99); it is, an appetite for whatever complements, fulfills, and satisfies the system that was built from temperament, training, and associations. No matter how an individual might try to behave altruistically, whether the individual is awake or asleep, this Master Passion always puts together, sees, or chooses what most gratifies it, regardless of whether it is good for the whole person or for humanity in general, whether it is "good" or not. As the Old Man talks of it, it assumes a kind of existence that is independent of the individual in which it resides, even though in fact it constitutes as much of an "I" as the individual can be said to have, which according to Twain's Old Man is not much. In its independence, it is, therefore, something like an invisible presence over which a person has no control.

Its invisibility is further enhanced by the "misleading names" mankind has given it:

> Y.M. What do you call Love, Hate, Charity, Revenge, Humanity, Forgiveness?
> O.M. Different results of the one Master Impulse: the necessity of securing one's self-approval. They wear diverse clothes and are subject to diverse moods, but in whatsoever ways they masquerade they are the *same person* all the time. (p. 18) . . . Compassion, Avarice, Benevolence . . . we attach misleading *meanings* to the names. They are all forms of self-contentment . . . but the names so disguise them that they distract our attention from the fact. (pp. 28-29)

The portion of Twain's essay that is relevant to Wright's story is contained in this passage. Like Stein and Wright's grandmother, the Old Man is altering language in light of his own viewpoint. Present also is the sense that something exists behind the ostensible form or meaning, just as Wright felt that something existed behind the external forms of his grandmother's religious logic and behind the artistic logic of the Afro-American blues and jazz folk musicians.

Explaining how self-approval is the motive behind these nominally other-oriented virtues, Twain uses an illustration that is particularly applicable to Wright's grandmother. The Old Man tells a parable of an "Infidel" resident in a Christian widow's home. Her little son is ill; the infidel entertains him and uses "these opportunities to satisfy a strong longing of his nature—that desire which is in us all to better other people's condition by having them think as we think" (p. 24). He succeeds in converting the boy and is happy until, at the moment of the boy's death, the boy and his mother reproach him for having taken away a faith that had sustained and gladdened them and their family for centuries. The infidel now suffers a remorse that softens his attitude toward Christianity and leads to his own conversion. As a believing Christian, his remorse over what he had taken from the boy is greater than ever, and to secure peace, he becomes a missionary. The story then repeats itself in reverse as he converts a dying infidel boy and is berated by the boy and his mother for what he has taken away from them.

The Old Man develops the point of the story:

> in both cases the man's *act* gave him no spiritual discomfort . . . he was quite satisfied with it and got pleasure out of it. But afterward when it resulted in *pain* to *him*, he was sorry. Sorry it had inflicted pain upon others, *but for no reason* . . . *except that their pain gave* HIM *pain.* Our consciences take *no* notice of pain inflicted upon others until it reaches a point where it gives pain to *us* . . . many an infidel would not have been troubled by that Christian mother's distress . . . many a missionary, sternly fortified by his sense of duty, would not have been troubled by the pagan mother's distress. (p. 28)

The fact that self-approval can be considered another symbol for the "something" behind Grandmother Wilson's bizarre (to Wright) religiously framed linkages is brought out by the following passage and its bearing on the dragon/furnace scene excised from *The Man Who Lived Underground:*

> O.M. . . . we ignore and never mention the Sole Impulse which dictates and compels a man's every act: the imperious necessity of securing his own approval, in every emergency and at all costs. To it we owe all that we are. It is our breath, our heart, our blood. It is our only spur, our ship, our goad, our only impelling power. . . . Without it we should be merely inert images, corpses; no one would do anything, there would be no progress, the world would stand still. We ought to stand reverently uncovered when the name of that stupendous power is uttered. (p. 29)

The borderline sado-masochistic, threatening tone and the religious imagery relate this passage to Daniels's experience in the theater basement. That experience, in turn, reflects the above passage in that Daniels derives an ultimate self-approval from the experience: he comes to realize that reality and worth are within him, to the extent that his notion of superiority acquires a vague tinge of divinity. Grandmother Wilson's idiosyncratic combinations, as well as those achieved in other Afro-American folk expressions, are assertions of self-approval understood in this manner, an approval or confirmation of Self that the objective world does not provide. The hunger remains;

but Wright's grandmother formulates a world on which she confers a reality, an "objective" world that conforms to her, reflects her vision, her reality, and hence confirms her existence.

The dangers, the less sanguine aspects of such self-approval, were recognized by Wright and will be discussed later.

Differences exist, however, between Twain's Master Passion that is constructed from an unchangeable, predetermined disposition of possibilities called temperament, actualized only by influences from outside the individual, and what seems to be motivating Daniels. However, even these differences bring into further relief the nature of the "something" that Wright is attempting to express. Wright seems to want his image of Man to be much less mechanistic than Twain's. He uses the concept of organicism and, in several places, forms of the word itself, in both the novella and "Memories of My Grandmother," to indicate the nature of relationships. To be sure, the behaviors he describes are often difficult to distinguish from the mechanically motivated behaviors discussed by Twain's Old Man. In addition to the organicism Daniels perceives as characterizing the relationship between himself and others, an organicism that is the essential thrust of Wright's entire story and is expressed by him as characteristic of his experience while writing the story, Daniels is presented as more than a victim of circumstances. He, like most of Wright's protagonists and Wright himself, seems much less passive than an outlook such as Twain's would encourage. Wright's pre-civil-rights-era, Afro-American experience in both the southern and northern United States, as well as his sympathy with communism and his plain common sense, did not deny the role of external influences, however much his grandmother might have resisted them. Yet Daniels does not act solely in response to what comes from the outside. His normal life aboveground has subjected him to traditional notions of responsibility. Wife, child, job, church, all imply something outside himself to be lived up to and, conversely, the feeling of guilt if he does not. He also knows that as a "Negro" he has additional responsibilities placed on him from without, expectations he must live up, or down, to but that impute guilt whether or not he behaves as a "Negro." The way Wright depicts him in the first part of the novella, his temperament would seem to have the possibility, as Twain would say, the interest or susceptibility, to receive the training extended to him. He does normally live up to, find satisfaction and self-approval in all of the expectations, all the values derived from associations with others aboveground: he does try to be a good husband, good church member, good worker, even a "good Negro." The reception of the training shows up in his longing to go "home" to his normal life, as the police beat him and even after he enters the underground. He does, in fact, experience at least twinges of guilt when Rachel/Lily berates him for not being with her in her time of need and when Murphy complains that he has caused the policeman a great deal of trouble, however ironically Wright intends both. Just as Twain's essay does not indicate that outside influences need be narrowly oriented to a specific effect—a worldly warrior can become a great saint through the mischance of a broken leg—so Wright's story does not permit the impulse to go into the sewer to originate full blown in Daniels's head. It is related to the accident of a rain storm that caused overflowing water to dislodge a manhole cover. Going back further, the treatment he receives from the police activates his desire to hide, a behavior that would not have come into his mind spontaneously from his own resources. Underground, Wright has him muse on the ease with which people accept guilt, as though they were predisposed by something they had done so long ago they could not remember what it was. The training in guilt is extensive and deep in Wright's story.

Even aboveground, Daniels is motivated to resist this imputation of guilt, even when the training gets as forceful as the beating he receives from the police. He feels the weight of the accusation bearing down on him, but his whole drive is to avoid it, get out from under it. Once underground he almost immediately perceives all of the guilt in human life—the crime of not looking in the right place for the self-approval that all crave—but rejects it. He is free, and his sense of freedom is repeatedly stated by Wright. All are guilty, but all are innocent because no one has told them the truth, no one can tell them the truth; there is no one or nothing that can provide that degree of compassion, such approval as is needed. No one, it seems, except themselves, as he comes to understand in the theater basement.

Nothing in the story indicates Daniels has had any training that would activate any potential to act differently from what the outside world urges on him. Wright seems to insist that Daniels's initial assertion of self is not derived from any experience until he encounters the dragon/furnace, and that experience does not in its exterior components contain any elements that speak to him directly of self. It could even be said that the experience does not give him his sense of self; it clarifies this sense through terror. In addition to repeated references to Daniels's treachery, Wright underscores the self-initiated quality he wishes to give Daniels's experience by having him sense that he cannot give this intensity to anyone else. Each one has to come upon it on his own. The experience is enclosed. It begins and ends with Daniels, giving him a self-sufficiency, as though nothing else could even happen to him. Even later, when he has the experience of organic oneness with the church group and with all people (in the earlier manuscripts that retain the dragon/furnace episode), he is vaguely aware that this experience, rather than coming from the church group, owes its power to the intensity that is the self that he had contacted earlier.

Wright also indicates a sense of the primacy of self-priming in two episodes dealing with what seem to be external causes that motivate Daniels. While Daniels does not feel that the intensity he has experienced can be handed over bodily to other human beings, Wright shows what the experience creates, the expressive forms it gives rise to. Daniels's second satori reveals to him his unity with mankind, a unity made veritable in and by his intensity. This conviction is immediate, with "an assertion of personality," in the form of an undeniable urge to "go forth and devise some means of action by and through which he could convince . . . people of the death-filled quality of their lives. . . . He had to tell them because he loved them, because his life was theirs, and theirs were his."

While it is of great interest that the only means he devises is himself—he is his statement, he thinks—and his action is finally the death that literally fills his own life, the point here concerns what occurs during his first foray aboveground after this illumination. Sitting on the floor of the grocery store, watching people pass by in the dying daylight, he feels a remembrance of this urge to go out to them. Then it strikes him that "his compassion toward them was not as full and generous as it had been when he had imagined the reality of their lives . . . the collective futility of their lives—of their hopes. Now, as he looked at them in the flesh, he was bewildered. Why had he felt with such tenderness toward them?" He realizes again that what is really pushing him to return aboveground is something within himself, not emanations from the people that lure him.

What finally propels him outside is, in the earlier manuscripts, the collage he has constructed. As he stands looking at it, he first has a kind of vision that is itself a mental collage, composed of his own remembrances: disconnected images of all he has encountered underground; as he looks again at what he has put together, the reader becomes aware of a symbolic transmutation of the remembered images, themselves unrealized symbolic expressions of external reality impinging on Daniels. "Those four walls were holding him prisoner; those baleful watches winking their round eyes at him; those glittering diamonds mocking him; those glints from the floor taunting him; that gun defying him with [its] evil sheen, challenging him. . . . He had to get out of here or be crushed by these images of death; he had to get out into the open and wrestle with them, fight them, spread the word of their menace."

It is not, of course, the material reality of these items that is crushing him but the value with which he has imbued them. This passage reiterates, while fulfilling, the promise in Daniels's earlier experience of his own creative work: "other forces . . . stemming not from his body . . . but from without, from the yellow light, these shimmering coins, these fiery walls, this bloody steel . . . he felt that the identity of these forces would slowly reveal themselves not only to him but also to others." The reality of these forms—whether they are purely mental convictions or external, materialized conceptions—a reality derived from the self, is greater, more compelling than any reality exerted by merely physical humans. Yet later, in an ironic statement that will be explored later, Wright has Daniels convinced that the return to the aboveground to which he is impelled "satisfied the deepest passions of his body, blood, brain, nerve, and bone." There is no doubt that Wright, like Byron, feels that "in creating we live a being more intense." In fact, as he says in "Personalism," images and symbols can lift "the warring, conflicting, paralyzed, and frustrated impulses" of daily life and make them into "a new, fortifying and positive experience" by means of an imaginative "exaggeration, informity and manipulation."

Wright's emphasis on the auto-derivation of this self-approval dovetails with the characteristic of imperiousness that Twain ascribes to the Master Passion. In Wright's scheme, this imperiousness is the reverse of resistance to a superior power. Although Twain's references to it as "insolent absolute Monarch," "Master," and "Sovereign" indicate an enslaving, domineering quality exercised primarily over oneself (as Daniels feels it in the basement), Wright must have responded to it as also saying something about his grandmother's attitude toward him. The irresistibility of the experience, of its ultimateness, its certitude—especially when, as in Wright's view, it owes nothing to anything or anyone outside one's self—gives rise to a form of aggressiveness and makes clear its amenability to totalitarianism. On the one hand, as Wright had said in "How Bigger Was Born," this experience of primal reality is the source of religious ecstasy, which is a form of abject surrender of self. One who has had the experience is led, as Daniels marvels, to a humility so deep that he is thrown speechless to the ground. Twain's essay also advocates a humility, but on the basis that anything of any merit that man possesses is, after all, given him by God and not self-originated. Any pride in self is, therefore, a decking of one's self out in false plummage, but Twain's essay also says that this appetite for self-approval is "blind, unreasoning . . . cannot and does not distinguish between good morals and bad ones, and cares nothing for results to the man provided its own contentment be secured." (*What Is Man?* p. 99) When given sight—the forms determined by the person's temperament, in and through which its satisfaction is achieved—it has "the Truth." If an individual, or rather his Master Passion, should find Truth or fulfillment "in the proposition that the moon is made of green cheese nothing could ever

165

budge him from that position." (p. 75) He will defend it against all challenges, with a bludgeon if necessary, sacrificing everyone and everything that this form of self-satisfaction be preserved, usually satisfying self under the guise of bettering other people's condition by having them employ the same form. Wright gives Daniels, especially as he is consciously experiencing a sense of something greater than himself, such an awareness of his own dignity and worth that he knows he will never grovel before anyone or anything again. Daniels's self-approval at first finds satisfaction in the form of underground life, as Grandmother Wilson's found it in her religion. Midway, he toys with the idea that "any action any man took to satisfy himself—theft—murder—robbery—was a fundamental right." This imperiousness also shows up in the callousness to individuals that Wright saw so characteristic of his grandmother's behavior and that he wrote into Daniels's attitude toward the night watchman. He at one moment pities him for his life wasted guarding meaningless baubles, and at the next, he entertains the fond notion that he has power over the man's life, can with impunity put a bullet into the watchman's head and so end his empty existence. Wright's grandmother would have killed him, he says, if, from her perspective, such an action would have saved his immortal soul. At the end, Daniels is determined to take others underground with him so that they too can see "the Truth." This is just as Grandmother Wilson imposed her abstract religious views on everyone; as the church and government, in Wright's eyes, urged themselves on the people in fascist Spain; as the Japanese admired by Bigger urged their truth on the Chinese; as Wright's letter to Nkruma so strikingly urged militarism on the Ghanaians; and, perhaps, as Stein imposed her will on language. In the area of Wright's poetics, this aggressive quality of the experience of intensity appears when Wright, in "Personalism," states that the theory he is propounding promotes artistic expression as a weapon of attack: "Beauty will consist in the power of a given work to influence. The greatest novel will be that one which will turn the world upside down." In this story, Wright's emphasis on the greater activity of the individual and his ability to impose meanings not derived from experience on phenomena implicitly asks the same questions he had explicitly asked earlier: if external conditions do not account for this norm of attitude and behavior, what does? He also seems to want to give the same answer: that which lies at the heart of all black human folk values.

If the contour Wright gives to the "something" at the heart of his grandmother's attitude, the contour that is his story, alters Twain's ideas concerning the totality of the individual's determination by outside forces, it undoubtedly retains the general issue of Twain's concern with the relationship of the individual to what is outside. In another shift from Twain's idea, away from Twain's insistence on the mechanical structure of humanness to a view of it as organic, Wright reintroduces the influence of the outside, making it not only internal but innately so.

Twain's proposal that Man is only an arrangement of juxtaposed systems, like so many gears meshing, not only diminishes the human individual's self-powering capability but totally and explicitly eliminates the "I," the personal center. When the Young Man complains that the Old Man's "elusive terminology" divides a person into a number of separate personalities, each with its own "authorities, jurisdictions, and responsibilities"—unlike his own reference that is always to a man as *the whole thing in one*," to "a common property, an undivided ownership, vested in the whole entity"—the Old Man replies for two pages, concluding that

> We all use the "I" in this indeterminate fashion. . . . We imagine a Master and King over what you call The Whole Thing, and we speak of him as "I," but when we try to define him we find that we cannot do it. The intellect and the feelings can act quite *independently* of each other; we look around for a Ruler who is master over both and can serve as a *definite* and *indispensible* "I" . . . but we have to give up and confess that we cannot find him. . . . Man is a machine, made up of many mechanisms, the moral and mental ones acting automatically in accordance with the impulses of an interior Master . . . a machine whose *one* function is to secure the spiritual contentment of the Master, be his desires good or be they evil. (pp. 95-96; 98)

The Master Passion is not the unifying center; it is found only in the subsystems, each acting to achieve its own satisfaction. Since one of the Old Man's tenets is that machines can originate nothing on their own, themselves presumably included, Twain readily has him posit a God as the ultimate fabricator of, the ultimate influence on, this technological marvel. The center is, as it were, displaced to the outside.

Wright's novella quickly dispenses with the notion of any efficacy attributable to such a quarter. While his terminology may at times be as reminiscent of deism as Twain's, the "something" that motivates his grandmother and that he felt he could define or contour is definitely something he surmises as being within her. Even if Wright's antipathy to conventional religion was not known from other sources, details in this story—from the ineffectuality of Daniels's church membership in his dealings with the police to his attitude toward the church congregation, his thoughts when confronted with the dead baby and the corpses in the mortuary, and his whole response to death, whose only consolation comes from the cold ground—make it amply evident. Daniels's experience of the reality that is self may be immediately tied to his experience of being in a greater presence, but Wright makes it explicitly clear that, even though Daniels retains a sense of invisible presence, this greater is not God in the usual sense but is mankind.

Wright's principle of organicism as it occurs in his original version of *The Man Who Lived Underground*, like the "God is dead" theology that was to come in the 1950s, secularizes the "old man in the sky" conception of the deity, humanistically relocating him in the human entity. Images do occur in the story which suggest a physical basis for the unity Daniels comes to intuit as existing between him and other people: for instance, his contemplation of the "primeval" slime from which he imagines the human form taking shape. Elsewhere the unity is implied as existing on a more cosmic plane: Daniels is glad to return to where he can hear the water rushing in the sewer because "the musical rustling at his feet brought him back to the free but measured swing of planets, to the vast but charted course of the stars, to the wild but orbit-bound glide of solar systems."

While Wright indicates biological and physical roots to this organicism, roots that will be discussed more fully later, he makes Daniels aware of his oneness with others primarily on a psychological level. Early in Daniels's underground sojourn, Wright ascribes to him intimations of the unity of the phenomena, and he observes: "*All* these things meant one and any *one* of them meant all." The meaning, however, and hence his organic awareness, eludes him. It is in the realm of feeling that his oneness with all comes through to him.

Jung's description of a primal experience summarizes what Daniels goes through in the theater basement as he is led to organic awareness. Jung starts with a definition that would have delighted Twain's Old Man, a definition of the "collective unconscious . . . a relatively thin layer immediately below the threshold of consciousness" composed of the archetypes and instincts; it is "a potentiality handed down to us from primordial times in the specific form of mnemonic images or in the anatomical structure of the brain." The archetypes, "inborn possibilities," are the "psychic residual of innumerable experiences . . . in our ancestral history." Under normal conditions, this unconsciousness never becomes conscious nor does it even exhibit a tendency to do so; like a river that has etched a deep canyon in the psyche, the waters of the life it contains usually flow along "in a broad but shallow stream." "Whenever that particular set of circumstances is encountered which over long periods of time has helped to lay down the primordial image," this unconsciousness, in the schema of the archetypes and in whatever form imagination may give them, "swell[s] into a mighty river": "The moment when this mythological situation reappears is always characterized by a peculiar emotional intensity; it is as though chords in us were struck that had never resounded before, or as though forces whose existence we never suspected were unloosed . . . we suddenly feel an extraordinary sense of release, as though transported, or caught up by an overwhelming power. At such moments we are no longer individuals, but the race; the voice of all mankind resounds in us . . . transmutes our personal destiny into the destiny of mankind." (Jung, *The Spirit in Man, Art, and Literature*, pp. 80-82)

Wright's own description, both in the novella and in "Memories of My Grandmother," is more convoluted, involving not only the two stages of Daniels's experience but also the intermediary of a symbol as the agent of the second stage. His emotional unity with others is revealed to him as he listens to the church group singing. The words they sing are joyful:

> Glad, glad, glad, Oh, so glad
> I got Jesus in my soul.

What he responds to is the music, in which he finds a profound emotion, melancholy. Several of the manuscripts contain the title "Secret Song," either as the title of the entire story or as the subtitle of the section in which this episode appears; that, plus the fact that Wright kept the image of the singing girl in the final, published version, indicates the expressive, symbolic importance he attached to the episode. Like Stevens's woman on the beach at Key West or Wordsworth's solitary reaper, this girl sings meanings that her conscious mind does not know; eventually the whole congregation is doing likewise. The point here is that it is not an abstract conceptualized meaning that is symbolized by words to which Daniels responds, but a more immediate intonational music, a symbol more immediately related to the self as impulse, as assertion. As subjective and uncommunicative as this sounds, Wright effectively establishes Daniels's sense of communion.

While other passages in the manuscript indicate that Daniels feels that music in general is the only thing that bridges the gap between what he has come to know underground and the aboveground "truth" (he is listening to a waltz on the radio), Wright does give this kind of priority to the spirituals and the blues, even though Daniels has rejected them earlier as merely distractions that white people allow blacks to keep their minds off the real problem, the meaninglessness of their lives. This efficacy, attributed to the symbol music, reiterates the underlying note in the story: that human constructs can incarnate the active, expressive nature of the self. This attribution of such an efficacy to symbols also forms a bridge between what Wright seems to imply about the meaning of organicism in the story and his discussion of what, in "Personalism" and "Memories of My Grandmother," he calls "tradition" and its relationship to what *The Man Who Lived Underground* is contouring.

In "Personalism," Wright introduces tradition when he attributes the flawed denouements of much proletarian fiction in part to "the attempts of [writers] to ignore their own tradition." In that essay, tradition is implicitly linked with "those defeated impulses of the collective individual consciousness." The expressive forms for these "impulses" also have a collective origin; the impulses are to be "resolved"—heightened and transmuted—in "*readily accessible* images, images taken from the common life of the people." According to this theory, the ability of the personalist writer to experience this tradition in himself provides one of his chief "sources of strength."

In "Memories of My Grandmother," tradition shows up in contexts that expand Wright's meaning. Fairly early in this essay, as he is beginning to analyze what went into the novella, he states that a writer has to assume many things. What is assumed he speaks of in the same terms he uses to discuss the basal rhythm that serves as the reference point for all of the incidents, images, and metaphors that ride on the surface of the story. What is assumed without explanation is the same as the underlying emotion, the "something" he wants to contour. Creating variations on that emotion—contouring, expressive formulations—spawns an extremely intellectual and emotional compactness and a resulting tension. Wright then provides a context that equates tradition with the idea of a collection of individual psyches and a less-than-full consciousness. In a rather circular fashion, he has to assume what he is trying to make visible, the "something" that is characteristic of a racial, cultural way of viewing reality, of doing things—that is, tradition in the deepest sense.

At one point, he compares Daniels's way of seeing events to the religious rituals of unindustrialized cultures. He then compares both what Daniels does and the transformational effect of these religious rituals to what takes place at sports events or political rallies, where individual enthusiasm adds to, and also draws from, the emotional whole, increasing the individual emotional force. What permits this translation and transformation is an unconceptualized grasp of a commonality of purpose or of acceptable, permissable, even expected behavior. In the same passage, in somewhat lyrical prose that contains some of the ambiguity of poetry, he compares tradition to dreams, both in the sense of phantasies or imaginings and of sleep versions. Without them, people cannot be in touch with their history and hence lack the springlike tensity that makes for the kind of action—including, one presumes, symbolic action such as writing—that brings about the future. Tradition is for Wright not so much a set of specific actions but a mind-set, all those unspoken, often unrecognized assumptions that undergird a culture, so pervasive and invisible that they seem inevitable, that they form a second nature that seems a natural commonality.

Referring to tradition as a dream, Wright also indicates that normal consciousness is not aware of, although colored by, it; it can be reached only when consciousness is somehow altered. Especially in a post-King era, a black American's calling it a dream can only reinforce the sense that only action can make it meaningful. Wright's meaning is revealed later in the essay when he writes about ritual, which he equates with an incongruous condition of wide-awake dormancy. What he means is that, in such ceremonies, the past, in its preservation as tradition, is vitally reanimated: the symbolic expressions—images—of the past, as it is experienced in the feelings of the people, received yet a new significance from the presently forcefully experienced "something" in the celebrants. All of the old, the now, and the new come together, are unified by this "something," which is the reality of, and gives it to, the tradition.

Insofar as tradition and its symbolic enactment—ritual—are the combination of past and future in the present and yet are none of these separately, they are other versions of that core of reality that is a process, a movement, a "now" common to all, a present energy or dialectic that bonds the myriad possibilities Daniels experiences in the dragon/furnace episode. It is also a point of constant, continuous decision-making or willing, as symbolized by Wright in Daniels's hanging between the two worlds and his sense of having to choose between them. As such an energy, it is similar to what Jung calls an archetype, with perhaps more emphasis on an active or actual element than on the purely potential quality speculatively assigned to it by Jung. It is also the energy that the music (not the static words) of the black church singers images. In Wright's grandmother, this inner "something" is expressed in the archetypal symbol she formed, the seemingly odd linkages with which she bound phenomena and clothed them in the religious garb that was available to her consciousness.

In the novella, this meaning of tradition is presented in the image of "guilt." Daniels's being accused of murder and having the accusation repeatedly drummed into him became a bass line. The novella is no more a story about guilt than, as Jung says, the historical or mythical events that Dante and Wagner employ are their real subject matter. "Guilt" is not what Wright sees behind his grandmother's behavior or that of other Afro-American folk. Similarly, Wright considered it a mistake to see the kind of God his grandmother envisioned. What she really was expressing was an archetypal process, a tradition—an active sustaining of possibilities in the face of all external actualities. Unlike Twain's idea of temperament, this assumed, unproven, accepted tradition or "something" at the heart of Wright's poetics needs no external God. Mankind passes it on to individuals, culturally through symbols and/or, as Daniels feels it, in bone, blood, nerves, and brain, which in turn give rise to the expressive symbols and patterns that, in an endless cycle, reimpose the pattern in the psychic potential of individuals.

The core of subjective reality, actively pressing it outward and becoming the essence of human creativity, is thus also a core linked essentially to what is outside the individual as well. Unlike Twain's passively determined Master Passion, Wright's central reality is as active and determining as the reality that comes to it from without. Objective and subjective are points on a loop that has no beginning or end, no divisions of cause or effect. Wright undoubtedly found support for his modification of Twain's notion of man in what he learned from Kenneth Burke's theories, which also played a role in the development of Wright's poetics.

7

ORIENTATION:
USES OF
KENNETH BURKE

Wright owned and presumably had read, by the latter part of the 1930s, Kenneth Burke's *Permanence and Change*. It contains, among other pertinent matters, ideas similar to those in "What Is Man?" but offers an extensive counterview to Twain's mechanistic view of the human psyche and human creativity. It was probably not the first thing of Burke's that Wright encountered, and probably not the last, nor was its counterbalance to Twain's mechanistic view the only service that Burke provided Wright.

Wright and Burke attended the First American Writers' Congress in 1935, where Burke received much attention from the faction-ridden group because of his provocative paper "Revolutionary Symbolism in America." Wright later owned a copy of the proceedings of the conference which contained Burke's essay. Both also attended the Second Congress in 1937, and during this time, both moved within the intertwined circles of leftist intellectuals, writers, and other artists. Wright was undoubtedly aware of, and also may have studied, Burke's three other books that were written prior to 1941—possibly even *The Philosophy of Literary Form*, published that year, while Wright was working on "Memories of My Grandmother" and *The Man Who Lived Underground*. Burke certainly knew and was moved by Wright's work: in addition to his reference to *Native Son* in his *New Directions* article on Surrealism, Burke refers to *Native Son*, in the foreword to *The Philosophy of Literary Form*, as offering "a whole new avenue to follow" in the development of his own speculations on "the ambiguities of power" (p. xxi); and he also mentioned *Native Son* several times in *A Grammar of Motives* and *A Rhetoric of Motives* to illustrate his points.

It is probable that Wright's first exposure to Burke's theories at the First Writers' Congress would have been to the pragmatically simplified theories that Burke placed, by his own admission, in the interests of Communist propaganda. At the same time, Burke was able to include a critique of the shortcomings of proletarian writing, a feeling that Wright shared because of his mother's reaction to samples of Communist literature that he had brought home. (*American Hunger*, pp. 65-65) Burke discussed this practical issue against a general background of symbol and myth. What he said about these entities would have struck a nerve in Wright, his puzzlement about his grandmother and Afro-American folk religious attitude and procedures, although in its major point, Burke's essay urged tactics opposed to Grandmother Wilson's. Symbol or myth, Burke says, defined as a "subtle complex of emotions and attitudes," "may be wrong or they may be used to bad ends—but they cannot be dispensed with." Myths, he contends in a remark that he developed at length in *Counter-Statement* and in *Permanence and Change*, are as real as any tool, as real as food or shelter, although they deal "with a *secondary* order of reality." They are not illusions but appear so only when "they survive as fossils from situations for which they were adapted into changed situations." (*American Writers' Congress*, 87-88)

The main thrust of Burke's comments on American revolutionary symbolism is that pro-Communist writers who are intent on actually effecting social change need to change the myths they have been utilizing. "The worker" is not a myth attuned to Americans (or perhaps to anyone); few people really want to be mere cogs on an assembly line or spend their lives picking fruits and vegetables on truck farms. Depictions of such a form of life may arouse sympathy, Burke says, but they do not arouse the ambition of those who read about it. In order for the imaginative writer to convince the people who are able to improve socioeconomic conditions implicit in the image of "the worker," he needs to appeal to, to utilize, the values held in common with those who are not workers. Burke suggests that, for "the worker," these artists substitute the ideal of "the people."

In such a symbol, the writer uses the vocabulary, the values, of those whose orientation he wishes to reach in order to alter it. The artist must leap over the bounds of class divisions if he wishes to bring about a society that is free of class divisions; he must indicate that he is focusing not just on improving the condition of a socioeconomic class but the condition of mankind. "The people" is a more effective symbol for a revolutionary writer because it indicates a

> greater breadth in a writer's allegiance. . . . He shows himself alive to all the aspects of contemporary effort and thought (in contrast with a certain anti-intellectualist, semi-obscurantist trend among some of the strictly *proletarian* school, who tend to imply that there is some disgrace attached to things of the mind). . . . [He should] take an interest in as many imaginative, aesthetic, and speculative fields as he can handle—and into this breadth of his concerns . . . interweave a general attitude of sympathy for the oppressed and antipathy towards . . . oppressive institutions. In this way, he would ally his attitudes with everything that is broadest and fullest in the world today. And he would argue for his political sympathies, not literally and directly, but by the intellectual company he keeps. (pp. 90-91)

In the last paragraph of the essay, Burke characterizes the attributes of "the people" as a symbol by reiterating a simile from his discussion of symbols in *Counter-Statement:* "the people" is "Janus-faced." (p. 93) Unlike "the worker" or "the proletariat," it contains overtones of both oppression and unity; it links aspects that are in conflict. This latter quality is particularly worthy of note, not only because of the underlying idea that is central to Burke's whole theory, but because of that idea's pertinence to Wright's observations about his grandmother and the Afro-American folk mentality. In Burke's context, rather than forcing compliance with a new outlook, such a symbol is an appeal from an alien viewpoint to a seed of destruction that the "old" viewpoint has bred within itself. While what he advocates is within the process of the dialectical method (in *Permanence and Change* he cites Sidney Hook's contention that Marx often phrased his arguments in a way that would gain a favorable hearing from a particular audience), Burke claims that such a symbol also indicates his own class, the petty bourgeoisie.

Burke, of course, was not the only speaker at the congress, not the only source of probable inspiration for Wright. There were those whose work Wright definitely knew and admired, such as Langston Hughes and James T. Farrell. The latter and others, such as Edwin Seaver, as well as Burke, had reservations about proletarian fiction and what was missing in its efforts, what was affecting the quality of their literature. But Wright was concerned with the problems of transposing political and economic-class frames of reference into a racial context, and Burke was saying things of direct importance to this issue which were of particular personal concern to Wright. Wright was pondering more than the problem of the essence of Afro-American folk expression and how to contour it in a nonreligious way. He was also, as Constance Webb reported in her biography, involved with how to make the ideal of communism—its self-fulfillment in the oneness of humanity which was an emotional reality for him—more apparent by devising more effective expressions of it, not only in literature but in programs and activities.

Furthermore, considering that Wright was then working on "Big Boy Leaves Home," Burke's "the people" would have been closer to what he had begun to do in fiction than in the poetry he had been writing. His poems for the Communist publications were often proletarian in the sense that was being deplored, concerned more with the Cause than with art. His short story, on the other hand, and those which were to follow in *Uncle Tom's Children*, would begin with lines from contemporary word games and songs of Afro-American folk, the kind of lore that white American audiences had generally found unthreatening, even charming. He would finish this story by the end of May in 1935, after the April congress. His finishing touches, possibly reflecting Burke's suggestions in "Revolutionary Symbolism," seem to have been the toning down of its language and the violence. According to Fabre, at least some of the audience had walked out on his limited public readings of it before publication, possibly an indication to him of the validity of Burke's recommendation. Negative suggestions of his response to Burke's ideas include his 1940 complaint in "How Bigger Was Born" that his stories in *Uncle Tom's Children* merely had stirred the sympathies of readers rather than moved them to any action regarding the kind of racist horrors depicted. If he had taken Burke's suggestion, it had not worked. Much later, in 1955, in an interview he gave to a young Indonesian at Bandung, Wright was to describe writers and their relationship to politics in words with Burkean undertones, even in the somewhat disparaging stress on the persuasive power and role of the literary artist:

> the more we find all concepts from God down to the concept of marriage to be simply man made artifacts. . . . When values, traditions, customs, habits, can no longer lead or guide us in life, then some leaders spring forward with ideologies and at the point of a gun organize society by force . . . the writer, at that moment, becomes something terribly important. He takes the place of the priest. . . . He is hired by the new rulers to write to persuade the populace to follow the dictates of government. . . . But where God reigns, where marriage is sacred, where traditional values rule, the writer is reduced to writing ads for Lux soap. ("Writers and Their Art")

The strongest positive indication of a relationship between Burke's ideas, even as they are presented in abbreviated form in "Revolutionary Symbolism," and Wright's is in his 1937 "Blueprint for Negro Writing." Far more culturally specific than Burke's, Wright's essay, nevertheless, could not be more in agreement with Burke's statements about the communicative value of a broader intellectual scope nor more explicit in its call for a synthesis of differing elements in, and by means of, a third entity.

Like Burke's congress paper, Wright's blueprint is a reworking of other expressions of his thoughts on literary theory. One version is found in an apparently very early, aborted essay, "On The Future Of Literary Expression," in which Wright declares that in its efforts to communicate "socialized emotional consciousness," literature will rely on personal emotional experience, but also on the "findings of science . . . to give a collective or racial, national sense of life . . . in its highest reaches, or collective sense of man['s] struggle on earth." Even a new form, beyond the traditions of the novel, poetry, and the drama but a dialectical merger of the three, will be created, and all schools will be drawn upon. Between 1935 and 1937, Wright's longer fledgling poetics, which he described in "Personalism," suggests Burke's stimulation. The personalist artist at the center of this artistic credo is no doubt a depiction of Wright's own ideal posture, but the entire manuscript can be read as a shrewd picture of the theorist Burke as he revealed himself in *Permanence and Change.*

"Personalism" is an attempt to reconcile the demands of art and of ideology. Wright's artist is specified as petite bourgeois; like Burke and his symbols, he stands between two orientations or myths, fluid "tendencies" rather than clearly defined states. Wright gives Marxist labels to these tendencies: the "proletariat," which conceives the "social order as changing and sensitive to control" and urges "the fulfillment of the individual through struggle, through the attainment of the scientific hopes of the 18th century"; and the "fascist," which "postulates the social order as changeless and eternal" and is "infused with religious ideology [and] seeks to lull and pull the individual back to the past." Wright's petite bourgeois personalist holds the theory of art for art's sake (Burke in his youth was impressed by Pater); he has sought "to pour into his artistic expression all the meaning of religion, all the denied satisfaction of social life," but he realizes that all the collapsing spiritual values that theory was intended to buttress are "dead beyond recall" and "the very world they gave birth to is dying." Moreover, in a Burkean manner, Wright does not call for the total abandonment of such a position. Rather, he questions how this older stance or orientation can be reconciled with new social conditions. He gives a number of answers; the one most relevant here is that, since the personalist artist's is the ultimate in communication, all techniques of expression— not only realism but symbolism, imagism, dadism, surrealism—in toto or in part are usable and "the subject matter can be drawn from whatever sphere of life the writer chooses." The "perfect personalist" thus solves the problem of universality; he "ceases to be a personalist and becomes an artist writing and speaking to mankind." Two short paragraphs stating this idea nod emphatically in Burke's direction: "The social value of personalist creation lies in its power to evoke definite and positive responses and attitudes, and to create psychological conditions amendale [sic] to political and moral suasion. The MISSING LINK in Proletarian writing—The forced resolution which ends the majority of . . . proletarian efforts at fiction does not come off. I believe this arises from the attempt of the writer to ignore their own tradition." ("Personalism")

Even more than "Revolutionary Symbolism," Burke's *Permanence and Change* and a good part of *Counter-Statement* are replete with ideas that parallel and illuminate Wright's early speculations and his fiction to a great extent. Examining them in the light of Wright's work, one feels that Wright either absorbed Burke's ideas to a remarkable degree—transforming them into something of his own, as he did with newspaper accounts or conversational anecdotes that he converted into stories—or that he had an equally remarkable, experientially achieved affinity with the core of Burke's scholarly well-developed and well-supported theory. Occasionally the relationship between these two writers is literally discernible in the writing. One example is found in "Memories of My Grandmother" in connection with his youthful desire not to understand English so that he could actually hear it, a wish that was to be fulfilled in his discovery of Gertrude Stein's prose and its role in his perception of Afro-American language and the "something" that lay behind it. In *Permanence and Change*, Burke advocates precisely the same deliberate defamiliarization with language for the purpose of gaining such a new knowledge:

> Imagine that you had long studied some busy and ingenious race of organisms, in the attempt to decide for yourself, from the observing of their ways, what inducements led them to act as they did; imagine next that, after long research with this race which you had thought speechless, you suddenly discovered that they had a vast communicative network, a remarkably complex arrangement of signs; imagine next that you finally succeeded in deciphering these signs, thereby learning all this race's motives and purposes as this race itself conceived them. . . . Imagine, then, setting out to study mankind, with whose system of speech you are largely familiar. Imagine beginning your course of study *precisely by depriving yourself of this familiarity*, attempting to understand motives and pur-

poses by avoiding as much as possible the clues handed you ready-made in the texture of the language itself. (p. 121)

Another example of this type of relationship between Burke and Wright is found in a long footnote in *Permanence and Change* which reads like a close analysis of the connection between *The Man Who Lived Underground* and "Memories of My Grandmother" and also of the relationship of these works to the genesis of *Black Boy* a short time later:

> Once a set of new meanings is firmly established [such as Wright felt he had gained in the writing of *The Man Who Lived Underground*], we can often note in art another kind of regression: the artist is suddenly prompted to review the memories of his youth because they combine at once the qualities of strangeness and intimacy. Probably every man has these periods of rebirth, a new angle of vision whereby so much that he had forgot suddenly becomes useful or relevant, hence grows vivid again in his memory.
>
> Rebirth and perspective by congruity are thus seen to be synonymous, a process of conversion, though such words as conversion and rebirth are usually reserved for only the most spectacular of such reorientations, the religious. The evangelizing tendency that usually accompanies rebirth, the need to tell others what one has seen, is interwoven with the whole program of socialization, the tendency to justify one's change by obtaining the corroboration of others. Evangelization is the obverse side of guilt—and when we realize that the new way of seeing often vows one to a divergency from his group, we can understand why the founders of a line may often seem not merely to endure persecution, but to court it.
>
> The artist is always an evangelist, quite as the religious reformer is. He wants others to feel as he does. . . . (p. 154)

The ties between Burke's ideas in these books and Wright's thought and practice are deeper and more extensive, however, than these instances show. A small book would be required to detail the various ways in which Burke's theories have relevance to Wright's works and what he was seeking to do in his fiction. In this chapter only two of Burke's key concepts in *Permanence and Change*—orientation and perspective by incongruity—will be discussed, along with the process of symbolization or expressive consciousness as he presents it in *Counter-Statement*.

In Burke's theory, orientation is a tool. Seeking fulfillment, the basic impulse of being—and in particular, in Burke's teleological theory, of life—devises it. Burke calls it by a number of names: "purpose," "interest," "a critical capacity" for developing new meanings; also, it is sometimes "motive." He refers to orientation as a "way" of giving signs and phenomena their "character," of interpreting them to the advantage of the organism. Orientation also blends into his meaning of symbol and of myth. The relevance of *Permanence and Change* to Wright's problem, as he had framed it in terms of his grandmother and Afro-American folk mentality, must have become apparent to Wright when Burke writes that orientation, the organism's system that guides it toward those phenomena that will best enhance it, is involved with "one's ideas of relationship," with the "process of linkages." (*Permanence and Change*, pp. 9, 11, 14)

Also appealing to Wright's interest would have been Burke's further delineation of orientation as not merely applied to the individual but to a cultural, traditional outlook, a schema. The way in which things can be seen as linked can become literally, in Burke's theory, second nature: reality, but of a second order (the secondness most often forgotten); habitual, to an entire group because the linkages offer a *"general view of reality"* (p. 3), a taken-for-grantedness that seems to work to the advantage of the entire gens—or simply because the group knows of no other way to view reality. This climate of opinion is, then, not necessarily a visible whole, an assumed ambient "knowledge" in which any particular text is experienced and given its meaning.

Of particular interest to Wright would have been Burke's discussion of the three major rationalizations that have occurred in history (he follows Frazer's *The Golden Bough*): the magical, the religious, and the scientific-technological-utilitarian. Wright would have understood the first two as prominent features of Afro-American culture, giving him a clearer understanding of his own experiences. Burke's opinion on the problems caused by the fossil-like existence of these older orientations in a changed situation confirmed the difficulties the culture had caused Wright and the difficulties it was causing itself. But the most reassuring and inspiring point of this discussion for him was, no doubt, Burke's ability also to see something valuable in the religious orientation—and for a secular reason that was compatible with Wright's own experience.

Afro-American's religious orientation, and that of most of the Third World, may not be "right" in the eyes of science, but "a given process may manifest itself in a surprising number of different guises, not all of which are identified in the vocabulary of common sense." (p. 108) "Orientations can go wrong . . . [but] the devices by which we arrive at a correct orientation may be quite the same as those involved in an incorrect one." (pp. 6-7) Burke's "given process" and "devices" are very like Wright's "something."

Wright's search for a new contour for the "something" in Afro-American expression is another way of saying he wanted to establish a new, more "correct" orientation for it. In *Permanence and Change*, Burke, too, wants to establish a new orientation, a "humanistic or poetical" one, a "philosophy, or psychology, of poetry." (p. 66) As the religious outlook had been a corrective of magic and science a corrective of religion, Burke wants a corrective of the modern scientific-technological-utilitarian viewpoint that pervades the modern era with some unfortunate consequences. Modern mentality, conceiving the universe metaphorically (and forgetting, as orientations are wont to do, that a metaphor is involved) as a machine, "may," Burke ironically suggests, be lacking something, ignoring "an important aspect of human response. . . . For man is essentially human, however earnestly he may attempt to reshape his psychological pattern in obedience to the pattern of his machines." (62-63) The religious orientation took as its model human capriciousness or freedom, humanity's organic, productive power to change, to merge; therefore, "any point of reference by which a philosophical corrective of the scientific rationalization (which emphasizes fixed laws) would be guided must almost necessarily show some superficial affinity with the religious orientation." (p. 63) Wright's emphasis was more strongly on "correcting" a religious orientation and enhancing a secular folk mentality that seemed at times to have more than a superficial affinity with the objective, utilitarian rationalization. From Burke's viewpoint, the outcome would not have differed greatly: both orientations would change, synthesized by this dialectical dance into a new myth, a new and more nearly accurate interpretation of reality.

The goal for both Wright and Burke was the same: in Burke's terms, to establish "the center of authority," a "concentration point" that sanctions the linkages of what goes with what in the best interests of humanity. Burke locates this point in "our soundest . . . human desires." Just what these are can be discovered in poetry because "the devices of poetry are close to the spontaneous genius of man." For Burke, this means not only that they are free but also that they are " 'biologically' grounded," the "organic, productive forces of the mind-and-body itself." In turn, as he implies elsewhere, these are the human form of the ever self-creating *"poietic"* quality of the universe. (p. 99) However, Burke would contour this center not in a body of poems ("the poetic medium of communication is itself weakened") but in terms drawn from psychology, biology, and other relevant forms of the scientific psychosis because "any new rationalization must necessarily frame its arguments as far as possible within the scheme of 'proprieties' enjoying prestige in the rationalization which it would displace." (p. 66)

Wright would, in the realm of art, of fiction, attempt to give an orientation to "human desires," the "spontaneous genius" he sensed as the symbol unifying, giving genuineness to Afro-American folk utterances. But prose fiction enjoys more prestige in the current climate than poetry; even more so do essays, journalistic articles, and autobiography, forms of "fact," if not of hard science, forms that he frequently came to employ. He was also, like Burke, concerned with developing an orientation for these central human desires, or from these desires, in more than the realm of theory or art; he wanted social, economic, political institutions to express and fulfill these desires. He, again like Burke, was concerned with a *"rationale* of art—not however, a performer's art, not a specialist's art for some to produce and many to observe, but an art in its widest aspects, an *art of living." (Permanence and Change,* p. 66)

Burke's theory, approached from a study of Wright's poetics, sheds light on what Wright saw as the chief characteristic of Afro-American folk expression. Its penchant for juxtaposing discordant elements, which Wright makes the starting point of his "Memories of My Grandmother" and places at the heart of *The Man Who Lived Underground*, is matched by Burke's lengthy discussion in *Permanence and Change* of "perspective by incongruity." Burke cites Nietzsche and Bergson as the main sources of his ideas about his *"state of transition"* (p. 69) between two orientations.

When one point of view regarding linkage is "questioned" by the presence of an alternative, Burke says the new, inappropriate (from the viewpoint of the dominant orientation) linkages appear as "gargoyles"—sometimes humorous, always grotesque—as revolutionary combinations because they violate accepted categories of "fitness." The actual medieval gargoyles, as well as paintings by Dadaists and the "Super-Realists," are examples of "planned incongruities": the image of "a watch dripping over the table like spilled molasses" is in juxtaposition not only to the everyday sense of watches as rigid but also to a *"different symbolism of time"* itself. (p. 113) In words remarkably similar to those used by Wright in describing his grandmother, Burke says that the "symbolism of both dreams and dream-art makes gargoyles of our walking experiences, merging things which common sense had divided and dividing things which common sense had merged." (p. 113)

Not all alternative views of how things are connected are planned; the dreamer sees no incongruity in his odd linkages. Burke's account of what naturally encourages these alternative formations, planned or unplanned, is quite applicable to the condition of Afro-Americans; what he says about individuals can be read in terms of a group within a larger society:

> Grotesque inventions flourish *when it is easiest to imagine the grotesque,* or *when it is hardest to imagine the classical.* . . . One sees perspectives beyond the structure of a given vocabulary when that structure is no longer firm . . . at any time in history, there may converge a set of factors which strongly differentiate [an individual's] situation from that of his group. Great liquidity in one's personal life may lead one to see "unclassically" even in an era generally classical. And similarly today, some men have enjoyed cloistered conditions which enable them to retain fixities not there for most of us. (*Permanence and Change,* p. 117)

Recognizing that their "cloistered conditions" have not always been "enjoyed" by Afro-Americans, they would have made possible the retention of older orientations such as magic and religion. Undoubtedly the isolation established by slavery and Jim Crowism also fostered a sense of liquidity, of the contingent nature of existence, of the Rinehartian need to be something else, to slip the yoke, to keep on the move. The degree of liquidity thus fostered would reinforce a retention of older orientations that saw reality in terms of movement, of transformations from one state of existence to another, a seamless interaction between realms.

Such orientations are seen not only as incongruous and illogical within themselves by the other viewpoint, but by their very different interpretation of reality, they can be seen as incongruous with the other orientations, especially those pervading the larger culture. They can therefore be seen as "impious," threatening, humorless, revolutionary, and they are reacted to accordingly.

Burke, like Wright, is concerned with more than just the intellectual meanings that orientations provide. A "deep emotionality" is involved in each orientation and, consequently, in "the search for new meanings." (p. 70) Burke's *Permanence and Change* is concerned with establishing a "poetic" corrective to the presently dominating scientific-technological-utilitarian schema that, especially in its economic and political structures and objective procedural methods, ignores this aspect of human response. Burke's discussion, at times, suggests that the most common gargoyle is the juxtaposition of emotion and intellect. It rears its disconcerting head when one is between orientations, and it can prevent the total effectiveness of a new orientation on a culture. People may accept intellectually, more or less, an orientation that is emotionally unsatisfying or, conversely, as in the case of Wright's grandmother, cling to an emotionally satisfying one that is intellectually opposed to the rationalization of the era. She used emotional, rather than rational or scientific, categories as the basis for what might be called her metaphors, and the linkages that were emotionally appropriate became inappropriate to an individual like Wright who had a rational eye. Burke makes his point with a Wright-like example involving a grandmother. A son-in-law frightens a great-grandmother with a tobacco pipe that he points at her like a gun while saying "Hands up!" She shouts at him to put the gun down, and when he shows her it is only a pipe, she answers, "Yes, I know—but that's the way people get shot." Her verbalization, juxtaposed to his explanation is incongruous because it is based on her complex and subjective emotional reaction; it is not based on the perceived external threat nor on the practical joker's rational explanation. Her resentment at being duped and, especially, her discomfort with feeling such resentment, both omitted from her words, are the motive, the tenor of her rejoinder. (*Permanence and Change*, pp. 85-89)

Like Wright's attempt to recontour the reality, the "mood," behind his grandmother's statements, Burke's explanation is in effect, misnaming the grandmother's response, as much as the grandmother's response itself can be called a misnaming. He is reverbalizing it, what one does, he says, when creating new meanings. His own book is a prime example of his theory in this respect; contrary to biblical injunction, he, like the poet he is, puts the old wine of ideas into new verbal bottles and succeeds in refreshing their meaning. Wright does the same when, in "Memories," he jars emotions, and he explicitly comments on the shock many will feel when he juxtaposes the practices of untutored Afro-American folk with those of the ultra-modern, sophisticated Surrealists or equates the methods of the wicked secular blues composer with that of the holy, spiritually saved Christian. Such a renaming, an "attempt to offer two concepts where the language of common sense, [i.e., the dominant point of view controlling a person's or society's interpretations] had had one, or to offer a merger where the language of common sense had discriminated, naturally requires an artificial manipulation of . . . linguistic properties." (*Permanence and Change*, p. 110) Afro-American folk expression, even as "folk" art, is art, and it was, for Wright, at least a heuristic device, a mislabeling by Afro-Americans that led him to the perception of an uncategorized feeling, just as irregularities (natural, but irregular in terms of regularity imposed by a widely accepted interpretation) in physical phenomena that were not explainable (categorizable or nameable) by the accepted formulas lead astronomers to posit the existence of an unseen, unverified ninth planet. If Wright could name the emotion in logically acceptable, twentieth-century terms, he could verify it, take it from the realm of the mystical, of science fiction, as it were, into the realm of science.

Burke speaks of emotion in conjunction with orientation in several contexts, not all of them concerned with an amorphous central feeling but that do have counterparts in Wright's work. The most notable such emotion in *Permanence and Change* is guilt, the same emotion that Wright felt was needed in *The Man Who Lived Underground* and that he considered to be one form of its unifying symbol. In Burke's book, guilt is taken from its religious signification and becomes the emotional equivalent of the "state of transition," the state of being between orientations. If piety is, as Santyana broadly defines and Burke accepts it, a sense of loyalty to the sources of one's being, then violation of an in-place orientation—a second nature, which seems to satisfy for most the sense of how things are and ought to be—produces a dis-ease, especially when one is not yet regrounded in the new orientation. A potter, in one of Burke's illustrations, is pious when he molds his clay to the exact form that "gratifies his sense of how it ought to be. (p. 71) A failure to achieve that form results in a sense of failure or impiety—guilt—in Burke's way of thinking, a limbo between the intention and the act.

It is guilt in this and not in the traditional, moral sense that Wright attributed to Fred Daniels, as mentioned earlier. Daniels has committed no crime, yet he is guilt-ridden even though he does not know why. In his underground locus, he is involved in an in-between situation; he is himself in-between; he is, psychologically speaking, a gargoyle, consisting of a new view of the old aboveground. Daniels is, therefore, also guilty because he is away from the old ground of his being (his return to the police at the end of the novella expresses this desire to atone, to be at one with what has seemed the basis of one's reality), driven from his familiar, commonsensical notion of what it is "to be" to a new realization, yet not able to fully grasp and articulate his own consciousness, emotions, behavior, and the new way of being.

Wright's novella is about more than Afro-Americans, as the shortened published version made clear. One implication is that to be an Afro-American, to have an Afro-American folk mentality, is not only to be in this in-between state but to be somehow more in touch with that state. The novella embodies the psychology of Afro-Americans like Wright, those aware of being doubled-visioned as a result of living in two external cultures. It is also Wright's metaphoric depiction of what is going on within the Afro-American folk psyche itself, a psyche not occupied by the views or practices of white people.

Another clearly defined characteristic, if perhaps not exactly an emotional equivalent of Burke's "state of transition," as it is found in Wright's theory and practice, is violence. The intermediate stage between orientations is analogous, Burke says, to the " 'rending and tearing (or sparagmos in tragic ritual," involving "a shattering or fragmentation." In Hegalian terms, it is a "logonomical purgatory." (Permanence and Change, p. 69). Wright, in "Personalism," spoke of his theory as producing a literature that would attack the world, that would be a weapon; Burke speaks of Nietzsche, who "we learn, in his Will to Power, was interested in the establishment of perspectives" (p. 88), in terms reminiscent of those Wright applied to Mencken. Nietzsche wrote pages that "are certainly a battlefield of thought," constructed "pages that put the raging of his brain before us," his style "like a sequence of darts . . . the sentences . . . forever striking out at this or that, exactly like a man in the midst of his enemies" or a predatory animal suddenly leaping on its prey. (p. 88) Burke speaks of the violence suffered by Saul on the Damascus road in a way that illuminates Daniels's experience of the dragon/furnace. Saul, deeply pious in his loyalty to the Judaic orientation and strongly given to activity in line with his piety, is "struck down" when a new way of seeing comes to him: "Old linkages were ripped apart, new linkages were welded, brutally, in accordance with the new creative device. . . . In that dramatic interim between the loss of his old self and his rebirth as Paul, we may expect to find his structure shaken to its very roots." (p. 156)

The violence that is transition need not show up in physical action; it does in Saul-Paul because he is characteristically a person of action. In one not so prone to act—Daniels, a poet, or an Afro-American in the first half of the twentieth century—the violence can be "confined to the symbolism of mood and imagery." (p. 156)

In words similar to those used by Wright in "Memories of My Grandmother" to describe his sense of the Afro-American folk expressive process and the sense of accomplishment that *The Man Who Lived Underground* gave him as a new configuration to that process, Burke says that, like the process by which a "chosen one" is selected, in "the writing of a great poem, or of a bad one, as we prefer . . . we find the two aspects of the poet's certainty: the poem is a sudden *fusion*, a *falling together of many things formerly apart*—and the very force of this fusion leads one to seek further experiences of the same quality." (*Permanence and Change*, p. 158)

Burke was writing, however, to an audience steeped in dualism and was attempting both to correct the notion of dualism and sway his audience to his more monistic view. This two-fold objective leads him to find conflict and combativeness at the basis of all civilization. Burke admits even within his advocated strategy of persuasion that "*cogency* becomes a mature form of *compulsion* . . . the militaristic, or combative element, and the attempts to remould it into something qualitatively different, lies at the roots of civilization." (p. 81)

Eventually he suggests that his pattern of cultural conflict is a kind of "spiritual projection" (more than merely a crude sublimation) of a pattern inherent in the biology of consciousness itself. The very equipment an organism has for achieving its nourishment, for reaching satiety and hence quiesence, is itself "military," quintessentially unquiet. To maintain consciousness, "one must exert oneself in "warfare," abiding by the competitive [and spontaneous] genius of mind and body . . . fanaticism, tenactiy, and even pugnacity, observable in the efforts of the scientist, artist, explorer, inventor, teacher, or reformer . . . militaristic patterns [that] may sometimes have bad results, sometimes good, but all cultural activity as we know it is erected upon them." (p. 198)

A force exists in the fusion of two orientations, a tension, Burke says, that must be maintained if the "*problematical new*" is to be "glorified" by means of the "*unquestioned old*." This maintenance calls forth the "*basic* military equipment in man" (pp. 87-88), that "something" that balances the appetite for unity, for fulfillment, for quietude, with separation, dissatisfaction, and restlessness.

Burke disclaims, however, glorifying raw combat or situating "the essence of human relationships in the sphere of the brutal." (p. 172) He disagrees with the modern emphasis on success as expressed in "the feeling of triumph which an eagle must feel in swooping down upon a lamb" (p. 174), an image Wright, in 1955, proposed developing in "Celebration of Life." While all action in Burke's scheme has underneath a combative element, "action can be qualitatively very different from combat." (p. 198) What he is getting at by this distinction is his key notion of symbolic action.

In light of Burke's ideas about violence and Wright's probable knowledge of these ideas, Wright's celebrated use of violent images in his fiction—as well as the violent figures of speech he used to describe, in "Memories of My Grandmother," his sensations during artistic creation and his advocacy of militarization in his letter to Nkrumha—acquires a significance other than that of sublimated rage stirred by racism, or mere sensationalism derived from his early exposure to pulp fiction. These violent images become a manifestation of the state of transition between two orientations, but they also tie together that idea with the personal condition of the artist as the source of literature, as Wright described, in "Personalism," and with the condition of his characters (and no doubt often of himself), a psychological condition that "symbolizes," as Burke says all psychologies do, a metaphysical—or metabiological—situation.

Perspective by incongruity, it must be remembered, had two loci for Wright: one within the Afro-American folk orientation itself; the other in the relationship between the black and white races in America, a juxtaposition as much of interpretation of reality as of skin color. Upon occasion, his protagonists represent the linkages within the folk orientation itself; they are contours, metaphors of the "mood," the unity that characterizes the folk mind. Daniels was, in Wright's expressed opinion, his most complete sign of this symbol. At other times, his protagonists stand for the transitional state between the dominant white attitude and its perceived-as-threat black outlook, or, as in *The Outsider*, between the individual and a larger concern.

Wright's most obvious use of planned incongruity to initiate the process leading to a new orientation is in *Native Son*. As *How Bigger Was Born* indicated, he deliberately created a character whose orientation, whose linkages and interpretations of reality were as different from those of the majority—including blacks as well as illiberal and liberal whites—as he could make them. He wanted to create between his readers and his book the kind of tension the book depicted, a perspective, an awareness, of differences; he sought the destruction of old linkages, associations, and "understandings," thereby setting the stage for the establishment of new and more realistic associations.

Each of Wright's first four stories in the original edition of *Uncle Tom's Children* is also an image of this transitional state, but he does not dwell on the different orientations themselves. The first three—"Big Boy Leaves Home," "Down by the Riverside," and "Long Black Song"—begin with a traditional, even quaint, view of Afro-American folk, playing traditional word games, singing spirituals and lullabies, concerned with the river, Ol' Man or Jordan. They begin with familiar images of blacks: the happy-go-lucky boy, the black sharecropper, the black mammy. In the fourth story, "Fire and Cloud," in several ways somewhat different from the others, the central and first character introduced is still a familiar one, the black preacher. When the white woman comes upon the naked black boys at the pond in "Big Boy," puts her hand to her mouth, and says "Oh!" a whole schema is expressed, a tradition, an "unquestionable old" is present, unspoken. In the first three stories, this orientation seems more or less shared by blacks and whites; it is the way everyone knows things are. Any distinctly black orientation is suggested even more minimally: the boys' mild complaints among themselves concerning the prohibition of swimming at the hole; Mann's concern for the well-being of his family. The vagueness of the Afro-American orientation and Wright's attempt to conceal it are highlighted in such story-ending images as Big Boy, Mann, and Silas unconscious—asleep or dead—and Sarah's running "blindly," shrieking a denial of her husband's assertive action.

What Wright emphasizes is the violent nature of racial contact. By doing so, he implies very clearly that, whatever a black orientation may be, it is distinctly different from the one that is dominant. It involves something over and above a desire to swim in the only available swimming place, to have adequate hospital care and food, and to possess one's own property. These are only aspects that, according to Burke, would be understandable to the white orientation. The book's epigraph indicates this black orientation would be quite different from "the cringing type who knew his place before white folks;" without the image of the Reverend Taylor in "Fire and Cloud," this might suggest that the "problematic new" could have been figured as a black proto-Rambo. However much such a figure might have achieved as wish-fulfillment (the reaction to Joe Louis's victories suggests the mass appeal that such a figure had), the stories would have had the hollow ring Wright discerned in the proletarian literature that ended with the worker triumphant in a fantasy denouement that, as Wright saw it, ignored the writers' tradition. Such a figure could not have been believable to any realistic, sophisticated black or white.

The stories, as stories, indicate that raw physical violence between the races was not in itself what Wright wished to extol. Like sex, while a physical action, it also represents something else. Rather, he is doing what Burke says Thomas Mann and André Gide, did: in order to glorify, gain acceptance for the new, however vaguely presented, he stressed in the central character-images the transitional quality, the tension itself. Big Boy lashes out but pulls back into unconsciousness; Mann, too, asserts himself, both in killing Mr. Heartfield and in his final decision to bring about his own death before the whites kill him. He atones for his impiety by dying. The stridency of the rebellious, murderous, suicidal Silas in "Long Black Song" is softened by the focus on the organic female figure, Sarah. The Reverend Taylor is an overt negotiation between old and new racial linkage patterns, and he is the image of violence, not by committing it or causing it, but by suffering, absorbing it, by holding together the voltage generated by the juxtaposed incongruous orientations. These figures are all logonomical purgatories. They are like the image of hunger in "Fire and Cloud," with its positive and negative poles. It is a force that unites white and black peacefully, although it is just as capable of producing antagonism, a force that, however reluctant or even apologetic, rends the old, dominant white interpretation of the linkages between black and white. Wright, like Mann and Gide, it seems, gives this attention to violence and the state of tension because such states appeal to something fundamental in humans, a something that Burke refers to as man's "*basic* military equipment." Particular points of view require the kind of prior perspective called consciousness, which itself comes about only when incongruous elements are juxtaposed. As Keats observed, however deplorable a fistfight may be, the energy exhibited by both parties is fascinating. Wright's practice in *Uncle Tom's Children* suggests he had some sense of gaining a foothold in substituting his new interpretation of black Americans for the old orientation by getting those of the old view to see the new in terms of something they instinctively approved because of its universality.

Another reason for Wright's emphasis on violence, in the process of conversion from one mode of conceiving reality to another, is that he is presenting characters who are not aware of the nature of their own orientation. Their language does not provide self-analysis, does not permit expression of its awareness in terms other than the awareness itself. They are folk, which, in Wright's view, is both their glory and their limitation; what they have and what they have to offer the dominant orientation is the very thing that prevents them from communicating it in cogent terms. Wright was dealing with the same problem Toomer described in *Cane*, but he saw its import in a sociopolitical rather than an aesthetic context.

In *American Hunger* he writes of the Negro Communist speakers—or shouters—in Washington Park. He admired their "emotional certainty," their "readiness to act," but he found them "lost in folly, wandering in fantasy." They did not know, he says, the complexity of the task facing them: "they had rejected the state of things as they were," meaning both black and white orientations, without realizing what they rejected and why and without realizing that the organic relationship of the Negro to American civilization required him to solve the problem of how America and the Negro were to lead full human lives. (pp. 39-41) This black problem, as Wright saw it, was analogous to the general American and, perhaps, entire Western problem, as Burke describes it: "The accepted terms of authority having fallen into disrepute, [people] seek in the cosmos or in the catacombs some undeniable body of criteria. . . . Unclear both as to what they are against and what they are for, they become confused as to their selection of means. And the tragic proportions of their predicament often lead them by sympathy to seek a tragic solution." (*Permanence and Change*, pp. 173-74)

What is needed, and what both Wright and Burke were engaged in, is "an attempt to return to essentials, to get at the irreducible minimum of human certainty" (p. 172); to get to the hearts of their respective orientations in order to correct them, while still retaining them as ballast and compass during the correctional journey.

In Wright's case, Bigger Thomas and Fred Daniels are his fictional formulations of one term of the black-white jux-taposition, of the Afro-American orientation per se, as well as of the tragic problem. They are Wright's symbols of this orien-tation coming to a realization of itself. Daniels is purer than Bigger in this regard because of the decreased attention given to the two races as the incongruous elements being juxtaposed. Neither of them, like the Negro Communists, know their orien-tation, although Daniels comes closer to doing so than Bigger does. As Burke and others have observed, *Native Son* is the development of consciousness from the unreflecting grasp of self and emotions to an increased near-conceptual, verbaliza-ble grasp of them; a development set forth in the image of the cornered rat at the beginning and the image of the highly articulate, yet still somewhat obtuse, Max at the end, as well as in the image of Bigger. "What I killed for," says Bigger, indicat-ing, even at the end, his uncertainty as to what he wanted, what new orientation he hoped to establish. What he did establish— the killings, the kidnap plot, calling a tune to which Chicago dances—is an erroneous orientation, a wrong interpretation of the way things are linked. It will, therefore, not lead to the fulfillment of the "something" that makes Bigger tick. Nev-ertheless, "it must've been good" for "it" was both himself and the making of himself"—"I am!" The criterion of its goodness was that he felt it strongly; "knew" by the sense of it that killing and violence were in some way the pattern of "it," and hence the way to use the environment to his advantage.

What he has felt is himself, even apart from racial confrontation, a perspective issuing from incongruity. As such, he is in a state of transition between " ⸲hings," the link, the continuum, yet a violent ripping apart, a basic militancy. Yet his militancy is reconciled in the transition. This condition is also, in Burke's theory, human existence itself. The racial imagery of the novel reiterates this perspective by incongruity. Bigger comes to feel that "it" so strongly partly because the dominant viewpoint, with all of its shortcomings, which has been superimposed as a feeling on his own, intensifies his sense of conflict. It sets up more conscious feelings equivalent to what Burke would call a critical, as opposed to an experiential, view of himself. This view is incongruous with his sense of self; it tells him that what is juxtaposed in his constitution does not go together, just as it tells him he does not fit with the dominant orientation on a social level. The new perspective that results from this incongruity is that of himself struggling to hold these two orientations together, yet rejecting each in light of the other. Rejecting both, without quite knowing why, he sympathetically, through his feelings of the uncomprehended combat at the core of his orientation, gravitates to a tragic solution in an effort to blot out one of the disparate elements.

At the end, however, he has accepted his fate, his condition of perpetual transition between necessarily incongruous elements. His acceptance of himself as a link missed, overlooked, because of society's interpretation of him, removes his fear, the emotional equivalent of his misunderstood awareness of his self. The viewpoints of the larger society have been closed out, not so much denied as dismissed as irrelevant.

Fred Daniels is likewise an image of this acceptance of self as transition, as linkage. His emotional equivalent was guilt as well as fear at the initial moment of awareness of himself as this Janus-like tension between incongruities. When he surmises that everyone is guilt, he is recognizing that everyone is bringing to bear within himself a something else that does "not go" with it. He has to leave the aboveground orientation (in Bigger's story, the white orientation) in order to see this, to see that what does not go is essential to what it does not go with, that while everything is the interaction of heterogeneous elements, war, conflict, and self-obliteration are not the only figures for their interaction, even though in at least one manuscript version, war is breaking out as Daniels reenters the underground and is killed by the police.

Both Bigger and Daniels thus ends up as figures, contours, of the folk mentality that Wright took as his point of departure. The expressive forms of that mentality—its folklore—reveal the sense of self as a perspective generated from elements that, according to other attitudes, do not go together. Taken objectively, Grandmother Wilson's religious pronouncements do not add up, make no sense, but she and other black folk, immersed however unconsciously in their own orientation— their subjectivity, their own identity—do not see incongruity at the heart of identity; identity is a battle constantly being won. Personalists, as Wright tried to theorize this folk attitude, are marked by "intense emotional consciousness." Their certitude, the criterion by which they estimate reality, derives not from experience of the cosmos as a system of linkages "out there," but from the catacombs of self, hidden below even unconsciousness in the very rock of life. Like all orientations, the folk mentality tends to make the world over in its own image.

While Burke does not speak in terms of folk mentality, the poetic orientation he would develop to correct the current scientific-technological-utilitarian orientation is analogous, a kind of metafolk-orientation. It is not like that of the innocent folk but is a restoration of the fallen folk orientation (such as that of Wright's Afro-Americans) which, traduced by the modern outlook, causes the folk mind to see itself through the eyes of another. Retained traces of its old view of itself can be seen as both exhilerating and horrendous. To adapt Burke's terms, this "something," this linkage, is seen as a fearsome gargoyle, a "staggering disproportion between man and no-man," a condition that is, as Wright was to have Daniels think while observing the green slime from which he imagines human form emerging, "no place for purely human boasts of grandeur." This perspective, and the one whose mind and life it is, is imaged as the "Eternal Enigma," the "abyss" that unites as it separates. It is aware of itself as the "preposterous fact"—as the "unthinkable"—shared alike by the incongruities of existence and nothingness. (*Permanence and Change*, p. 272)

Such, certainly, is the universal condition that Wright conveys in the figure of Bigger, who is emotionally aware of teetering on a brink, hanging over a void. The world tells him blackness is nothing, and he struggles to avoid his blackness, to assert his existence. He is specified as a great tension.

Both Bigger and Daniels have another tragic flaw in addition to this universal human gap between essence and existence. It is not that they reject their orientation when they realize emotionally that reality is, like themselves, a reciprocal flow of identity between elements, but they are held captive in this orientation. They are not able to get out of themselves. It does not provide them with a language—something of the other orientation, a technique—to communicate, with psyches permeated by the abstract, utilitarian, and technological values shaping the world view of the majority of people. The Chicago waitresses in *American Hunger* "knew nothing of hate and fear, and strove instinctively [orientationally?] to avoid all passion . . . lived on the surface of their days . . . thoughtlessly, serenely . . . none . . . possessed the insight or the emotional equipment to understand themselves or others . . . my language was a different language from theirs." (pp. 12-13)

Or, in Burke's phrasing of it, there are those who are susceptible to only "a few simple groups of stimuli, not highly complex at all, such as the lure of a new refrigerator, the fear of losing one's job, the distinction of smoking a certain brand of cigarette, etc." (*Permanence and Change*, p. 33)

The pattern of life, however, *Permanence and Change* emphasizes, is organic: living components do not remain in isolation; the motive of life is merger. The Bigger Thomases and Fred Danielses, therefore, are impelled by vitality to meld their viewpoints, their conviction of subjectivity as the touchstone of reality with the widely accepted belief that objectivity is to be the criterion. Without a bridging vocabulary, they can only juxtapose their orientation to the other. The result is not communication but an anterior stage, perspective by incongruity, a state like *sparagmos* in tragic ritual.

Perspective by incongruity informs not only *Native Son* and

The Man Who Lived Underground but also *Black Boy,* especially in the section (pp. 272-77) in which Wright so vividly describes his discovery of reading. The novels he devoured in Memphis did not interest him so much because of their technical aspects, their "plots and stories," but in "the point of view" they revealed. He would "read hard, discarding a writer as soon as I felt that I had grasped his point of view." The books were "new ways of looking and seeing," contained "something that made the look of the world different." This viewpoint enabled him to see, for the first time, the way in which the white world linked things. Misremembering *Babbitt* as *Main Street,* he says Lewis's novel "made me see my boss. . . . I had always felt a vast distance separating me from the boss and now I felt . . . that I knew him."

This viewpoint also provided, by its incongruity with his own life, "what being a Negro meant." The result is a heightened awareness that takes him beyond Negro and white, a perspective described in terms of a great and terrible transitional unsettledness: "buoying me up, reading also cast me down, made me see what was possible. . . . My tension returned." For all of the insight the books gave him into both white and black orientations, "My reading had created a vast distance between me and the world in which I lived and tried to make a living. . . . My days and nights were one long, quiet, continuously contained dream of terror, tension, and anxiety." As Burke would expect, Wright felt "vaguely guilty," that he "carried a secret, criminal burden" about with him, "guarding and hiding the knowledge that was dawning."

He also says that what he got from these novels, this new knowledge, was a feeling that had been denied him. It was of "vague, unformed yearnings"; more specifically, it was "the very breath of life," "the sense of life itself."

His problem was how to contour this new knowledge, how to complete it by shaping it into a new orientation. To have discussed his reading and what he got from it would have been "too painful"; it would have meant revealing himself, which survival irrefutably ruled out. The various Negro life-styles he inventories are rejected as orientations not conducive to the fulfillment of his sense of life: they result in death or death-in-life negations of his thoughts and feelings.

He tries to provide a contour, an orientation for his "new moods," by writing, but "nothing would come" or else was totally inadequate to his sense of life. He wanted to write, but he did not have the language—in this instance, specifically English, specifically a formal, technical language, involving more than grammar and vocabulary. This situation is identical to what he attributed to Afro-American orientation and expression in general—the subjective, interior power of imagination providing an imaginative realization of objective "signs," sensing in them the marks of one's vitality and reality, and his view of that orientation's inarticulateness with regard to the world at large.

In Burke's *Counter-Statement*, especially in the sections entitled "The Poetic Process" and "The Status of Art," Wright would have found a theoretic formulation of the expressive process as he knew it from experience and in Afro-American folk. Burke, in his attempt to ground symbolic expression and knowledge in irrefutable reality, hypothesizes something very like the "mood" that Wright sensed in Afro-American expression and was trying to contour in his own work.

Interpretively, and without full justice to the scope of Burke's ideas and none to his style of presentation, human expressive art, symbolization of any kind, including everyday language, is always real because it is in its nature reflective of the basic "universal texture." Implicitly employing the principles of evolutionary biology and science in general, that a phenomenon is never merely a singular occurence, Burke arrives at primal consciousness (including un- and pre-) as an assertion, as a psychical mode of the generic human physical condition, a transparent emotion informing the whole and repeating its motile pattern, but with a difference. It is, in Burke's theory, a natural symbol of that physical condition, a rhetorical version of it.

This assertive, externalizing process synchronically occurs over and over: the primal consciousness mode—or mood—projects its own symbol or emotion of itself; language, in the sense of "mind," is a reflection on, but at one with, generic consciousness. And so on, along a continuum to positive conventional language to science, art, and religion, each symbol-state being something "added on," over and above, yet sub-

200

suming all that is contained in the anterior condition—a symbol of a symbol of a symbol . . . "until everything was rainbow, rainbow, rainbow!" . . . of the universal texture.

All of these stages and the universal texture behind them are the self or, as Burke defines it in *Permanence and Change*, "our ultimate motive, the situation common to all, *the creative, assertive, synthetic* [synthesizing] *act* (p. 259): a dialectic. At every stage of the continuum, the pattern of movement is expressive, asserting itself from the universal texture, thereby establishing an incongruous element, the individual. Between the individual and the whole is a "perspective" that is negotiated into the next stage. The movement becomes, in orientation and in expression, commonly understood as an act of reunion with the whole. Combining the essentials of this self-fulfilling reunion involves not only knowledge but communication as well. At every stage, emotion translates itself into a kind of autobiography, into an "invention of details" that are drawn either from past experiences of this same emotion or, if no such experiences are "clustered" about this emotion, are simply invented. It is a translation; the emotion is not caused by the details but rather it is the principle of selecting which details will be used to externalize the mood. The translation, therefore, always preserves a "ratio" between the details and the emotion, the equivalent of the suitability of the ends that orientation seeks to select in order to fulfill the needs of the entire organism. The clustering or linkage of details explains something about the emotion seeking expression and regarded carefully, tells something about the generic human condition and ultimate, universal reality itself. In the expressive or poetic process, the emotion and its externalizing details together constitute a symbol in what Burke calls its "emotional form."

Just as orientation can interpret things erroneously, so the "ratio" is never exact. Every symbol, each stage on the expressive continuum being a translation, is also a "compromise"; it involves a Wordsworthian recompense of "new virtues of its own, virtues not part of the original [experience]" (Burke, *Counter-Statement*, p. 54), yet something is surrendered. Burke exemplifies the consequences on the symbol level of "emotional form" by citing "the reminiscences of old men, who recite the facts of their childhood, not to force upon us the trivialities and minutiae of these experiences, but in the for-lorn hope of conveying to us the 'overtones' of their childhood, overtones which, unfortunately, are beyond reach of the details *which they see in such incommunicable light,* looking back . . . upon a past which is at once themselves and another." (p. 51, emphasis added)

The details, the reminiscenses chosen by the old men, are a kind of symbol, but of a type that Burke was, in *Permanence and Change,* to call "purely mimetic." (p. 253) Such details may denote the existence of something, but they are individualized, of the individual and not of the group. When they are taken by the speaker as self-denoting and also recognized by the listener as peculiar to the individual speaker, these forms "point to something about which we have no great emotional concern, they necessarily fail to reveal any marked underlying pattern." (p. 52)

The expressive process, as Burke conceives it up to this point, is analogous to what Wright says he saw in Afro-American folk expression and what he depicted in Bigger and Daniels. What they have to communicate is an emotion, one that, in his fiction even more than in his references to his grandmother, he makes clear expresses the "something" at the center of their being, a "something" revealed in the dialectic of their actions, words, or stories, whatever details they choose to give form to that emotion. Religious terms; murderous, belligerent acts; a variety of experiences, from a dead fetus to an unjustly accused suicide, are linked by them in the light of a subjective mood. They see the connection between the details because they "see" the link, the mood, that selects the details. This individualized and subjective mood is incommunicable to, incongruous with, the more external, scientific-technological-utilitarian orientation, which is inclined to take the material forms, after abstracting the emotion that gives them their significance, as the reality.

If these characters (and Burke's old men) were in a culture that was oriented to subjective processes as the criterion for the reality of an expression, the emotion linking the details would not be communicated but assumed. Leopold Senghor gives a model of "communication" as it exists in a society oriented to the assumption of the oneness of the individual with himself, his fellows, his environment: "In African-Negro poetry it is quite plain that the abstract word is rarely encountered. . . . 'Once upon a time,' and the audience responds 'as usual' ['Amen'?]. The story and the fable are interwoven with events of the day because African-Negro ontogeny is existential. There is no place in it for the merely anecdotal or the "slice of life" type of story. Facts are imagery." ("African-Negro Aesthetics." (pp. 32-33)

In such a society, whether Burke's old men attempt to communicate the feelings of childhood or dreamers try to convey the reality of their dream, it is as though everyone listening is an old man with the same childhood or a dreamer who has had the same dream. Everyone already knows what is going on. Communication here is closer to what Burke calls "utterance," a utilization of the type of symbol he calls an emotional form and that is mimetic of its "burden."

Stephen Henderson, in his *Understanding the New Black Poetry*, seems to intend such a mimesis when he speaks of "saturation." Whatever the theme or discernible structure, the verbal expression, whether humorous, tale-like, or "heavy," is permeated with a quality that an experienced reader intuits, however subliminally, as faithful to that experience, as having the right "feel," the right spirit. This is "telling it like it is," although to the uninitiated, the culturally illiterate, it may appear as merely inexplicable. Everyone knows what is really being expressed, regardless of the words. Everyone grasps the "symbol" beneath, or perhaps indissolubly at one with, the facts. Whatever it is about, even if it is a known lie, it indicates the right kind of lie, that the writer or speaker is in contact with his in-the-grain culture, interfacing with its pervasive, if not consciously expressed, sense of self as motion and fluidity, his very dialectic.

But Bigger and Daniels do not live in "utterance" cultures, although both are Wright's figures of, among other things, what Saul Bellow describes as "soul," a description that has its own relationship to Burke's theory and Wright's practice. "Soul" is "the deepest part of ourselves . . . that part . . . which is consciousness of a higher consciousness by means of which we make final judgments, and put everything together." (Foreward, *The Closing of the American Mind*, by Allan Bloom, pp.

16-17) This "primal point of balance" is often hidden, over-grown with the confusions that arise, but

> the independence of this stricter consciousness, which has the strength to be immune to the noise of history and the distractions of our immediate surroundings, is what the life struggle is all about. *The soul has to find and hold its ground against hostile forces, sometimes embodied in ideas which frequently deny its very existence,* and which indeed often seem to be trying to annul it altogether. (pp. 16-17; emphasis added)

Bigger and Daniels find their souls. They are able to communicate with themselves at the end; they have come to an "understanding" of the emotion that is themselves; they have translated it into details that externalize it to themselves, actions and experiences that the subjective emotion has chosen. This is a positive unfolding but, like any orientation in Burke's theory and apparently also Wright's, it is not the terminal point, nor should be. In the fate of Bigger and Daniels, Wright presents his critique of the Afro-American folk reliance on utterance and its discounting of technical, "socializing" forms when it is carried over into a new and "hostile" situation.

Utterance or mimetic symbolization is, in Burke's view, not the whole of self-expression. In addition to handing one's experiential self over directly, one can express self by attempting to "provoke emotions in others." This self-expression differs from that of Burke's old men. Theirs, as in a dream, is concerned only with the relationship of the chosen details to the emotion that has chosen them. In Western culture, with its emphasis on abstraction and separation, art, as conceived by Burke, is a kind of self-expression that involves "an arousing and fulfillment of desires" which is also his definition of poetic form. (*Counter-Statement*, p. 124) The fundamental dialectical act that is "self" is, after all, assertive in one phase if synthetic in another, but in art, as in a religious orientation, one becomes unified with the other by a type of ingratiation, by getting into the favor of the other. Western art or communication, like Western orientation involving knowledge, is the acknowledgment of the recalcitrance of others, the adjusting of strategies to the emotions of those to whom one wishes to communicate.

The complete symbol—of whatever stage—is characteristically Janus-like in that it "faces two ways." (p. 61) One face or form looks toward subjective life, offering a pattern of individual bioemotional experiences. Its other face is directed toward other aspects of psychic life, including what Burke considers the abiding, unchanging "forms of the mind," "universal patterns" derived from experiences of external phenomena, and which are potentials for certain kinds of additional experience. He offers "crescendo" as an example, a pattern formed in the very "germ plasm" of humans (thus part of their orientation) after aeons of experiencing analogous patterns in physical events, such as the growth and maturation of crops and the process of the sex act. Other examples are given, "contrast," "balance," and "repetition" (pp. 46-47), as he further develops his notion of rhetoric. If one wishes in a twentieth-century Western culture to express self by evoking emotion in others (the only way one can communicate self), the emotional form or cluster must be arranged according to these universal patterns or, as Burke calls them, these "technical forms . . . *conditions of emotional response.*" (p. 47) Expression with the "addition" of technical form becomes more artful, however, and the original emotion is compromised again.

At this point, one is reminded of Wright's early essay "Personalism," in which he states that the work of the personalist artist, with only himself and his emotional consciousness to draw on, ceases to be personalist and speaks to all, achieves the power to influence "the world," not in terms of his subject matter but "psychologically," from his "mode of presentation. Those works in which the element of time predominates will carry the atmosphere of universality . . . those in which space, that is, character, predominates, will carry the atmosphere of universality."

One should also recall the stories of Bigger and Daniels. Bigger's actions and Daniels's experiences follow no recognized pattern, if seen from without. Wright emphasizes the spontaneous quality of movement from one action or experience to another. His narration in *Native Son* is formed by crescendo, of course, peaking at the end of each of the sections; abundant crescendo is also present in the manuscripts of *The Man Who Lived Underground*, which possibly was one of his problems with the story's composition. What he is trying to image in both stories is a single emotional form "choosing" the details that surround, contour, give it expression—and leave it incomprehensible to people like the police, the Daltons, and even a number of "liberal" readers. He indicates that Bigger's killing Mary is no logical climax to the series of emotional steps leading to the accidental event. When Daniels repeats his visits to certain locales, the repetition is merely random occurrence among a limited number of options. The collage he constructs, with its surrealist overtones, is a figure of this escape from technical form, the items arranged "playfully" by Daniels. His jumbled verbalizations to the police, a collage repetition that is Wright's technical formation, stress his lack of logical form, as does the lack of connection between the scenes he has experienced, his appearance, and the rather jubilant feeling he exhibits to the police. The fact that the story attempts to depict a gathering of happenings that have only an emotional consistency accounts for Wright's difficulties in writing the story.

The cultural expressional mode that Bigger and Daniels represent (among other things, that of Afro-American folk) is not, as indicated above, totally without the kind of technical form Burke describes. Repetition, for example, is clearly one characteristic, and crescendo clearly structures verbal exchanges such as "the dozens." Wright's view would seem to be that emotional form takes precedence over these technical considerations in Afro-American folk expression. Wright's understanding of this expressional mode is very close to the description of black American folk psychology developed in the 1960s and 1970s as part of the Black Aesthetic.

This model of black expression was a psychology of poetry, and like the new orientation Burke proposed in *Permanence and Change*, it was concerned with the art of living, with living as an art. Allegedly based on the realities of Afro-American perception, the aesthetic spoke of black Americans as extremely subjective people; objectivity was only a myth, especially in the minds of those white scholars and critics who used it as a justification for denigrating Afro-Americans and their culture. To study any subject accurately, especially human social entities, only an intimate, experiential knowledge of it can provide authoritative understanding. Reality is felt, revealed in one's sense of events rather than in concepts.

Since interiority is not peculiar to any one human consciousness, the subjectivity of black American psychology does not mean per se an eccentric solipsism. What it does mean is that black Americans tend to see in terms of "impacting on" or "connected with" them. The further from interiority, the more devoid of connection with self, a procedure is, the more it is rejected as an "airy nothing." As Haki Madhubuti puts it, "reality is whatever is real to you" (*Dynamite Voices I*, p. 76), which is not unlike Burke's remark that reality is what things do to and for one, or Wright's insistence that only his own personal responses and feelings had any meaning to him.

The Black Aesthetic holds that what feels right to a black American's perception is that which moves. Numerous black writers, even before the Black Aesthetic's formulation, have pointed out the continuous innovation or improvisational adaptability characteristic of black American life. This sensitivity to movement is, in turn, related to interiority, the feel of one's being, and being in the Black Aesthetic is equated with existence, which is characterized by change. Unlike essence, the conceptual cornerstone of classical Western thought, existence is unfixed, fluid, organic, impermanent, and hence unthinkable in Western terms. Black consciousness is, therefore, more closely linked to the sense of self as a dialectic. (See Stewart's "The Development of the Black Revolutionary Artist.")

This orientation, this general and pervasive, if not always fully conscious, attitude of self as ever a *natura naturans* (similar to Burke's phrase, a "making rather than a made"), develops a culture far different from one that thinks in terms of discrete, noncontradictory categories and sees reality as it is determined by what is separate from the perceiver. In such a culture, black life is itself a poem, but the art form that best reflects this psychological sense of the fact of existence is music. Black folk music for the black aestheticians "has always been the most dominant manifestation of what we are and feel, literature was just an afterthought, the step taken by the Negro bourgeoisie who desired acceptance on the white man's terms. And that is precisely why literature failed. It was the case of elite addressing another elite." (Neal, "And Shine Swam On," p. 654)

Specifically, it is music performed by black musicians who

embody this subcultural (in terms of the dominant society) or folk attitude; it is not printed music that reveals it as an expression of the profoundest reality nor is it something learned, but it is "passed on as a secret blood rite." (Jones, *Black Music*, p. 13)

In terms of Wright's poetics, amplified by what he read in Burke, black American music is an emotional symbol or cluster and this is, in black perception, why it is so highly valued. It comes out of such utterances as the "hollers," extremely close to the experience that lies behind them. To be sure, there is, using Burke's terminology, a technical form, a kind of rhetoric, to black music, "an attitude about the way the music is made" (Jones, *Black Music*, p. 130), but this attitude is never regarded as important in its own right, and certainly not as something "added." According to the Black Aesthetic, the negligible, non-importance attached to technical form, its irrelevance to the reality of black music, is the reason that white musicians, however sympathetic to the difference they hear in black jazz, can never really play it. Normal musicology cannot account for this music's spirit, its genius, its deep form, or, as Wright might say, its mood. Musicology cannot explain the "something" that a jazz piece means over and above its musical notation, cannot account for the notes' coming-into-existence meaning. For one of a Western mind-set, it is the nonmusical quality that constitutes this music.

For many years, and possibly still today in some quarters, this was the judgment passed by the dominant society on spirituals, blues, and jazz and their influence on all forms of music and art. The presence of some degree of technical form, as Burke defines it, does allow for some degree of communication of the symbol to those not attuned to the emotional experience being expressed. Wright, in *The Man Who Lived Underground*, gives even the hostile policeman Lawson the sense to recognize that Daniels could "wreck things" if his viewpoint were allowed to spread.

These different views are succinctly brought out in a comparison of two quotations concerning music. One is from Burke, who, during 1928-29, was music critic for the avant garde and influential *The Dial* and, later, contributor of a music column in *Nation*. He believed that "Mozart is music";

he never wrote about jazz and consistently, if genially, belittled "impressionistic" music. In *Counter-Statement* he notes certain anonymous modern artists who "have attempted, without great success, to eliminate the symbol, and thus to summon the *emotional* cluster without the further limitation of a *logical* unity. This is also true of modern music. Compare . . . the constant circulation about a theme in classical music with the modern disregard of 'arbitrary' unity. As story today gravitates towards lyric, so sonata gravitates toward suite." (p. 61, n.)

To a Black Aesthetician, although he recognizes the presence of such primary technical forms such as repetition and contrast, increased attention to logical unity appears an unsuccessful development, altogether too much "symbol": "The symphony . . . is a dictatorship. There is a rigidity of form and craft-practice—a virtual enslavement of the individual to the autocratic conductor. . . . But music possesses properties of being that come closest to the conditions of life, of existence . . . music comes closest to being. That is why music teaches. That is what music teaches." (Stewart, *Black Fire*, p. 9-10)

This disinclination of the Afro-American folk orientation to stray from the experience of interiority, to compromise its expression in a fog of symbols is referred to elsewhere. Eugene Genovese alludes to it: "the slaves' notion of order assumed a special aspect: it personalized everything." Told that they must obey the government and then that Lincoln had been assassinated, the freedmen were "stunned . . . they had great difficulty in imagining that the government, which was protecting them, could survive or indeed had ever existed apart from his person." (*Roll, Jordan, Roll*, pp. 118-19). Joseph L. White, in *The Psychology of Blacks*, says that "complex mentalistic explanations of Black behavior should be avoided when a ·more straight-forward observational cause-effect sequence derived from Black experiential-phenomenal perspective will suffice." (pp. 18-19)

Wright's critique of this Afro-American folk orientation is expressed in the fates of Bigger and Daniels. He is not without admiration for it. He says in "Memories of My Grandmother" that, while the knowledge Daniels is trying to impart is faulty, Daniels does assert his freedom in his decision to carry what he has come to realize to the aboveground. He, like Bigger, is certain of death, but both decide to die, acceptance of death being the ultimate in self-determination. Understanding, in the sense of possessing one's reality by means of something outside that reality—confirmation by "the other"—is not necessary to what one is. Willing, even by consent to the inevitable, one's death is an Erzuli-like act in its luxurious liberality, something done without hope of further gain, the *ne plus ultra* image of one's fullness. Like Gabriel Prosser in Wright's review of *Black Thunder*, Bigger and Daniels represent the fullness of folk value, a simple assertion of, almost by resting in, self as something by right of itself.

While this Afro-American emotion or sense of self is admirable, especially in its determination to stand its ground, and while Burke's brand of dialectical materialism would have increased Wright's awareness of this lore's potential in solving the American problem during the course of solving its own, extinction was its only fate. Total extinction, in the sense of sterile isolation and ineffectualness, in the larger world was in store if it was unable to find modern forms with enough force in the dominant orientation to effect cross-fertilization and the origination of a new species of orientation.

A new orientation, a new organic synthesis, however, also implied the demise of the original components, and there were other dangers. Burke's theory of communication, of overcoming the violence of the transition between incongruous, merely uttered perspectives, requires a compromise in the mood by its development into a more universal form, one that can evoke the requisite emotion in others. This translation, or, in an Afro-American context, the adaptation of the masks that allow the ingratiation of one's own viewpoint, can result in the loss of the original emotion that was intended for communication. Burke uses an example that could have provided Wright with a cautionary comment on his proposed blueprint for Negro writing. He cites Twain, who started out wanting to express his bitterness but who "again and again transformed [it] . . . into the humor he *could* evoke." (*Counter-Statement,* p. 55) As artist, Twain had a desire to call up emotion, a desire so much stronger than his urge to utterance that he could change what Burke calls "the burden" of his message. In other artists, the emotional-form symbol that is the generative force can be submerged by the technical communicative form; the interest of the artist "in his own emotion transcends into his interest in the treatment" of that emotion. The means of communication thus becomes the end.

The problem Wright wrestled with, as he came to realize, was not only that of Afro-Americans' relationship to a dominant racist United States society but the even broader concern of the individual's relationship to himself and to any society, of colonialized peoples' to Western civilization, and of the modern writer's to his audience.

That an intelligent person in the twentieth century should have, as Bellow says, the "channel to the soul" overgrown with "some of the wildest thickets"—the "noise of history . . . the distractions of . . . immediate surroundings," as well as the "hostile forces" embodied in a demonstrably effective scientific outlook—is not surprising. Wright's channel was never completely blocked as is witnessed by his writings and ruminations in the early 1940s and by the work that occupied him at the very end of his life. His experiments with haiku and his plans for a Proustian magnum opus are his last attempts to express this "soul," this "deepest part," this "theme," this "something."-

8

THE COSMOS:
USES OF ORGONE
AND HAIKU

The tracing of Wright's poetics, of the uncodified principles guiding his translation of feeling into form, leads to the question of whether Wright was, to use Jung's terms, a writer in the visionary or the psychological mode. The sources of his stories, his open interest in psychology, his preference for the pragmatic and what he considered the rational, his life-long preoccupation with the concrete political-social-economic conditions of black people around the world, his eschewal of religion and mysticism; his lack of concerted attention to "schools" of literature in general and to Surrealism and negritude in particular, all suggest the answer, "psychological mode." Also his statement in "Memories" that he had long sensed the "something" he wanted to contour in the expressions of his grandmother and other blacks implies that this distinguishing characteristic was not within his own immediate experience of biologically grounded reality. His avowals, also in "Memories," that none of the images in *The Man Who Lived Underground* has meaning except in relation to other images seems to suggest a deconstructed text, words circling around a center of no objective, "other" referent.

It is possible that the "something" being contoured or referred to was experienced but had been mediated by a structure of language, Wright's undefined mental and emotional reconstruction. He says in "Memories" that, while he had never experienced the deep appeal of religion, he was convinced that he both intellectually and emotionally grasped the significance of it to those around him. As a structure of language in the broader sense, it could have been a part of what Fabre calls Wright's "unshakable belief in the power of words," his inability (admitted in connection with the writing of his autobiography) "to tell whether he had imagined or had actually experienced certain events." (*The Unfinished Quest*, p. 292) "Imagined" here would be more like "fancied," a close encounter, but of the first or second rather than the third kind, leaving a corrosive gap between experience and expression.

Conversely, both circumstantial and more direct evidence indicates at least a desire on his part to go beyond the level of concepts to that of unmediated vision. There is the image of a fiery furnace and its recurrence, whether the dragonlike threat to Daniels, the hot kiln that shelters yet entraps Big Boy, the Dalton furnace that consumes the remains of Bigger's crime yet contains the evidence that will undo him, the house fire in *Black Boy* that satisfies his curiosity but almost results in his death, or the dance hall conflagration in *The Long Dream* which destroys Fishbelly's world and prompts his removal to the larger, unfamiliar world beyond Mississippi. Images of this type are recognized by Jung as extending beyond merely psychosexual significance concerning the ambiguous feelings toward one's mother and hence all women. He saw it as archetypal, like the Faustian realm of the Mothers an involuntary expression of the deeper than unconsciousness source of psychic reality, the process of rending and tearing, the generative issuance of new life, of meaning, of value. Such archetypes suggest that Wright had glimmerings of what he was after, glimmerings that whetted his intellectual and emotional appetites, arousing them to the kind of active pursuit that would not permit their satisfaction. Journal entries in 1945 spell out such a "spiritual hunger" and the need to "assuage my hunger for some sort of unity in my life. . . . Oh, God, how lonely I am with this burden of consciousness. . . . Why do I feel so deeply that this theme I want to write is so important? . . . What has happened to me that makes me feel the necessity of stating so vast and broad a statement of life? Some deprivation? . . . Somewhere, yes, in the life of the American Negro lies a clue, a cue for me. I must seek it more fervently than ever." (Fabre, *The Unfinished Quest*, pp. 273-74)

Later, Fabre says, Wright's "meditations took a metaphysical turn"; the "theme," while particularly important in Afro-American terms, has the power to introduce Afro-Americans to a much broader context: "there is something universal about it and something that lifts it above being a Negro in America. Oh, will I ever have the strength and courage to tell what I feel and think; and do I know it well enough to tell it?" (p. 274)

There is a self-consciousness about these statements implying that, while Wright still believed in a "something" and had viewed this Promised Land from afar, he had never been able to enter. These statements could also be taken as indications of a Keats-like sense of dismaying shortfall between an actual experience and his command of the techniques required to fulfill it in expression. In the same 1945 journal entries, he speaks of wanting to write a work like Proust's *Remembrance of Things Past*, in that Proust, "in touch with all the latest developments in art and science . . . found that associational thinking and memory, which he borrowed from psychoanalysis, could form the scaffolding of his massive work; and so he took it for his own and used it. I must find something likewise to hang my theme of Negro life upon." (p. 273)

The "theme" that possesses him is an Hegelian journey of the spirit, a "subjective voyage spanning centuries . . . a spiritual journey . . . not a material one." The imagistic or conceptual scaffolding, the orientation he proposes for it here, is psycho-historical: the wrenching of the Negro from the oneness with his African tribe, his dehumanization by the Middle Passage and the slave system "to the level of random impulse and hunger and fear and sex," his subsequent adaptation of a religious and then an urban-secular orientation, and finally his creation of a new world for himself. Particularly important to Wright is the image of the voyage. If this entry is read in light of the manuscript versions of *The Man Who Lived Underground* and Wright's blueprint for Negro writing, and also in light of Burke's theories, it seems clear that Wright is attempting to express the black American experience as an organic movement, a unified action from biological stirrings in the universal texture to emotional and intellectual externalizations.

It is also similar to the Burkean state of transition between juxtaposed, incongruous perspectives to a new interpretive frame of reference. Fabre's estimation of Wright's remarks further supports such a reading: "This is Wright in his entirety—his insatiable longing to find unity and identity by rejoining his ancestral heritage inspiring him to live elsewhere so as to contemplate America from a distance, and the painful realization of the solitary nature of his task combining with an almost mystical need to capture the meaning of life in his work. . . . To bridge a gap was the leitmotif of his work." (*Unfinished Quest*, pp. 273-74) Wright is concerned with discovering his roots, but not in historical terms. They are only a contouring means. It is explicitly a spiritual voyage that he wishes to chart, one that suggests a vision beyond the means of expression at his command.

As late as 1955, in his responses to the young Indonesian at Bandung, Wright speaks of the quality of personal visions and reveals his ability to doubt the import of his deepest feelings:

> [Concerning] Subjective and Objective and Synthetic modes of expression . . . mystic visions or synthetic visions which are found in art . . . Mysticism is generally such a vision as that painted by El Greco [in "The Burial of Count Orgaz"] but without the support and sanction of the State or Church; it is a personal vision. The drawback of such visions is that they are mostly held together by arbitrary elements selected by the artist, and not agreed upon or approved by the society. Sometimes such vision[s] carry great validity, such as the visions of Blake; at other times they are just simply the dull day dreams of men out of touch with reality. ("Writers and Their Art")

His reference to the arbitrary glue that holds such visions together recalls not only Daniels's collages but also Burke's description of the emotional symbol before it is inspired by a technical, socializing form.

Earlier he had expressed the conviction that, in *The Man Who Lived Underground,* he found a perfect frame in which to hang such a journey. No doubt the critical response to that story affected his later evaluation and caused him to doubt the validity not only of the technical, socializing form or frame but also of the "something" he was experiencing at the center of his psychic life as a black American artist. The deeper such intuitions are, the less objective certainty one has as to exactly what one knows. The deeper such an intuition, the more primal it is, the more, according to Jung, it strikes consciousness as chaotic and, in any case, more inexpressible. In Wright, this kind of inhibition was compounded by the desire of a strong intelligence to be objective, by checks to personal expressiveness inflicted by racism, by a temperamental shyness and privacy, and, as his journal entry indicates, by a great sense that no one else seemed to have any inkling of what he was in contact with. Had he had an Ezra Pound to edit *The Man Who Lived Underground*, perhaps the "something" he was attempting to express there would not have retreated into his psychic recesses.

However frustrated he might have been in trying to state his private visions, the haunting concern for the "something" that was of the essence of Afro-American folk reality showed up again in his studies of Ghana, Asia, and Spain. More directly it surfaced in the two renewed attempts at imaginative writing that occupied him during the final five years of his life: his aborted "Celebration of Life" project and his haiku poetry.

Between mid-1955 to the beginning of 1956, Wright outlined for his editor, Ed Aswell, and his agent, Paul Reynolds, a literary project that he meant to occupy his attention for the next several years. As Fabre has said, the work proposed was not an entirely new plan. Wright had talked about it first in 1941, when he envisioned *Twelve Million Black Voices* as a kind of prototype of what he wanted to do. Again, in 1945, the idea recurs in a journal entry concerning the spiritual voyage of Afro-Americans which he wished to depict. In 1955, he moved from "voyage" to "celebration," and rather than concentrating solely on an Afro-American soul journey, it was "life" that was to be affirmed. The work was to be a static, synchronic but evolutionary panorama, a sage of the cosmos from primal inorganic bases to a flowering, however grotesque this might be because of errors and repression, in the man-made world of society and civilization.

The project, in addition to its predecessors that Fabre mentions, in both its content and the form proposed, also harks back to what he says he wanted to explore in Afro-American folk expression.

The work was to include a number of novels or novelettes. Modeled somewhat on Proust's interconnected "remembrances," they were not to be united by continuity of character, by setting, or by continuing saga. Just what was to connect them Wright had difficulty explaining. This thread, in his rather lame statement to Aswell, was to be an unspoken sense of the relationship of individuals to their societies, specifically an exploration and an implicit critique of mankind. With its ability to create a society intended for positive humanization, it, nevertheless, has produced forms—governments, traditions—that provide limits, imposing more and more requirements on individuals and dehumanizing them by restricting the impulses, imagination, and actions that spring from these subjective sources. In Burkean terms: why does humanity come up with such apparently faulty, erroneous orientations when what is behind orientation is so "right," so real in itself? Or, in the Wrightian context developed in this study, it was to be an exposure of various human attempts to find the right contour for the human elán.

The technical structure of "Celebration of Life" was to involve a device superficially similar to that used in his two apprentice novels, *Tarbaby's Dawn* and *Lawd Today*. In those works, supposed by such scholars as Margolies to be modeled on Dos Passos's novels, material not directly involved with the story line was inserted (juxtaposed) to present an alternative vision or viewpoint (orientation) that by implication produced a commentary on the main line or orientation expressed in incidents, behavior, and values of the characters. In "Tarbaby's Dawn," this inserted material was prose-poetry, a chorus-like represention of Tarbaby's unconscious, dream-revealed reaction to his situation; in *Lawd Today*, it was, for the most part, snatches from a fictional radio program celebrating Lincoln's birthday. This time, what rejecting editors had found as a technical flaw in the form of those two earlier novels, a lack of plot, Wright seems to have taken up consciously as central to his opus. In some ways, it was also a throwback to his discovery of literature in Memphis, where he read not for plot or stories. Point of view was his focus then, and that, in the form of perspective by incongruity, would be the focus of this new project.

In a July, 1955, letter to Reynolds, Wright refers to the novels as being concerned with "the highest and most intense moments" in human lives, "moments that show the individual in violent conflict with his environment." But what will really connect them is an attitude. (Fabre, *The Unfinished Quest*, p. 427) In his letter to Aswell, Wright emphasizes the connective device as a *mood*, a term he had employed in "Memories" to indicate what he saw as linking the utterances of Afro-American folk and wanted to contour in *The Man Who Lived Underground*. It also sounds like what he had called, in his review of *Black Thunder*, the essence of folk value: it urges on an organism's potencies, the expression of its interior experiences of all kinds—mental, physical, emotional—when external conditions obstruct such expression. Conversely, it denies and avoids experiences that would act against the exercise of an entity's organic powers. He states that he wants to champion feeling as the criterion by which actions are to be judged. This connecting device, it becomes clear, is an attempt to overcome the gap between feeling and the expressional form he sensed in his fiction. He had long been plagued by knowing, only too well, what he wanted to say in his novels; he was too impatient to allow it to come to him in images, rather than in his own didactic commentaries that damaged the existential power of his narratives. This problem had recently been recalled by reviews of *The Outsider*. He presents this mood as functioning in the way he had seen mood, feeling, the intense emotion—personality—functioning in Afro-American folk expression. Since it, rather than plot or any technical form, would link disparate actions and characters, he could, therefore, introduce any subject matter he wished between the mood pieces.

One tentative outline of the series reveals how varied the scope of materials was to be. There was a long, Whitmanesque blank verse monologue by the mood itself, describing its relationship to all natural things and actions, as well as to humanity, which Wright sees as natural but peculiarly so. Then there were brief descriptive pieces dealing with the workings of nature and having nothing to do with people. Wright exemplifies these descriptions by a peculiar dramatic prose composition, neither short story nor essay, in which he attempts to express the sensations of an organism less conscious or articulate than even Bigger Thomas or Fred Daniels—a seed potato dissolving underground, its rot the other side of its act of giving life to new plants. After the dissolving potato, an eagle seizing a lamb was to be the focus, then a zoo lion copulating. The first actual novel to be introduced was one that Wright had published previously, *Savage Holiday*. The preceding conjurings of mood, by their mere juxtaposition to the novels and prose pieces and without further comment by Wright, were to form a point of view and elicit from the reader an evaluation of people like Erskin Fowler and the shape he gives to the mood within himself.

Eight more planned novels or novellas are listed by names of apparent main characters, sources, or titles, only two worked out in any detail. Both of these deal with the inevitable destructiveness of orientational encounter. In "A Strange Girl" or "Strange Daughter," a strictly reared American girl, whose resultant sexual repressions are overcome by a sexually brutal Nigerian who also gets her pregnant, is murdered by him because of his tribal prohibition against reembodying one's ancestors in the white race.

A story about Montezuma, "When The World Was Red," comes across as a fable involving the conflict between the incongruous Aztec and Spanish cultures. Montezuma is seduced because, in a Burke-like scenario, his indigenous orientation contains fifth-column aspects to which the juxtaposed conquistador's is amenable. While Montezuma watches his psychic suasion lead him willingly to accept this "modern," inevitable, wave-of-the-future outlook, he is horrified at the emotional price such "advancement" demands, the only value prized by his people. He is ridden, like most of Wright's characters, and as Burke says advocates of new orientations are, with guilt, that emotional equivalent of the terrible freedom one possesses as he abandons his roots, his parent, for a new orientation that he knows is better but does not satisfy old emotional dependencies. Like Daniels, he moves in his freedom to embrace that which must be embraced, even though it is fatal; prepared to do so by prophecies of a new religion to come, new gods, which his own, self-validated religious beliefs have set up for him; and by a rational admiration for the efficiency and precision exhibited by the Spaniard. However much influenced by contemporary events in Africa, Algeria, and Indo-China and such works as Manonni's *Prospero and Caliban*, the pattern of juxtaposed, disparate items, whether as broad as different cultural orientations or as mundane as items taken from everyday life, had been familiar to Wright for at least twenty years.

As the view of a man who had, in his recent past, protested (and would again within a year emphatically protest) any identification with mystical visions, claiming for himself a world-shaping imagination based "strictly on the materials of the world in which I live each day" (*White Man Listen!* p. 48), this declared mood seems a paradox. The style of the mood's declaration also raises questions. It is an incongruous combination. The content is new, purportedly special to Wright, a content he feels that he must define in a new "word" or symbol, as Flaubert created his Madam Bovary symbol for a particular insight he wished to name. This newness comes through in the intensity that Wright generates by means of the sheer length and multiplicity of versions of what the mood says it is. However, striking across this intensity and dashing the sense that a very special expression is seeking to emerge, are Wright's numerous clichés. The cumulative effect (like Fred Daniels) is of throwing himself, without adequate technical forms, against the preconceptions of the established orientation in an attempt to succeed by means of strength of passion and conviction alone. He is writing, as some critics had observed of his earlier work, psychosomatically. As he indicated to Aswell, Wright hopes to communicate the meaning of this mood by mythologizing it to the reader. The monologue in which the mood expresses itself is incantatory, not discursive, following an emotional sequence of details as they occurred to him, rather than employing such a "technical" arrangement as repetition or crescendo.

This mood is not a person, although Wright has it speak in the first person singular. It does not esteem the person, displaying characteristics of Twain's Master Passion, seeking only its own fulfillment and following its own purposes, impartial as to what it inhabits or whether it brings happiness or misery:

. . . no flesh am I, and no blood;
And though I am of myself persuaded to dwell for swift
    moments
      in the breathing temples of men, I am not man, and with
      his
    ways I have I am not to be confounded.
Yet I live; yet I have my being; yet I haunt the whole of
    this and
    other worlds without number and without end;—
At home in the rock's deep heart, in the still, old depths of
    the
    ocean's sand . . .
In the icy stretches of stellar spaces . . .
My hot will belching upward from the tall tops of
    mountain peaks,
    sending lava sliding and smoking down the ragged
    slopes,
Nestling eternally at the cores of burning suns . . .
Everywhere and nowhere, visible and invisible, felt and
    unfelt,
    there and not there, in all and in nothing, I hover,
    seeking to
    enter . . .

Like Tennyson's Nature, it brings to life and to death indis-
criminately:

Controlling the fluttering of a baffled and curious child's
    eyelids,
Relating the heart's beats, each to each,
Structuring the bones of men and women . . .
Exulting in flexed and tensed flesh,
And equally,
Suffering I am, pain, the compulsive rasping in the
    choked throat . . .
Ecstatically aching in flaccid muscles . . .
Escaping slowly as foul scent from corpses, seeking
    release,
Issuing in screams from contorted lips while tugging new
    life from wombs . . .

Proclaiming victory when the body gives its last heave
   and lies
still. . . .

(Fabre, The Unfinished Quest, pp. 428-29)

Nevertheless, this mood has an almost compassionate, desparate preference for mankind. But while begging pusillanimous humans to allow it entrance, once it finds an amenable human, it becomes a juggernaut. In its rapacious eaglelike descent into its human host and in its restlessness, it sounds like Shelley's Intellectual Beauty. Its kinship to this Shelleyan source of inspiration is also bourne out in that, while concerned only with itself, not with improving the person it comes to inhabit or assuring him of success or happiness, it is extremely concerned with finding forms that can realize it emotionally, thereby somehow giving it a liberty inherent in self-consciousness or self-possession that it otherwise does not possess.

Wright had long wanted to get this emotion into his works, to communicate "it" but he was hampered by what he considered the limitations of traditional techniques of fiction. In early 1940, in his lecture "On Literature," he had called for an infusion of this mood in the egregiously realistic, journalistic, proletarian novel so that these novels would "*cut deeper . . . present as yet unrevealed aspects and looks of reality*," shed "sudden beams of light . . . upon the familiar to make them seem strange"; "*to link unusual relationships, to grasp in unity that which is disunited.*" In this lecture, he refers to the power accomplishing this as "imagination." To incorporate this into such works, he suggests that the "writer now begin to project *himself*—objectively of course—more and more into his work." He is not "arguing for the return of the subjectiveness of a Proust or a Joyce." He wants "an act of acceptance by the writer *himself* as a kind of subject matter not literally, but imaginatively." He sounds somewhat like Burke, who also found the character and plot requirements of the realistic novel more a hindrance than a help in efforts to express his sense of modern life. Burke had developed, in *Towards a Better Life*, a kind of essay-novel, which allowed his personal, subjective self to emerge but in a fictional form. But it is Hemingway's *To Have and Have Not* and Steinbeck's *Grapes of Wrath* that Wright cites; Hemingway's novel, he says, should have ended with Harry Morgan's death, but it is at that point that Hemingway really opens up and tells what he means, throwing overboard the technique of characterization. Wright ends the lecture by call for "bolder, more intricate character types . . . to take the novel into new fields and at the same time retain what is best in the technical achievements of the old fiction." ("On Literature")

Boris Max was, of course, a form of this projection of the writer imagistically—imaginatively—into the work; Cross Damon was an attempt at a more "intricate" character type that would "objectively" allow Wright into his fiction. The mood monologue of "Celebration of Life" was to be the most intricate form of this imaginative character type yet to appear in his fiction.

The mood, as well as the entire literary project, thus begins to emerge as collage. The literarily expressed mood is the visible glue between the variegated sketches and novels, and the "something" is what is uniting the disjointed verses of the expressed mood itself. Both the part and the whole can be seen as elaborate, analogous jazz or folk blues pieces, in Wright's view. The individual lines of the monologue and the prose novels and vignettes in the overall work correspond to riffs or lyrics, and the mood, as stated, corresponds to the steady bass beat that Wright refers to in "Memories." Each line of the monologue and each novel would be entire, self-consistent wholes, but like the events, episodes, experiences, and images he combined in *The Man Who Lived Underground*, each would have its greatest significance and meaning only in the schema of the provocative, machinelike, yet vital mood. The mood was to be heard only indirectly, as Wright had picked up what lay behind his grandmother's and other black American folks' expressions; its objective is to call forth imaginative or recollected linkages in the reader. Clearly, though its form is closer to that of what Burke calls an emotional symbol, mood serves a function more like Burke's technical form in that it is "correcting" the view of society expressed by the characters in the fiction. It is also an attempt, especially in conjunction with the disparate prose pieces, to say the unsayable, or at least to know what is said best if left unsaid.

As both the title of the project and Wright's remarks to Reynolds make clear, the central point of the series is to be "a depiction or a dramatization of what, for the want of a better name, I'd call the 'life force.' " (Fabre, *The Unfinished Quest*, pp. 427-28) What Wright means by "life," however, clearly goes beyond biology alone. It has more in common with Burke's "universal texture." It transcends the opposing categories of animate and inanimate, organic and inorganic, natural and artificial. It is in sperm, cracking seeds, trembling leaves, abscesses and maggot-producing decay, as well as in rocks, volcanic eruptions, columns of light, the tints of clouds, the cold of interstellar space, lightning, silence; it is in the heart of the criminal and the condemned facing the firing squad, as well as in fantasies and music.

Fabre makes the observation that "Wright was certainly as indebted to Wilhelm Reich's "orgone" theory as to Whitman's poetic and philosophical vision" for this notion of mood (p. 427), and he has found that Wright owned four of Reich's books: *Character Analysis; The Function of the Orgasm; The Mass Psychology of Fascism;* and *The Sexual Revolution.* Reich's work enjoyed a certain celebrity and credence in the 1940s and 1950s. His reputation as a successful if unorthodox psychotherapist—as well as the creditability of his experimental methods and some plausible orgone successes with cancer retardation (which also caused his problems with the FDA) and with rain-making—earned him a number of loyal followers. Arthur Koestler, with whom Wright was acquainted knew Reich and his ideas as early as 1932, when both Koestler and Reich were members of the same Communist party cell in Berlin. Koestler was not uncritical of Reich's ideas, but he was apparently impressed enough by them and/or Reich's reputation as a clinical psychoanalyst to mention Reich twice in his writings: in his 1952 autobiography, *Arrow in the Blue,* and earlier, in his contribution to *The God That Failed* in 1949, to which Wright had also contributed.

Apart from any of his specific theories, Reich seems to have shared some basic attitudes with Wright. One Reich scholar describes him as having "a deep cosmic sense" but as unable to accept "true spirituality." Reich grew up in Austria and Germany at a time when spirituality was represented by "low-level spiritism," which Reich considered "rank superstition." For Reich, anything labeled "spirit" or "soul" was relegated to "distorted mysticism," an escapist behavior in mankind that split the unity of human function. (Mann, *Orgone, Reich and Eros*, p. 15)

Reich was a devoted disciple of Freud, early in his career a part of the inner circle of Viennese psychiatrists, but from the mid-1920s (and until his death in a United States prison in 1957) his eccentric espousal of Freud's early notions of libido and the sexual nature of all human psychological drives and disturbances eventually alienated Freud. In spite of Freud's modification of his own understandings of these hypotheses and his rejection of Reich's eccentric, or brilliant, views, Reich was convinced that all psychic illnesses result from a deficiency of what he called "orgastic potency." This is the power to give oneself over completely to full genital gratification, to become at one with the involuntary nervous and muscular contractions and expansions that constitute orgasm, eliminating the fog of symbols or fantasies during the experience.

Reich's development, however wrongheaded, of Freud's ideas appears today rather commonplace. What remains of the titillation and controversy that Reich's work stirred, even as late as the mid-1950s, is centered on what Reich's theory of orgastic potency led him to in the areas of biochemistry and biophysics. It is also this area of Reich's work that is of most possible relevance to Wright's concept of mood.

Reich came to believe that orgasm represents the expulsion of a "surplus" biological "energy," of a "something," as he calls it in *The Function of the Orgasm*, that he at one time did not understand but of whose existence he was aware in somatic phenomena characterized by movement. These movements, like their opposites—certain muscular rigidities he observed in a number of his psychiatric patients—were not symptoms, causes, or results of " 'psychic processes,' but were actually themselves those processes or functions in the somatic realm" (p. 272), a unity of mind and body. The energy blocked in the muscular tension is, Reich believed, the very source and essence of life, even though its normal condition—or orientation—is movement, not stasis.

His first clue to its nature developed from his attention to sexology in his attempt to understand the physiology of the sexual act. He combined an awareness of the friction involved in sexual intercourse with the findings of a German internalist that "the body is governed by electrical processes. It is made up of countless 'border surfaces' between membranes and electrolytic fluids, having various densities and compositions. According to a well-known law of physics, electrical tensions develop at the borders between conducting fluids and membranes. Since the concentrations and structure of the membranes are not homogeneous, differences develop in the tensions at the border surfaces, and, simultaneously, differences in [electrical] potential of varying intensity." (p. 273) Ideally, a kind of current develops, which is the release of this bioelectric energy from areas of higher to those of lower energy concentrations. Since the body is composed of billions of such membranous surfaces, this bodily, electrical energy is constantly moving.

Reich is emphatic in his belief that this energy is not identical to the body fluids or their movement; such fluids and movement may be an essential means of physical/psychic excitation, but an additional "unknown something" produces sensations such as anger, anxiety, and pleasure. He coined the word "bions" to refer to the elemental units of this "something" that he claimed to have detected in laboratory experiments. These amoebalike entities were transitional forms between animate and inanimate matter, spherical, vascular, pulsating quanta of this bioenergy. Their pulsating, expansive-contractive movement is the basic life movement. It contains a four-beat rhythm: double buildup of tension, first through the mechanical increase of fluids along the periphery of the bion, and then the buildup of bioelectric energy, followed by a double discharge, first of the excessive energy and then of the mechanically moved fluids. This movement is found in all major somatic systems—cardiovascular, digestive, alimentary. It is found also in the pattern of the autonomic nervous network, a system that works through the antithesis of parasympathetic or expansive action "'out of the self—toward the world,' pleasure and joy" and a sympathetic or contractive "'away from the world—into the self' sadness and unpleasure" action. (p. 288)

Eventually Reich came to perceive this energy beyond biological organisms. In laboratory experiments, first involving organic but sterilized hay and mosses in sterilized water, he observed the formation of his bions. The energy in these minute semiliving packets, while it shared some characteristics of the "charge" in what is traditionally called static electricity, also produced a kind of radiation; its presence could be registered not only on an electroscope but on a Geiger counter. Reich's experiments with bion production involving inorganic materials bore results particularly startling and revelatory of the nature of this energy. Beach sand, intensely heated and injected into an egg and gelatin medium, produced bions that were not only larger than those produced by the hay but gave off an intense bluish light. In the room in which a large number of these bions were stored, various items and even the walls appeared to be emitting bluish dots and lines that merged in a blue-grey or violet haze. When working in the room, Reich and his colleagues noticed that their hands, hair, and clothing also emitted such a haze, which followed their bodies about like an enveloping vapor. Reich concluded that this radiant energy had "charged" the organic substances, acting to produce an emanation that could be registered as electricity, or as visible phenomena if the energy working on the organism was sufficiently strong.

Reich built variously sized boxes in which to isolate the SAPA (for "sand packet") bions for further, more controlled study. He and his co-workers found that, even after the SAPA bions were removed and the boxes treated to remove traces of their effects, and even in new boxes before SAPA bions had been placed in them, the same visual effects of a moving, bluish vapor were observable. Reich made the deduction that the energy first detected in man-made bions was actually present everywhere in the atmosphere and in everything in existence, and nowhere was this more evident than in entities that were strongly "vegetatively active." He "verified" this conclusion by looking through a wooden tube at the dark sky between stars. He observed the same flashing dots and lines of bluish light or radiation that he had witnessed in the boxes with the SAPA cultures. He also claimed to see this flashing radiational phenomenon in the daytime, on white clouds, or white tables, and on white doors.

This hitherto undetected, unremarked, and certainly undefined universal energy Reich named "orgone." Unwittingly, perhaps, he had moved from being a disciple of Freud into the ranks of such controversial figures as Paracelsus, Galvani, and Mesmer, men whose work fell into that gray area between science and occultism. He came eventually to believe that orgone was the identical "something" that had inspired, in such ancient philosophers as Democrites, the atomistic theories about the nature of the universe. These theories had been nullified, however, by the mechanistic or scientific attitude, and the study of nature now relies heavily on artificially constructed experiments that rule out or discredit simple, "natural" observation. For Reich orgone was practically identical to life and its processes; it comes from the sun and is the equivalent of sunspots. It thus became present in the atmosphere and soil, and all animate things absorb and release it. Regarding the latter, it is found even in decaying matter, just as, on the psychic level, it will, if otherwise blocked, orient itself in psychic, physical, and even social mischiefs.

In addition to some shared basic attitudes, Wright's impressions of Kenneth Burke's ideas would also have enabled him to be receptive of some of Reich's theories, since strong analogies exist between what Burke had said in *Permanence and Change* and what Reich indicated his scientific methods had developed in a logical, step-by-step empirical way. These similarities exist, no doubt, because of the modernity of both men's thinking and its debt to such common sources as Freud and the influence of Marx. The similarities are both general and particular. For example, Burke, while writing of the organic wholeness, unity, of reality in its "universal texture," as opposed to its fragmentation in human epistemological structures such as cause and effect, uses the example of the "progress of an electrical current from cathode to anode." Neither of these points is thought of as a cause but merely as a "logical convenience . . . for describing two organically interdependent points in a continuous series." (*Permanence and Change*, p. 231) He uses such an example recognizing full well that his "range of investigation," his "point of view obliges [him] to apply the organic metaphor" even to such phenomena as electric fields. Mirroring this is Reich's stipulation that expansion and contraction, the basic pulsations of life movement, are also found "in the primordial realm of nature." (*Ether, God and Devil*, p. 86)

More particular is Reich's explanation, in *Ether, God and Devil*, of how error is to be accounted for:

> New systems of thought are intended to overcome the errors of the old systems. As we well know, the former spring from the contradictions of erroneous thinking, which has become divorced from reality. Since it derives from this realm of thought, the new system carries some of the old sources of error into its new structure. The new thought grows in the logical, although incorrectly arranged, old one. The pioneering intellectual spirit is socially tied to his own time. To this is added a purely psychological factor, namely, that the pioneer does not want to discard altogether the erroneous conceptual system, with its comfortable, familiar features. He would like to be understood in his own time, without having to stand entirely outside it. Hence he neglects to use his critical faculties, takes over erroneous concepts, or disguises his innovations by using dated, sterile words. The new system vacillates, too insecure to find its own ground. But the old system which is under attack enjoys public applause and contemporary esteem; it is backed by organization and power. (p. 17)

This passage contains the equivalents of Burke's "perspective by incongruity" and the notions of recalcitrance and socialization of viewpoint. In other places, Reich, like Burke, encourages self-criticism of conceptual frameworks as a necessity, as part of the continuous effort needed to keep from locking one's mental processes into a fixed position. For both of these modern thinkers, reality is fluidity; stasis is the prime error of mind-forged illusion, the original sin that is foisted onto all existence.

Like Burke, and Wright in his "Celebration" letter to Aswell, Reich sees fit to emphasize that man is a part of nature, although just how he fits in is problematic. This doubtful status will remain until his nature, which powers both reflexive physiological activities and human thought that is frequently at odds with instincts and impulses, is recognized as a mode of "cosmic organic energy"—the primordial, universally existent, all-permeating; the origin of all matter, including all the galactic systems throughout the universe, and the origin of all change, motion, and all forms of energy, such as biological life, decay, human thought, and emotion. Both Reich and Burke emphasize the biologic as the model from which they build the comprehensive view of reality that each offers as a corrective to the confusions and evils of the modern world, which result from a rigidly mechanistic, scientific, technological orientation. As Burke posed a kind of evolutionary process, whereby thought—symbolization—is a version of biological behavior transformed into a different species of being (different but no less real and valid than the undeniable, scientifically accepted source from which it springs), Reich also stressed a connection between thought and the "natural functions" with which it deals. For Reich, even thought as "high" or "abstract" as mathematics can accurately describe "objective processes" because such abstract ideas are themselves part of the same natural function. Though mathematical symbols are "unreal and do not even pretend to mirror reality," they, nevertheless, are the products of a "vigorously pulsating orgonatic system." (Reich, *Ether, God and Devil*, p. 95) For Reich, mathematics is anchored in organ sensations, the experience, whether or not acknowledged, of the functioning, biological reality of the mathematician's being. He is "the living organism that orders, regroups, and connects its sensations before articulating them as mathematical formulas." (p. 95)

A central Reichian point that ties him not only to Burke but to Wright's view of Afro-American folk expression and the heart of his poetics is precisely this notion: only the existence within the perceiving subject of a variant form of the same reality makes possible the validity of the perception of objective reality. When Reich says that "*the organism can perceive only what it itself expresses*" (p. 69), he is not espousing solipsism any more than does Burke or Wright in his repeated emphasis on his subjective responses as the source of truth. For example, when Wright, in "On Literature," calls for the imaginative "projection" of the writer's self into his work in order to establish a closeness of the work with the artist, imagination, in his sense, shares some affinity with Reich's "sensation of orgonatic pulsations." It is thus both at the core of the individual and yet suprapersonal. The writer, in Wright's view, has to give this part of his life to what he observes; he cannot express the life, the reality of the objectively derived subject matter, simply by being as faithful as possible to those phenomena that are divorced totally from himself. If he can give objective phenomena something of his own life, he is giving it a variant form of the reality, the energy that it already possesses. Reich excoriates the "technologies" and "technicians" (science and scientists), those blinded by the convolutions, the "perfections," and the artifices of procedure. He would have more emphasis placed, as he did in his experiments, on natural, direct observations—experience itself, which always includes the experience of one's own external and internal organs that are sensing, responding to, the stimuli being studied. Reich's statement, "*The character structure and the senses of perception in the observer are major, if not decisive, tools of natural research*" (p. 157), is not a bad summary of Wright's view of how imagination should be more intensely projected into realistic fiction.

Other of Reich's ideas, related to his interest in the "something" behind Afro-American folk expression, could also have rung a bell of recognition in Wright. He would undoubtedly have been able to see and utilize Reich's explanation of the mystical or religious experience as an explanation of how the "mood," so valid in itself, that characterized his grandmother's form of expression could exist with an erroneous religious outlook. As explained above, in Reich's theories, the perception of reality involves the recognition of individual but suprapersonal reality in one's self. The core of this reality in living beings is movement, the pulsating, wavelike flow of orgonistic plasmic "fluid." But this unitary, natural, pleasurable movement, branches, for an undiscovered reason, into metaphysical/religious or scientific lines. Both treat the core of reality as something wrong. In Freudian and Jungian terminology, this is the incest taboo. Society, with its patriarchal, authoritarian, hierarchical orientation, exacerbated by the modern mechanistic, hyperbolically objective outlook, and the psyche itself, with its great fear of being absorbed into the ocean of orgone energy—into orgasm—have set up barriers that prevent direct contact with this source of individual genuineness. The pulsations of the life source continue, however; direct sensation of them is blocked, and they reappear in the form of supernatural powers: ghosts, spirits of various kinds, angels, devils, and God. This biogenetic core would be, therefore, the source of such a religious formulation as Wright found in his grandmother's outlook.

Reich qualifies his estimation of religion in a manner that also would have been familiar to Wright. If religion is, in Reich's words, a "grotesque distortion," it is so because it puts the wrong head on a right body. It is, after all, a form of thought derived from the biological variant of cosmic energy. Unlike the earlier, even more "primitive view of emotional life" known as animism, religion deals with unreal forms through which it expresses itself. Animism derives, as does all religion, from man's correct experience of his own very real sensations and emotions; however, the animist then makes the simple mistake of ascribing such functions to other objects, objects that are real and that in some way partake of the same orgone energy sensed in the animist himself but are incapable of having biologically based emotions. Such an attitude is not, in Reich's view, as far from "natural processes" as is the religious or mystical. The latter completely violates reality; it transforms subjective, vital, natural impulses and sensory and emotional realities into things "beyond this world" and therefore unreal. (*Ether, God and Devil*, pp. 87-88) Unlike the mathematician, however, the religious person says that his formulations do mirror reality.

While Reich sees a kinship between the mystic and the mechanistic scientist in that both pervert or ignore self-perception, which is something Wright wishes to avoid, he places the religious person in closer contact with the subjective experiences of life movement. Mechanist have no understanding of emotions or their functions, but for religious people like Grandmother Wilson, emotions—the sensed motions of protoplasmic orgonotic streams through the body—are the very material of their experience, though they do not or cannot face this fact because of their "armorings." Grandmother Wilson heeded her inner sensations and acted in concord with them, but she had failed or refused, for one reason and another—not the least of which would be racism and what it did for Afro-Americans' perceptions of themselves—to recognize their true source.

Along these same lines, when Wright had Daniels come to a greater liking for blues than for spirituals, because somehow the blues seem to belong more to the people who originate them, his thinking is compatible with Reich's ideas about the relative direct contact with life that different expressive forms indicate. Folk blues lyrics may not be animistic, but they do utilize facets of real-life phenomena with which to project the awareness, as mood or feeling, that they have of their own undeniable reality. The actual source may not be fully acknowledged, but neither is it ascribed to a nonexistent entity. Concurrently, Reich's theory would allow that the spirituals, even when taken as literal, bona fide religious expression, possess great truth. Distorted by armorings, and thus remaining farther from their real goal that is also their very motive, the real, genuine vital pulsations are discernible. Daniels faults the words he hears being sung by the church group, words that talk about being so happy, happy, happy in Jesus, but in the intonations of the voice of the girl singing them, he hears something to which he can readily respond and accept. Similarly, Wright could not accept his grandmother's words, but he was intrigued by the "music" of what she said.

Reich's work would have seemed familiar to Wright also because of the strong parallels between specific elements in his fiction and Reich's specific details concerning orgone. Although Wright probably did not encounter Reich's ideas until the late 1940s or early 1950s, Reich's neo-Freudian diagrams and talk of "armored character," its causes and effects on the orgonotic expansive movement in the human organism, at times seem to be a psychiatrist's abstract of Boris Max's courtroom speech. Reich says that he

> could write a ponderous tome on the numerous armoring mechanisms to explain the mystic, the politician, the criminal, the tactician, etc. . . . We must limit ourselves to the basic mechanisms that distinguish the truly alive organism from its distorted form of expression in the biopath. Furthermore, we have to confront these two alien worlds and penetrate to the social tragedies that have afflicted the human animal for thousands of years, ever since his organism became armored. In its realm, the unarmored organism develops an infinite variety of life forms. The same is true for the armored organism, which develops an equally infinite variety of biopathic reactions . . . the living core of the armored organism retained its impulses, but they can no longer find free expression. *In the desperate attempt "to express itself," every natural impulse is*

233

forced to penetrate or break through the wall of the armoring. The impulse must use force to reach the surface and the goal. While the impulse [the expansive or "love" orgonotic movement] is trying to overcome the armoring by force, it is transformed into a destructive rage, regardless of its original nature . . . whether [this destructive rage] spends itself or is inhibited, whether it turns into morbid self-pity or reaches its goal as undisguised sadism . . . it is the effort to express itself naturally and reach its goal that converts every biological impulse into destructiveness. (*Ether, God and Devil*, pp. 63-64)

Colors that Wright uses, in both *Native Son* and in the manuscripts of *The Man Who Lived Underground* in an apparently realistic, merely descriptive way, take on another significance in light of Reich's observations. As Burke has stated, all physical phenomena are "pseudo-statements"; stroking someone's hair carries with it a meaning akin to that in a statement such as "I stroke the hair of Cleopatra." Reich claimed that orgone energy is usually perceived as lumination having a distinctly bluish tinge, whatever its basic color. At the beginning of several of the manuscripts of *The Man Who Lived Underground*, Wright gave singular attention to descriptions of the clouds that Daniels sees in the summer evening sky. They are the source of the later rain that is instrumental in Daniels's discovery of the underground as a hiding place. Wright depicts the clouds as green, red, pink, but always purple. He was also to have the dramatized mood in "Celebration of Life" identify itself with the purple at the edge of clouds. Then, when Daniels is underground, his source of light is frequently the "orange-blue spurt of flame" from a match. The organic diamonds in his collage emit blue and white sparks; orgone was frequently observed by Reich as streaks and dots of blue or white light. The light that filters through the perforations in the manhole covers is seen by Daniels as "a hazy violet." The pool of green slime that he observes, and from which he imagines mankind first being born, pulsates "bluish-purple" bubbles that burst with an expiring sigh. It is also a blue light that suffuses Mary Dalton's bedroom as Bigger is increasingly moved to surrender to the involuntary sexual impulses rising in him. The pervasive, implicit association in Afro-American folklore of the color blue with sex coincides with Reich's comments, not only on the color orgone seems to elicit, but also with his views that the more unarmored, the more naturally and directly in contact with "organ sensations," one is, the more perceptive he is of orgone's manifestations in the cosmic environment.

Other similarities between items in Wright's fiction and Reich's writings are not particularly remarkable because of the common basis traceable to Freud or Jung. An example of such is Reich's explanation of intense anxiety and terror (such as Bigger and Daniels experience). These emotions are the reaction of consciousness to confrontations with a potentially overwhelming "something" (symbolized in Wright's fiction by devouring flames in a furnace, a house, or a dance hall). They are also the source of the armorings or protective barriers that consciousness raises against orgasmic absorption into the oceanic orgone.

Worthy of more comment is the obvious connection between Reich's orgonotic bioenergy and Wright's ideas of "mood" in "Celebration of Life" and of the "something" in Afro-American folk expression: orgone energy links all things, no matter how disparate, because it is that of which all matter—and for Reich everything is matter—both animate and inanimate, is constituted. Anyone of the right character (unarmored) and of sufficient sensitivity to the workings of orgone as the "life function" in himself will perceive the reality of the connections between an amoeba and a thundercloud; anyone only sufficiently sensitive to his life function will still have the impulse to forge connections between unlikely things, without being aware that the connection is "unlikely."

Whereas this kind of connection was referred to by Burke (occasionally), by the Surrealists, and by Wright himself as a juxtaposition of seemingly incongruous elements, Reich speaks of superimposition, a concept that might have offered Wright another perspective on the "something" that he had long sensed behind Afro-American folk expression and that linked it with the "mood" of his projected work. Reich's notion is his explanation of the functional identity of all things, especially of all living things. Wright, it must be remembered, had, in 1941, in "Memories of My Grandmother," spoken of the similarity between his grandmother's viewpoint and that of the blues singers, so different in content, as functional.

Reich's thinking about superimposition began with his work on the orgasm and the sexual embrace, but he gradually expanded his understanding so that the sexual embrace was only one manifestation of a basic pattern that ran through and revealed ultimate reality. The primal superimposition is the convergence of two, and sometimes more, currents of movement (or, in modern physics parlance, "strings") streaming in different directions in the ocean of mass-free orgone "ether." These streams, as Reich observed in the orgone accumulators, moved in a spiraling wave. When they attracted each other and converged, Reich assumed, according to the laws of physics, that a loss of kinetic energy resulted, with a diminution of the spiraling. The long, drawn out, forward spin, pulling back on itself, would become an in-place circular motion. The superimposed, "open" streams formed a kind of closed wheel-within-a-wheel, and orgone energy was converted into inert mass, which can be called an atom, an electron, a particle, or anything one wishes. Reich compares this pattern to the spinning, forward movement of planets and stars, the arms of galaxies forming massive material at their centers. He would, no doubt, have seen his theory confirmed also in the eventually discovered figuration of the double helix.

If the basic pattern of material reality is reflected in the double helix, it could also be said to show up in the looping, spiraling flow of Stein's prose and poetry. Although Reich did not dwell on this pattern as it exhibits itself in cultural expression, he does speculate that the human *"quest for knowledge expresses desperate attempts, at times, on the part of the orgone energy within the living organism to comprehend itself, to become conscious of itself. And in understanding its own ways and means of being, it learns to understand the cosmic orgone energy ocean that surrounds the surging and searching emotions." (Ether, God and Devil*, p. 279) As Wright's "mood" declares, while it is in everything and especially in every living thing, it seeks most of all the form of man. This form can feel and express, and thus it can set the energy free again in knowledge that is particularly human and yet has a cosmic universality.

The basic processes of knowledge, the basic processes of life, therefore, involve superimposition. It may appear to be mere juxtaposition if the functional identity between the two juxtaposed, enclosed forms is not sensed. Wright's blueprint for Negro writing is just such a description of two oblique streamings of energy converging and continuing on in a highly charged new system. Grandmother Wilson and Afro-American folk expressed this identity without exactly naming it. Burke, in his 1940 essay on Surrealism, discusses *Native Son* specifically in terms of "superimposition." Like Surrealism, Burke says, *Native Son* "combines two orders of logic." Reich says that the shape most revelatory of orgone movement is the looping wave, reflected in shapes such as the snail shell and in the characteristic sexual and orgasmic movement that is an effort to bring the mouth and the genitals together following the natural flow of orgone. In Burke's remarks on *Native Son*, he says that, in both Surrealism and ordinary experience, two orders of logic exist, but not merely side by side or alternating; in a clause he might have taken directly from Reich's later statement about the merger of basic orgonomes, he says "they *interpenetrate*." (*New Directions in Prose and Poetry*, p. 564) Similarly, *Native Son* contains an "associative logic (where the quality of the whole is implicit in the *introduction*) and an argument (where all is brought to a head in the *conclusion*)." That is, on the vector that is the image of the rat at the beginning of the story is superimposed the different logic that is Max's explication. Bigger and Max, if not Bigger and the rat, are in Burke's words "reciprocal functions of each other." While Burke finds that the second order—Max's conceptualizations—"shows some signs of being *superimposed* upon the first," it is the "shows some signs" that he protests. Superimposition is the way of art: Burke lauds Wright's superimposition of these incongruous perspectives as "nearer to completion than in the alternating levels of Dos Passos's trilogy or Steinbeck's *Grapes of Wrath.* (*New Directions in Prose and Poetry*, p. 564) This superimposition of logics, of the felt interior life on external events directly or indirectly experienced, would result in an expression that is simultaneously the fact of the writer's reality and of what he is depicting; yet all of it would be a fiction, a model of the functional identity of seemingly different facts.

However scientifically valid Wright believed Reich's theories to be, he most likely found in Reich's scientifically couched records of his visions a kind of modern mythology that bolstered Wright's sense of the "something" in Afro-American folk expression and possibly in himself, an energy he could not deny and yet feared to indulge lest he be regressing into subjective or cultural obscurantism. Wright had once said that if the Negro accepted what being a Negro meant, he would discover something universal in this knowledge. Reich's more or less scientific theories stirred remembrances of Wright's earlier urge to contour an Afro-American spirit as a voyage between two worlds, as a functional identification or linkage that was masked in the (real) metaphoric terms of creative African tribal emergence in a new world. With the encouragement of Reich's mythology, the images—the Whitmanesque language, the stories, and novels—the Symbol (etymologically, the "throwing together") in "Celebration of Life," would be even freer of stereotypical associations wth black American life and history than those in *The Man Who Lived Underground*. They would, like Reich's hypotheses, make one ponder a single force, such as physics ideally hopes to find uniting the stars, and the atom, macrocosms and microcosms, the one and the many, as a critical backdrop for the world's more observable ways.

Aswell and Reynolds discouraged Wright's project, in part, because of this central mood. Their objections were voiced ultimately on commercial grounds, whatever they may have thought of the poetic quality of the "Declaration." The poetry between the novels would, at best, have had little appeal to readers, given the generally low esteem in which poetry was held, and hence would be disastrous for sales. Wright seems to have gone along with their opinions for similar reasons, although the project and his poetic "mood" meant much to him. Fabre, whose biography emphasizes the antimystical, rationalistic, pragmatic aspects of Wright's cast of mind, indicates that, in his agreement to abandon the project, "his disappointment shows through; it was so difficult to reconcile what he had dreamed of accomplishing with what he could hope to publish." (Fabre, *The Unfinished Quest*, p. 431)

Mood, in its many guises and elusive meaning, was deeply ingrained in Wright's awareness, and its resurgence in his Third World books, researched and for the most part written prior to his outlining of "Celebration of Life," has been noted. Even after the negative reaction of his friends, it is still visible in the hard questions he raised at the 1956 First Congress of Negro Artists and Writers in Paris: to what use could black African and Afro-American cultural forms be put to counter the political, economic, and psychological ravages and abuses Western scientific ideology was inflicting, while allowing Africa and Afro-America to develop as twentieth-century equals to white Euro-America? The congress's overemphasis, in his opinion, on negritude failed to motivate a definite plan "to blend national traditions with modern nationalism." Fabre sees this as the ultimate point behind Wright's questions. The congress's fixation on negritude apparently prompted his overstress on the need to superimpose a rationalistic, technological, industrial orientation on these cultures in order to develop a chiasmatic, complex cultural mind that could link the two.

Mood definitely surfaced again in the late summer of 1959 when Wright turned to writing haiku. Fabre attributes the immediate cause of this seemingly unusual interest to a chance conversation Wright had with a "young South African who loved this form of poetry" and described it to Wright. (p. 505) His immediate fascination with this form, like his interest in Reich's theories, is probably attributable to the fact that the haiku struck chords of familiarity. Reich, for instance, had alluded to *prana* in oriental theosophy as an ancient expression for orgone energy. To be sure, this oriental sense of a fundamental vital energy is stated in Hinduism and yoga, neither of which directly contribute to haiku or the spirit behind it. Still, the haiku form is clearly an attempt to contour "something" that is never named. It is also certain that Wright was aware of a functional similarity between the haiku form and the lyrics of folk blues, both of which work by juxtaposing or superimposing disparate elements.

R. H. Blyth's four volume study, *Haiku*, which Wright read, begins with a volume-long description of the spiritual origins of this poetic form. In this background information, Wright would have heard similarities to Burke and Reich, not the least of which would have been the emphasis on motion, the fluidity of reality. Haiku "has as its (unconscious) philosophical basis the fact that all things are changing, unfixed, unfixable, contradictory." (1:197) Blyth's opening remarks seem, at times, to be taking up where Reich and Wright's "voyage" plan for "Celebration of Life" left off. He discusses, for example, the history of mankind as the history of its spirit. This historical progress is not, in his haiku-framed description, linear: it is a movement like that of Reich's orgonotic streamings; a movement outward toward another world and then a movement inward, a return to this world. If these dialectical, looping movements are thought of as occurring simultaneously, Blyth says, they describe human nature as it is understood by the haiku-oriented mind. In illustration, he offers the Burkean example of "a quite noticeable flow toward religion in the early world," which is repeated ontogenetically in the early life of almost every individual. In both realms, this flow is followed by an ebb, a retreat from religion as an escape, a return to "things." Apart from any familiarity such remarks may have had for Wright because of his familiarity with the theories of Burke and Reich, the initial emphasis on haiku's down-to-this-earthiness would have gained Wright's interest immediately.

This movement is, moreover, identified with life. It is the "spirit of life" that haiku commemorates. The spirit of haiku recoils not only from religion—or, at least, from "false religion, which is nothing more than magic disguised" (1:181)—but from the worlds of "false poetry" and of science as well. The haiku poet shares, to an extent, Burke's notion of art as something quite different from life, but only when it is, like religion, concerned with "a world of escape," "a world of literature, but not of life." (1:181) Science, according to the spirit of haiku, while it can save us from what is unreal, "cannot give us more than a mechanically correct universe in place of phantasy. It cannot tell us what life is, nor can it give it to us more abundantly." (1:181) Such a view parallels Wright's sense that twentieth-century rationalism and technology, for all their material advantages and however much he espoused their role in developing nations, left much to be desired in the realm of human emotional values.

"Haiku is concerned only with life" says Blyth (1:279), and life is change. Whether it be creative life, "the inflow and the outflow of object and mind in moments of poetic insight"

(1:280), or physical life, it is manifested in the particularity, the "'thusness' of things," which Blyth equates with "the becoming'" of things. As in Burke and Reich and as in Wright's declared "mood," this "thusness" is itself a variant and is found in inanimate objects in their *will to exist* (1:264), their constant striving or assertion, so that even rocks and clouds are not static entities. As Wright's "mood" describes itself, it is a "universal and identical Buddha-nature in . . . physically limited and specific outworking." Haiku is the expression of the individual's infinity within the limitation of finite things. The haiku poet sees that "the brush [pen] and the poet, all have their own 'personalities'; the spirit of life is working in all of them." (1:159) As both Burke and Reich would have it, and as Wright implied in his belief that he knew things only subjectively, this identity is, in haiku, perceived by one in contact with his nature because "life runs so freely between [perceiver and perceived] that we perceive things by introspection, and our experiences of the other world have the same immediacy, validity and certainty as have states of pure self-consciousness." (1:271)

The "thusness" of life, this Buddha-nature or Zen, is the central problem of haiku. It is similar to the problem Wright experienced when he tried to find terms for the "something"—the "thusness"—that characterized his grandmother's utterances, as well as when he attempted to articulate the inarticulate Bigger, a problem that he found indigenous to proletarian literature and that he discussed in "On Literature" in 1940. It is also the problem Daniels faces—how to find an expression, a symbol, a mental equivalent that is adequate to experience and does not destroy it. In haiku, what is essentially being expressed does not exist, at least not as a thing, though it exists only in things. As Wright's mood declares itself in mind-stopping, often contradictory and negative statements, so there is nothing that symbolizes what haiku wishes to express. "How indeed," asks Blyth, "should any symbol represent the activity which is beyond speech and silence?" (1:244) Blyth's formulation of what haiku is wrestling with articulates clearly the similarity of its concerns to Wright: "The problem for haiku, both in composition and in appreciation is the same as for life itself: how to retain and assimilate the intellectual elements that distinguish the upper from the lower animals, into the instinctive life common to all . . . the inchoate, chaotic mass of thought-emotion, which is the font of our existence, sometimes emerges, crystallized into words. In being expressed, it loses something of its primitive vitality." (1:204)

The primary phenomenon that haiku tries to express is interesting states of mind that have a particular significance; this significance lies in "a 'something' about the external things, a 'something' about the inner mind which is unmistakable." (1:vii) In these states, all entities are "united in the ceaseless activity of their Buddha-nature." (1:6) This activity is life, an activity present in both mental and bodily forms. In Wright's case, it is the process at work in his grandmother's religious utterances and the more secular vocal expression of Afro-American folk which he wanted to express. The minimalist strategy of haiku is a solution to the problem since what is being expressed is in one sense hardly anything at all and is not expressible in conceptual language. Wright, in "Memories of My Grandmother," had spoken at one point of his contouring effort, in the image of the whirlwind that a train stirs up as it speeds along, a whirlwind detectable only in the spiraling swirl of railbed rubbish. Blyth quotes a haiku, that employs a similar image:

> The train passes;
> How the smoke
> Swirls round the young leaves!
> (1:244)

Another point of contact between Wright's poetics, especially as expressed in his blueprint, and haiku, as discussed by Blyth, is that the Japanese poets, in their endeavors to express this state of consciousness and its significance, came to rely predominately on a kind of folk form. While not a form developed by the unsophisticated general populace, haiku was originally only a word game that was used by poetasters concerned with a humorous use of language, a humor derived mainly from puns. The term "haiku" means "sportive," and the form originally was not considered literary nor suitable for the expression of serious sentiments. Over a period of several hundred years, and especially under the hand of the poet Basho in the seventeenth century, it took on features of Zen and all its spiritual inheritance. It also incorporated aspects of older Chinese and Japanese forms of painting and poetry, keeping all the while its own laconic quality and its down-to-earthiness. The aim was to achieve "the setting to rights of the common parlance and ordinary language" (1:119), the most significant moments expressed in a most everyday, matter-of-fact way. Haiku thus took the way of salvation, and older forms of expressing it, from the realm of the etherial and the vague and tied them to ordinary, commonplace occasions. In so doing, Blyth says in words reminiscent of Burke's view of one of language's shortcomings, it obliterated the "poetic haze" between the perceiver and the thing perceived. Compared to older and more literary or poetic forms, haiku is "popular, democratic, plebian." (1:121)

Blyth's discourse also evokes a relationship of haiku to Afro-American folk expression when he compares haiku to music. Haiku, he says, "are songs," meant to be read aloud and, like many folk songs, "repeated aloud." (1:369) Elsewhere he points out haiku's relationship to music in terms that sound like Wright's mood when it declares that it is not music, yet is more like music than anything else in the universe. Blyth says that the haiku poet sees and expresses "the universe under the aspect of harmony, as rhythm and symphony; in the deepest sense of the word, *musically*. The relation of the elements of the haiku is that of phrases of a melody, and this melody is in counterpoint to, is a variation of the music of the spheres." (1:357)

Conveying the *satori*, the significant state of mind, is "the underlying rhythm of thought rather than the thought itself." (1:171) In the essence of how they "work" and what they convey, haiku are really "'Songs without words' . . . the melody and the rhythm remove the barriers of custom and prejudice between ourselves and the object." (1:117) Haiku, in its unitary reception of subject and object, is like the perfect union of form and content in music. Wright had, of course, used the image of Afro-American jazz in "Memories of My Grandmother" to describe the form he felt he had originally given to *The Man Who Lived Underground*, the unity that symbolized, as he put it, the "something" that was behind the multiplicity of specific episodes and events in the novella.

Terms like "rhythm," "symphony," and "harmony" imply a

243

diversity, a disunity; haiku's addiction to things immerses it in multiplicity, with elements incongruous to the very condition it is dedicated to express. The identifying essential character of this form is this paradoxical linking of disparate elements. As Wright's blueprint for Negro writing calls for the uniting of two different streams of outlook, haiku derives or expresses significance from setting the "prosaic life of little people . . . in the greater, the poetic life." (1:330) A haiku poet may combine effectively references to the artificial life of a Chinese royal court with references to an unrealistic historical event and with references to a very real, simple willow tree, or he may produce the following:

> How heavy
> The doors of the Great Gate,—
> An evening of spring.
> (p. 291)

This prompts Blyth's question, "what is the relation between the end of spring and the heaviness of the door?" As Wright had observed of his grandmother's statements and the blues, Blyth says of haiku: "there is a kind of syllogistic nature about the form which gives it the utmost clarity while actually containing no logical elements, often no intellectual connections between the parts." (1:327) The parts, so different and complete in themselves, are related by a kind of superimposition, as in the process of experiencing, self and thing are superimposed, producing the special or perhaps orgasmic quality that marks this state of mind, the "ah!" quality as it is sometimes called. In a haiku such as

> What was once the Barrier of Fuha,
> Now only fields and thickets:
> The autumn wind,
> (1:113)

"the autumn wind is the Barrier, is the field and thicket, is the very soul of the poet who gives the scene its meaning and value." (1:113) As Blyth says elsewhere, in terms that recall Reich's, the real import of the haiku lies "in the overlapping, in the interpenetration of one scene with another, of man with nature." (1:144)

To be sure, Wright speaks of the form of his grandmother's expressions and those of the blues lyricists as "juxtaposed" rather than as interpenetrating. Nevertheless, his references to an organic quality of linkages, a characterization of connection no doubt prompted by Burke's ideas, indicates his sense of the connection as vital, not merely mechanical. Had Wright managed not to see the similarities between all of his earlier thought and what he was now reading about haiku, Blyth offers a clue that cannot be ignored. He presents a long collection of "haiku" derived from a variety of Western writers, mainly of the nineteenth and twentieth centuries. He takes passages from their works which seem to embody the haiku spirit of Zen, the spirit of real poetry, and without changing words, he arranges the passages in the three-line format associated with haiku. Grouping them, as haiku often are grouped, according to seasons, he includes the following in "Autumn":

> The railroad bridge
> Is a sad song
> In de air.
> (1:306)

This is a portion of "Homesick Blues" by Langston Hughes, with whom Wright had, at one time, written a number of blues lyrics.

The most extensive study of Wright's haiku, Robert Tener's essay, "The Where, the When, the What," makes an effort to establish Wright's interest in this form as a sign of a "return to nature" on his part, an attempt to recoup the spiritual energies that had been eroded by financial difficulties, physical illness, the betrayals by friends, and the machination of foes. Because his "return to nature" is less than perfect in most of the approximately four thousand haiku he wrote, the two dozen that have been published and are available for study have been judged as seriously flawed. While a unity with nature is a very important characteristic of Japanese haiku, and while Wright's perennial outlook has, in spite of his emphasis on reason and technology, a highly romantic cast, an attempt to establish a "return to nature" motive for his interest in haiku is ill-advised wrenching that interest from its integral position in Wright's thought and career.

Wright's primary interest in 1955 was the integration of the individual with society, not nature. Haiku fit with his interest if they are seen in relation to the spatial knowledge in his psyche, spaces resulting from experience of Afro-American folk expression and the mentality Wright saw as behind it, spaces developed by his experience of Stein, Surrealism, Burke, and Reich. He never employed these sources literally but adapted them always to his own purposes. It is unlikely that he would have attempted to reproduce the Japanese haiku precisely. He would have known, from the first lines of Blyth's first volume, if not from some other source, that authentic haiku are intimately connected with a whole cultural tradition of which he was not a part. Constance Webb is undoubtedly correct in saying that Wright was trying to bring a black American consciousness and tradition to this distinctively Japanese poetic form. The life and consciousness of a black American, Wright felt, involved the juxtaposition or superimposition of disparate items that are held together by a subjective "mood," by the sense of one's own subjective life and reality. To know objective reality or nature is to know it in oneself, which shares the very process that constitutes objects. This attitude differs from the classical Western view that knowledge of self is posterior to knowledge of objects, and to the Japanese view that oriental effacement of the self is the way to knowledge and salvation. To know or become one with nature, or reality, in Wright's view of the Afro-American way, was to become one with oneself.

The adaptive change this attitude would make in Wright's haiku is recognized by Tener but passed over as a flawed variation or deviation from the Japanese haiku. Wright's approach to haiku interposes "between the speaker and the scene the poet's habit of subscribing meanings to an event. But the meanings come from within the poet; they are not part of the event and its things." (Tener, "The Where, the When, the What," p. 283) Tener's comment on Wright's haiku here is similar to Wright's initial observations concerning his grandmother's thought and speech patterns. Wright's haiku should be analyzed in the light of his own poetics, rather than be compared to the Japanese poems he used as models. This approach might not reveal them as any better poems, but it will reveal more about Wright as a creative artist.

Even had Wright not been inclined to this kind of adaptation (his interest prefigures a wider interest in the form among English-language poets which was to develop in the mid--1960s), Blyth's texts would have suggested its validity. Blyth emphasizes the evolutionary or accretionary development of classical haiku and the viability of the form, at least up to the early twentieth century when Japanese poets made attempts to widen the references and alter the form in other ways. Also, Blyth's inclusion of numerous haiku "touchstones" from Western poetry clearly indicates that this authoritative scholar saw the haiku form as applicable to expressions of sensibilities that were derived from vastly different traditions. Above all, as Wright became involved with Third World concerns, this non-Western form would have seemed worth exploring for its suitability to an Afro-American orientation, as a way of indicating Afro-Americans' links with forms other than those of Western colonizing civilizations.

Apart from Blyth's suggestions, Wright's long-lasting, if often submerged, concerns about the interpenetration of form and content, of consciousness and articulation with emotional awareness and inarticulateness, would have led him to this experimentation. Fabre believes that Wright's work with haiku is an indication that he was entering into a new phase of creativity, that the haiku represent a kind of foreplay as he launched into the production of newly powerful works, released from the creative eddy in which he seemed to be trapped at the time. During the time he was writing his haiku, he was reading Colin Wilson's *Age of Defeat*, noting Wilson's comment that "the final hero will be the man who has healed . . . self-division, and is again prepared to fling himself back into the social struggle." (Wilson, pp. 81-82) The title he gave his proposed publication of haiku, *This Other World: Projections in the Haiku Manner*, suggests that Wright saw them in a Sartrean way: as a "project" or plan by which to shape what one is to become. If history does repeat itself, spirally if not cyclically, such a scenario for Wright is plausable. In *American Hunger*, telling of the effect of his discovery of Stein's prose when he could not write sustained narrative, he says he filled up sheets of paper with disconnected sentences. The thousands of haiku he wrote at the end of his career bear a resemblance to those earlier, disconnected sentences. Like those sentences and their purported inspiration, his haiku may have a relationship to their model quite different from the most obvious one of superficial style. In the case of the haiku, the relationship is discernible only in light of Wright's entire poetic motive.

The proposed title for Wright's planned book of haiku indicates his intention that the poems be analyzed from the point of a schema that differed from Japanese Zen. His poems are haiku only in manner, but the groupings, as he has left them, do indicate the model of the Japanese haiku. On several large mat boards, he pasted his haiku under a variety of headings. Those he selected for possible publication came under the seasonal headings—Winter, Spring, Summer, Autumn—of traditional haiku. In addition to these, Wright provided additional categories like Blyth's subindexes, arranging the poems not only in the various volumes dedicated to the different seasons but also according to topics. For example, in the "Spring" collection, Blyth gathers the poems under such headings as "Fields and Mountains," "Birds and Beasts," and "Trees and Flowers." Wright's subcategories, however, are quite different from the natural phenomena Blyth says are so central to Japanese haiku. Wright's subgroups carry such titles as "Cryptic," "Relations," "Sensation," "Religion," and "Project." These titles, and especially that last, as well as the title of the proposed publication, imply that what Wright saw emerging from these short poems was a kind of autobiography, a projection of his feelings, of his self as another world, as it might be revealed in more or less spontaneously occurring images.

Somewhat like the automatic juxtapositions fostered by the Surrealists, and like Stein's spiraling waves of narrative flow, Wright's haikulike poems emphasize his subjective state more than the objective phenomenon that might have been instrumental to the realization expressed. Indeed, some of the topics seem to be taken not from immediate experience involving external stimuli but from memory, surrealist fancy, or folklore: jazz wafting from a run-down apartment house; black birds pecking at a discarded glass eye; a corpulent naked woman cooking and sampling applesauce; the movement of a dead body within its coffin after a week.

The original order in which Wright wrote these poems is not available, so the "mood" that tied the disconnected poems together as they flowed from his pen cannot be inferred. His groupings, however, suggest he was, indeed, looking for a pattern, looking for what these bits and scraps contoured, what definite yet obscure feeling. When he gives the title "Religion" to a certain group, it is clear that he is not thinking of a dictionary definition. They present scenes—an open barnyard gate, lice and moonlight in a cold room, the planting of turnip seeds, an abandoned canoe drifting in a fall rain, a deserted road under a threatening winter sunrise, and, finally, a cat yawning and steadily gazing past a fall sun. Does "religion" refer to what religion meant to him at the time? Does it refer to his sense of its role in the lives of others, in the world at large? Is it a sense of what it once meant to people or that it once had meaning? The poem about lowering his head to avoid seeing the new moon is clearly based on a folk superstition about looking at a new moon under certain conditions. The essence of these poems that makes them appear to him as "religion," whatever it means to him, is not semantic but rather a "mood" that can take on a "religious" configuration. Looked at from such a perspective, the poems become a nondiscursive expression of the name Wright gave to an apparently recurring form of feeling that he distinguishes as "religion," like and yet unlike the traditional understanding of that word. This gathering of poems is, therefore, not unlike *The Man Who Lived Underground*.

Individual Japanese haiku, as Blyth says, work by imagistic overlay within the few lines allotted; Wright, viewing haiku from the orientation of an Afro-American folk tradition, might have brought an additional consideration to such a conglomerate, seeing it as a series of stanzas in a blues song. In the individual, traditional haiku form, there is some carryover of image, but from poem to poem rather than within each poem. Occasionally in Wright's collection, images are carried over literally and are more repetitive than in Japanese haiku, where different images in each line interpenetrate each other. As occurs in the traditional Japanese form, Wright has made a season an important element in each of his "Religion" haiku, although, in the aggregate, they do not concentrate on a single season. The "lines" or stanzas of Wright's "Religion" contain recurring images of spring and autumn, as well as of cold and moon. "Empty" also occurs in two poems, and its presence, if not the word itself, is discernible in several others. Religion is, it seems, not "hot" in Wright's feeling, yet it does not seem to indicate an attitude like what Wallace Stevens has called "a mind of winter." His poems suggest an "in-between" state—late or early winter, bordering fall or spring, rather than the dead of winter.

The feeling he calls religion is not overwhelmingly negative, as might be expected in light of Wright's avowed quarrel with religion and its merits. It may be silent, empty, cold, yet the gate is open, seed is being sown, the moon is new and waxing, there is a dawn as well as a sunset. It is an expenditure that sustains lice, but also moonlight, and it is not without light-ness, humor. The entire collection might be said to suggest religion as an experience valuable in itself—deep, bracing, although devoid of content; a great yawn; a steady, calm, yet intense staring past rather than at something, or a staring that indicates a fixation on something within the starer. Similar analyses could be made of other groupings of Wright's poems in the haiku manner.

These haikulike poems were, in their experimental nature, probably surrealistic to Wright in that they were his attempts to discover what was going on in his psyche. Blyth points out that, for all their spontaneity, Japanese haiku were often re-vised many times; while the experience was always that of the human consciousness realized and revealed in things present, revision of the poems was a revision of the experience: the "experience had matured in the words of the haiku so that [the poet] *came to know what he should have wanted to say.*" (*Haiku,* 1:366) In spite of the presence of an apparently un-Zen-like self-consciousness and rationalization in many of them, these haiku are Wright's exercises in coming closer to his unmedi-ated experience of self. In this sense, Wright was, as Tener has said, attempting to recoup, to write from his psychosomatic state. They represent his approximations—light, without the heavier hand of his conceptualizing intellect—to an important source of values and meaning in himself, the focus of energy that would enable him to say what he meant and put the reality of himself into his verbal structures. The uncertainty he had felt concerning their value indicates that he had been expressing himself from a source he could not or did not care to acknowledge.

With the haiku, Wright's writing career came full circle: his search for consonant, integral contour of the "something" he sensed behind authentic, Afro-American creative expression; a "something" compatible with, but not identical to, religious form; a "something" that was the unity of even the most disparate of elements, essence and existence, in the dynamism that is a person. As his earlier Stein-motivated sentences gave little hint of what followed, the haikulike expressions are probably unreliable auguries of what content or form Wright's subsequent work might have taken. In the late summer of 1960, after he laid the haiku aside, he worked on one more novel. One of the characters is a young man who commits murders in order to be caught and punished, the punishment itself being an "attempt to communicate with others." (Fabre, *The Unfinished Quest*, p. 514) This pattern recurs frequently enough in Wright's work to make one wonder why he considered this last version to be different from anything he had ever done: the isolated person who resorts to inappropriate forms in order to force communication with others; the individual who, sometimes less and sometimes more, realizes the inadequacy of his chosen form to communicate but who cannot, or will not, have it otherwise. It was a pattern he attributed to his grandmother and Afro-American folk, a pattern he used in his fiction and found in such writers and thinkers as Stein, Burke, and Reich who appealed to him. It was also increasingly his own political stance at the end of his life, staking out his own pronouncements and line of thought on racial and national issues, avoiding communist as well as new-left associations and Western attitudes, and working to establish Africa as an independent entity. But there was something missing from this very prized, very Western, very American individualism, something that Wright knew, and yet did not know, was missing, although he attempted to discover it by contouring it: a view of the individual as community, of personhood itself as the model of the integration of the individual and society.

An essay by Michael Gorra in *The New York Times Book Review*, "The Sun Never Sets on the English Novel," though not about Wright, says some things that are most apropos to him and his gropings at the end of his life. Postcolonial writers, such as V. S. Naipaul, in an attempt to turn a non-native language into a fit medium for their own cultural expression, see the novel not from the perspective of avant-garde concern with form for its own sake but from an older traditional angle as an interpretation of society and culture, especially its political organization. They know, as did Wright, that "history is the nightmare from which they cannot awake." (p. 24) Their struggle with the role of the individual—the heart of the novel—in political systems, which operate ideologically regardless of social class and individuals, requires that language be shaped according to cultural and political values and concerns that are particular to the once colonized peoples, concerns not found in the colonizing culture or in its language. A V. S. Naipaul, in this context, like Wright a person with a minority-culture background from one country but living in another, attempts to write not about his egocentric sensibilities but to integrate "the worlds I contained within my self." Naipaul is said to write best "when he has something personally at stake—when he can acknowlege the fiction of objectivity upon which his work depends" (p. 25), when he can admit, for example, that the geographical areas he writes of in travel books also refer to conditions within himself.

Many of Wright's attitudes and utterances at the end of his life suggest that he would have welcomed and perhaps joined the scorching revolutionary stance of the black militant writers who were to emerge in the 1960s. But the haiku and their relationship to his sense of indefinableness hold a hint of another line of possible development. If Wright could have admitted—had he been allowed by publishers (World had rejected the submitted haiku) and by readers—things deeper in himself than even *Black Boy* had dealt with, this other line might have brought him finally, like Naipaul, to new terms with the matter of spirituality—or imagination—and its role in the unification of incongruities.

Works Cited

Alexander, Margaret Walker. "Richard Wright." *New Letters* 38 (Winter, 1971).

Alquié, Ferdinand. *The Philosophy of Surrealism.* Ann Arbor: University of Michigan Press, 1965.

Balakian, Anna. *Surrealism: The Road to the Absolute.* London: George Allen & Unwin Ltd., 1972.

Bellow, Saul. Forward. *The Closing of the American Mind.* By Allan Bloom. New York: Simon and Schuster, 1987.

Blyth, R. H. *Haiku.* 4 Vols. Tokyo: Hokuseido, 1949.

Bone, Robert. *The Negro Novel in America.* Rev. ed. New Haven: Yale University Press, 1965.

Breton, Andre. *Nadja.* Paris: Editions Gallimand, 1963.

Brinnin, John Malcolm. *The Third Rose.* Boston: Little, Brown, 1959.

Brown, Sterling A. "Negro Folk Expression." *Black Expression.* Ed. Addison Gayle, Jr. New York: Waywright and Talley, Inc., 1969.

Burke, Kenneth. *Counter-Statement.* 2nd ed. Berkeley: University of California Press, 1968.

———. *Permanence and Change.* Rev. ed. Los Altos, Cal.: Hermes Publications, 1954.

———. *The Philosophy of Literary Form.* 1941. Berkeley: University of California Press, 1967.

———. "Revolutionary Symbolism in America." *American Writers*

Conference. Ed. Henry Hart. New York: International Publishers, 1935.

———. "Surrealism." New Directions in Prose and Poetry. Norfolk, Conn.: New Directions, 1940.

Burley, Dan. Dan Burley's Original Handbook of Harlem Jive. New York: Dan Burley, 1944.

Carrouges, Michel. Andre Breton and the Basic Concepts of Surrealism. Trans. Maura Pendergast, S.N.D. University, Ala.: University of Alabama Press, 1974.

DeKoven, Marianne. A Different Language. Madison: University of Wisconsin Press, 1983.

Deren, Maya. Divine Horsemen: The Living Gods of Haiti. London: Thames & Hudson, 1953.

Dorson, Richard. Negro Folk Tales in Michigan. Cambridge: Harvard University Press, 1956.

———. "Negro Tales from Bolivar County, Mississippi." Southern Folklore Quarterly 19 (1955).

Fabre, Michel. "Richard Wright's First Hundred Books." College Language Association Journal, June, 1979.

———. "Richard Wright: The Man Who Lived Underground." Studies in the Novel 3, no. 2 (Summer, 1971).

———. The Unfinished Quest of Richard Wright. New York: William Morrow, 1973.

Fisher, Dexter and Robert Stepto. Afro-American Literature: The Reconstruction of Instruction. New York: Modern Language Association of America, 1979.

Freud, Sigmund. The Interpretation of Dreams. Vols. 4-5 of The Standard Edition of the Complete Works of Sigmund Freud. Trans. and eds. James Strachey et al. London: Hogarth, 1953.

———. Introductory Lectures on Psychoanalysis. Vol. 15 of The Standard Edition of the Complete Works of Sigmund Freud. Trans. and eds. James Strachey et al. London: Hogarth, 1963.

Genovese, Eugene. Roll, Jordan, Roll: The World The Slaves Made. New York: Pantheon, 1974.

Gorra, Michael. "The Sun Never Sets on the English Novel." The New York Times Book Review, July 19, 1987.

Haas, Robert Bartlett. A Primer for the Gradual Understanding of Gertrude Stein. Los Angeles: Black Sparrow Press, 1971.

Henderson, Stephen. Understanding The New Black Poetry. New York: William Morrow, 1973.

Hoffman, Daniel. Form and Fable in American Fiction. New York: Oxford University Press, 1961.

Hurston, Zora Neale. "Hoodoo in America." *Journal of American Folklore* 44, no. 171 (Jan.-Mar. 1931).

———. *Mules and Men.* Bloomington: Indiana University Press, 1978.

———. *Tell My Horse.* Berkeley: Turtle Island, 1983.

Jahn, Janheinz. *Muntu: An Outline of Neo-African Culture.* London: Faber, 1960.

Jones, LeRoi. *Black Music.* New York: William Morrow, 1967.

Jung, Carl. *The Archetypes of the Collective Unconscious.* Trans. R. F. C. Hall. Eds. Herbert Read, Michael Fordham, and Gerhard Adler. 2nd. ed. Vol. 9 of Bollingen Series 20. New York: Bollingen Foundation, 1968.

———. *The Spirit in Man, Art, and Literature.* Trans. R. F. C. Hall. Eds. Herbert Read, Michael Fordham and Gerhard Adler. Vol. 15 of Bollingen Series 20. New York: Bollingen Foundation, 1966.

———. *Symbols of Transformation.* Trans. R. F. C. Hall. Eds. Herbert Read, Michael Fordham, and Gerhard Adler. 2nd ed. Vol. 5 of Bollingen Series 20. New York: Bollingen Foundation, 1967.

Lee, Don L. [Haki Madhubuti]. *Dynamite Voices I.* Detroit: Broadside Press, 1971.

Levin, Harry. "What Was Modernism?" *Massachusetts Review* 1, no. 4 (August, 1960).

Lomax, John A. and Alan Lomax, comps. *American Ballads and Folk Songs.* New York: Macmillan, 1935.

Mann, W. Edward. *Orgone, Reich and Eros.* New York: Simon and Schuster, 1973.

Margolies, Edward. *The Art of Richard Wright.* Carbondale: Southern Illinois University Press, 1969.

Mitchell, Henry H. *Black Belief: Folk Beliefs of Blacks in America and Africa.* New York: Harper and Row, 1975.

Neal, Larry. "And Shine Swam On." *Black Fire: An Anthology of Afro-American Writing.* Eds. LeRoi Jones and Larry Neal. New York: William Morrow, 1968.

Olrik, Axel. "Epic Laws of Folk Narrative." *The Study of Folklore.* Ed. Alan Dundes. Englewood Cliffs, N.J.: Prentice-Hall, 1965.

Puckett, Newbell Niles. *Folk Beliefs of the Southern Negro.* New York: Negro Universities Press, 1968.

Reich, Wilhelm. *Esther, God and Devil: Cosmic Superimposition.* Trans. Therese Pol. New York: Farrar, Straus & Giroux, 1949.

———. *The Function of The Orgasm.* Trans. Vincent R. Carfagno. New York: Farrar, Straus & Giroux, 1973.

Rockwell, John. "Virgil Thompson's 'Saints' Goes Marching On." *New York Times,* Nov. 9, 1986. Sec.II:12.

Senghor, Leopold. "African-Negro Aesthetics." *Diogenes* 16 (Winter, 1956).

Sontag, Susan. *Against Interpretation*. New York: Farrar, Straus & Giroux, 1966.

Stein, Gertrude. *Lectures In America*. New York: Random House, 1935.

———. "Sacred Emily." *Geography and Plays*. New York: Something Else Press, 1968.

———. *Three Lives*. New York: Random House, 1958.

———. *Wars I Have Seen*. New York: Random House, 1945.

Stewart, James T. "The Development of the Black Revolutionary Artist." *Black Fire: An Anthology of Afro-American Writing*. Eds. LeRoi Jones and Larry Neal. New York: William Morrow, 1968.

Sutherland, Donald. *Gertrude Stein: A Biography of Her Works*. New Haven: Yale University Press, 1951.

Tener, Robert. "The Where, the When, the What: A Study of Richard Wright's Haiku." *Critical Essays on Richard Wright*. Ed. Yoshinobu Hakutani. Boston: G. K. Hall, 1982.

Toelken, Barre. *Dynamics of Folklore*. Boston: Houghton Mifflin, 1979.

Twain, Mark. *What Is Man? and Other Essays*. New York: Harper, 1917.

Wertham, Frederick. "An Unconscious Determinant in *Native Son*." *Journal of Clinical Psychopathology* 6 (July, 1944).

White, Joseph L. *The Psychology of Blacks: An Afro-American Perspective*. Englewood Cliffs, N.J.: Prentice-Hall, 1974.

Wilson, Colin. *The Stature of Man [Age of Defeat]*. Boston: Houghton Mifflin, 1959.

Wright, Richard. *American Hunger*. New York: Harper & Row, 1977.

———. *Black Boy: A Record of Childhood and Youth*. New York: Harper, 1945.

———. *Black Power: A Record of Reactions in a Land of Pathos*. New York: Harper, 1954.

———. "A Blueprint for Negro Writing." *New Challenge* 2, no. 2 (Fall, 1937).

———. *The Color Curtain: A Report on the Bandung Conference*. Cleveland: World Publishing, 1956.

———. "The Future of Literary Expression." File 395, Wright Archive. Beinecke Library, Yale.

———. "Gertrude Stein's Story Is Drenched in Hitler's Horrors. *P. M.* magazine, Mar. 11, 1945.

———. *How Bigger Was Born*. New York: Harper, 1940.

———. "Joe Louis Uncovers Dynamite." *New Masses* Oct., 1935.

———. *Lawd Today*. New York: Walker, 1963.

———. "The Man Who Killed a Shadow." *Eight Men*. 1961. New York: Pyramid Publications, 1970.

————. "The Man Who Lived Underground." *Eight Men*. 1961. Pyramid Publications, 1970.

————. "The Man Who Lived Underground." Files 205, 212-215, Wright Archive. Beinecke Library, Yale.

————. *Native Son*. New York: Harper, 1940.

————. "On Literature." File 507, Wright Archive. Beinecke Library, Yale.

————. *Pagan Spain*. New York: Harper, 1957.

————. "Personalism." File 515, Wright Archive. Beinecke Library, Yale.

————. "Roots and Branches." File 751, Wright Archive. Beinecke Library, Yale.

————. "Superstition." *Abbott's Monthly Magazine*, April 1931.

————. "A Tale of Folk Courage." *Partisan Review and Anvil* 3, no. 3 (April, 1936).

————. "Tarbaby's Dawn." File 906, Wright Archive. Beinecke Library, Yale.

————. *Twelve Million Black Voices: A Folk History of The Negro in the United States*. New York: Viking, 1941.

————. *Uncle Tom's Children: Four Novellas*. New York: Harper, 1938.

————. "What I Think Writing Is." File 511, Wright Archive. Beinecke Library, Yale.

————. *White Man, Listen!* New York: Doubleday, 1957.

————. "Why I Chose 'Melanctha' by Gertrude Stein." *I Wish I'd Written That*. Ed. Whit Burnett. New York: McGraw Hill, 1946.

————. "Writers and Their Art." File 811, Wright Archive. Beinecke Library, Yale.

Index

African culture: survivals in United States, 12-13; void created by its rupture, 13-14
Alienation: and Surrealism, 80-81, 82-84
Anima: images of, 134-35, 136, 137
Animus: imaged as old man, 131-33, 136
Aragon, Louis, 78
Art: Wright's attitude toward, 156; distance from reality, 204; Burke's notion of, 204
Asian cultures: and educated elite, 18-19
Automatic writing: Surrealist technique, 84; and jazz, 85, 86

Baldwin, James, 26-27, 46. *See also* Primal attitude
Bions, 226-27
Black Aesthetic, 77-78; and music, 206-07, 208, 209
Blessed virgin: in Spain, 44; and Erzulie, 54-55, 56
Blue: color, 53-54, 234; feeling, 145-46
"Blueprint for Negro Writing, A": and Spain, 20-21; and Wright's African experience, 27-28; and Jung, 130; and Burke, 178
Blues: and Surrealism, 79-80, 81; as contour, 83, 232-33; and haiku, 244, 245, 249. *See also* Music

Breton, André, 85, 88, 89, 90; essential Surrealist act, 83
Brown, Sterling, 35-36
Burke, Kenneth, 5, 146, 217; and Surrealism, 79; knowledge of Wright's work, 79; definition of psychosis, 96; and Freud, 128; essay-novel, 222; relationship of ideas to Reich's, 228-30

"Celebration of Life," 218-20. *See also* Collage; Jazz; Mood
Cezanne, Paul, 73
Chirico, Giorgio de, 92, 93
Chou En Lai, 30
Christ legend: as contouring theme, 114-19
Coleridge, Samuel Taylor, 110; "Rime of the Ancient Mariner," 114, 125; "representative I," 149-50. *See also* Imagination
Collage, 206, 215; structure of *Pagan Spain*, 22; Surrealist technique, 84, 106; Fred Daniel's, 155-56, 164; "Celebration of Life" as, 223. *See also* Juxtaposition
Collective unconscious, 169
Communication: Wright's disregard for, 32-33; African-Negro mode, 202-03; and violence, 210
Communism, Marxism: in Asia, 30, 31; its ideal for Wright, 177; and "Personalism," 179; *See also* Dialectic

259

Index

incongruities, 196. *See also* Symbol

Jazz, 208; as contour, 83; as surrealistic, 84-87; and "Man Who Lived Underground," 101-02; form of "Celebration of Life," 223. *See also* Music

Joyce, James, 58-59, 222

Jung, Carl, 153; theories and literary analysis, 130; view of sex, 130; theory as contouring theme, 130-31; nature of archetypes, 131; womb of the unconscious, 135; visionary mode of writing, 137-38; night world figures, 141; *dragon imago*, 143

Juxtaposition, superimposition, 32, 60, 80, 94, 167, 184, 186, 195, 217-18, 219, 220, 239-40, 246; as heuristic device, 187; process of reality, 235-37; Burke's critique of Wright, Dos Passos, Steinbeck, 237; in haiku, 244-45

Keats, John, 106, 194
Koestler, Arthur, 224
Ku Klux Klan, 44

Language, 180-81; Negro dialect and Stein, 67; "scat" or "jive," 70, 75; Stein's attitude toward, 72, 73; Stein's rebellion in, 74; Negro attitude toward, 75; lack of in masses, 198; as mind, 200; haiku's purposes regarding, 243

Lawd Today, 59, 63, 217
Leopold-Loeb case, 70-71
Lewis, Sinclair, 199
Libido: Reich's and Freud's differences over, 225
Loas: figurative presence in *Native Son*, 48-57; Legba, 48-49; Zaka, 49-50; Ogun, 51; Baron Samedi, 51-52; Erzuli-Freda-Dahomey, 53-57, 210. *See also* Door images

"Magical realism": in Morrison and Reed, 91

Master passion, 147, 153, 158, 159, 161, 173, 220; differences between Wright's and Twain's views of, 161-65; and imperiousness, 165-67, 169. *See also* Organicism

"Melanctha": Wright's estimation of, 62; imitation of, 64; discovery of, 67, 70; other Afro-American writers' estimations of, 67, 68; Negro workers' response to, 71-72; reflections of influence in *Man Who Lived Underground*, 153-54

"Memories of My Grandmother," 4-6, 7, 69, 70-72, 98-99, 100, 114, 119, 130, 161, 174, 212, 213, 235, 242, 243; and Freud, 125; and collage, 155-56; and *What Is Man?*, 157-58; and tradition, 171; and Burke, 180-81, 209

Mencken, H. L., 3
Metaphysical dimension: lack of in Western culture, 81, 93; to Wright's thought, 214

Militarization, militarism: as expressive form, 29-31; as contouring theme, 119-20; in Burke's theory, 190-91

Montezuma, 219-20
Mood, 22, 60, 87, 187, 200-02, 235, 236, 238-39, 241, 249; in "Celebration of Life," 218, 220-23; and orgone, 225. *See also* "Something"

Movement, motion, 145; structure of *Man Who Lived Underground*, 100, 142-43; creation as, 144; and mystical trance, 146; Afro-American orientation, 186; of symbol formation, 200-01; self as, 203; as existence, 207; in Wright's proposed great work, 214-15; emotions as, 223; in Reich's theories, 225-26, 228-29; core of reality, 231-33; in haiku, 239-40. *See also* Dialectic

Music: as folk expression, 4, 5, 6, 233, 243; in *Man Who Lived Underground*, 170; image of central reality, 172; in Afro-American culture, 207-08; in plan for "Celebration of Life," 223

Myth: use of in *Native Son* and "Man Who Killed a Shadow," 58-60; reality of for Burke, 175; "worker" as, 175; "people" as, 176. *See also* Symbol

Naipaul, V. S., 252